# Education, Democracy, and Public Knowledge

Interventions • Theory and Contemporary Politics
*Stephen Eric Bronner, Series Editor*

---

*Education, Democracy, and Public Knowledge,*
Elizabeth A. Kelly

*Unequal Struggle: Class, Gender, Race, and Power
in the U.S. Congress,* John C. Berg

*The Revision of Psychoanalysis,* Erich Fromm

*Corporate Society: Class, Property, and Contemporary
Capitalism,* John McDermott

*Television and the Crisis of Democracy,* Douglas Kellner

FORTHCOMING

*Social Regulation and the State,* Charles Noble

*Technical Fouls: Democracy and Technical Change,*
John Kurt Jacobson

*Crises and Transitions: A Critique of the
International Economic Order,* David Ruccio,
Stephen Resnick, and Richard D. Wolff

# Education, Democracy, and Public Knowledge

*Elizabeth A. Kelly*

*Westview Press*

*Boulder • San Francisco • Oxford*

*Interventions: Theory and Contemporary Politics*

Published in 1995 in the United States of America by Westview Press, Inc., 5500 Central Avenue, Boulder, Colorado 80301-2877, and in the United Kingdom by Westview Press, 36 Lonsdale Road, Summertown, Oxford OX2 7EW

Library of Congress Cataloging-in-Publication Data
Kelly, Elizabeth A.
  Education, democracy, and public knowledge / Elizabeth A. Kelly.
    p.  cm. — (Interventions)
  Includes bibliographical references and index.
  ISBN 0-8133-1633-2 — ISBN 0-8133-1634-0 (pbk.)
  1. Socialism and education—United States.   2. Critical pedagogy—United States.   3. Education—United States—Philosophy.   4. Public schools—United States.   5. Politics and education—United States.
I. Title.   II. Series: Interventions (Boulder, Colo.)
LC196.5.U6K45   1995
370.1—dc20                                                                94-27496
                                                                              CIP

Printed and bound in the United States of America

The paper used in this publication meets the requirements
of the American National Standard for Permanence of Paper
for Printed Library Materials Z39.48-1984.

10     9     8     7     6     5     4     3     2     1

*To Professor William T. Daly*
*of Stockton State College*
*with gratitude and affection*

.

... ignorance is the curse of God,
knowledge the wing wherewith we fly to heaven.

—Shakespeare
*Henry VI, Part II*

# Contents

Acknowledgments   xiii

*Introduction*   1

1   *Education, Democracy, and Public Knowledge:
Toward a Socialist Theory of Education*   11

2   The Education of Henry Adams *and the Transformation
of the Bourgeois Public Sphere: A Case Study*   27

3   *A Public Philosophy? Pragmatism and
Public Knowledge*   47

4   *Public Knowledge and the Paradox of
Democratic Education*   63

5   *Public Intellectuals and Public Knowledge*   79

6   *Literacy for What? Critical Literacy and
the Power of Public Knowledge*   97

7   *Framing the Question of Freedom:
Public Knowledge in Practice*   115

Notes   131
About the Book and Author   155
Index   157

# Acknowledgments

This book is dedicated to William T. Daly, an exemplary educator, mentor, and friend. In and outside of the classroom he is a model to emulate; for over twenty years he has inspired me personally and professionally. Were it not for his care and concern I would probably not have finished college. Thank you, Bill, for all that you have taught and shown me. Warm thanks are also due to Stephen Bronner, matchless adviser, mentor, friend, and critic, without whose guidance and support I would never have begun, let alone completed, this book.

I have been blessed with many memorable teachers and colleagues at several institutions, all of whom have influenced my thinking and teaching. I wish I could thank each one personally; if I tried, the list would probably be longer than this book. I must single out for special thanks Myron Aronoff, Dennis Bathory, and W. Carey McWilliams, all of the Political Science Department at Rutgers University, whose comments were most helpful at an early point in this project. In a variety of ways, each of them made it possible for me to continue writing at moments when it would have been easy to give up. Long ago and far away at Stockton State College, Joe Walsh and Allen Lacy spent hours outside of the classroom discussing philosophy and social problems with me. I have not forgotten our conversations; indeed, some of the ideas expressed in these pages had their genesis over coffee in the G-wing cafeteria.

Since coming to DePaul University in 1992 I have received warm welcomes and ongoing support from several colleagues, most notably Chris Mobley and J. Harry Wray of the Political Science Department; Sandra Jackson and José Solis of the School of Education; Associate Dean Lynn Narasimhan of the College of Liberal Arts and Sciences; and Marjorie Piechowski of the Office of Sponsored Programs and Research. Others in the Political Science Department, the Women's Studies Program, and throughout the university have contributed to the creative, challenging, and supportive institutional environment within which I completed this project.

The members of my writing group, Frida Furman, Mechthild Hart, and Kate Kane, have individually and collectively provided careful readings, cogent criticisms, and more moral support than I would have believed possible. There has also been rich, deep laughter when the work was done. A loving toast to you, my friends.

My students at Stockton State College, Rutgers University, Vassar College, and DePaul University have been my best inspiration; thanks to all of them for reminding me, over and over again, just why I became a professor and how much I love my work.

At Westview Press, Spencer Carr, anonymous readers, and an incredibly helpful, patient, and friendly staff have been a joy to work with. My gratitude to you is unrestrained.

I have been especially lucky to have loving friends and family, without whom my life and work would be empty. My mother, Maude Kelly, has encouraged me throughout years of graduate school and professional life, at times providing support from limited resources at no small personal sacrifice. Her generous heart has sustained me during dark times. Ila and the late W. Scott Burman both showed me, at an early age, that some of the best education takes place outside the classroom. Their abiding friendship and support over several decades is something I will always treasure. Our kinship may be fictive, but it is nonetheless dear.

Linda Williamson Nelson, "sister-friend" without equal, intellectual companion, and constant source of encouragement, has been at my side throughout this work despite the distances that have separated us. She has given wise counsel at points of crisis, patiently talking me through bouts of writer's block, and she has the phone bills to prove it. Uma Narayan has offered unstinting support, stimulating conversation, critical vision, and profound silliness—always perfectly blending the sublime and the ridiculous. Vicki and Norm Ervine have simply been there, through all the highs and lows of the past twenty years and more, offering love and friendship without qualification. So has Kevin Cathcart, to whom I owe much more than words can capture. I cannot imagine life without them. Nor can I imagine having survived graduate school without the friendship and support of Michael Forman, who read and commented on an early version of the manuscript at a time when he should have been working on projects of his own. John Martin, T Regan, and John Vail have been exemplary friends over the years; time spent at Rutgers would have been far less easily borne without these good comrades.

Carl Larsen has been a strong and steady force behind my sometimes wavering commitment to this project. He has put up with innumerable complaints, fears, frantic phone calls, and Internet messages with steadfast grace. He believed in me (and this book) even when I sometimes lost sight of my goals. His willingness to give time, compassion, and spirit has known few limits; my gratitude to him is beyond measure. I cannot count the ways in which our friendship is precious.

Finally, I must thank my Chicago "family" for being, individually and as one, a continuing source of love, friendship, delight, and joy. I could never have imagined that signing a lease for the first floor of a duplex would bring me such blessings as I have received from Jackie Taylor, Carol Sadtler, and Lucy and Grace Sadtler-Taylor. They are all bright lights on the horizon of home.

*Elizabeth A. Kelly*

# *Introduction*

A few years ago, as I began this project, Stephen Bronner suggested that I start thinking about the relationship between public knowledge, education, and democracy by describing the education I *ought* to have had, as opposed to the one I *did* have. At the time, this seemed impractical, beyond the pale of possibility. After all, I had been trained as a political theorist and thought I should appropriate what my friend Linda Nelson has dubbed the "haute couture" discourse of academia. Thinking, or writing, about personal experiences was simply out of the question. No reflections on my own educational history could possibly meet the standards of scholarly detachment, of the "objectivity," such discourse demands.

Now I see the wisdom of the advice I initially avoided. Any text is really a compilation of voices. Some remain impersonal and generalized; it is these which generally appear in ink on the printed page. Passion, personality, subjectivity are left to lurk in the interstices, the spaces between the lines. Yet they are there, even in the most apparently objective texts, if one learns to look carefully. Critical analysis of personal experience as a locus of theory construction has fallen out of fashion, a casualty of the postmodernist condition. For the moment, however, I want to resurrect the old insight about the personal being political and begin by sharing a series of snapshots. Imagine that you are looking through a sort of family album, where moments from one woman's life have been captured. Indulge, if you will, my brief lapse into the first person. Scholarly detachment will emerge soon enough.

*It is 1958.* My father, a master sergeant in the Air Force, has been posted to western Massachusetts. I am newly enrolled in the base's public elementary school; my first weeks there are rocky, marked by behavioral outbursts and notes sent home by my teacher almost daily. Finally the principal orders an evaluation by the school psychologist, with whom I am closeted for a few days before being pronounced "gifted" and placed in an accelerated third-grade class. Here, challenged academically for the first time, I begin to thrive, but I am the only child in class whose father is not an officer. A month or so later, a colonel's wife, the mother of one of my classmates, accosts my mother in the commissary. I do not belong in her son's class, the colonel's wife says. It is an outrage; an enlisted man's daughter has no place among the gifted children of commissioned officers. She talks on and on, insisting that my mother take steps to have me removed from the class. I hear all this as I stand beside the shopping cart. I hear, and to this day I remember, every word.

*It is 1965.* I am a sophomore at the public high school in the small, conservative South Jersey town where my parents have retired. My father's Air Force pension is small, not enough for the family to live on. He is permanently unemployed, a man in his late forties with a high school education and an inclination to overdo the vodka. My mother manages the florist's shop on Main Street. I endure an obligatory annual conference with my guidance counselor, a well-dressed, middle-aged woman who wears her hair in a matronly bun. She asks if I have thought about my future. I have a hard time thinking about what might happen in the next hour, but I make up a plan on the spot: I say that I want to go to Mount Holyoke and study French and Russian. Someday, I say, I want to be an interpreter at the United Nations. The counselor is surprised. She coughs gently and then suggests that perhaps I am "aiming too high," because "girls like me" should be thinking about getting married, not about college or careers. Typing and shorthand would be more "realistic" than college, "given where I come from." She does not say "the wrong side of the tracks." She does not need to.

*It is 1966.* My U.S. history teacher, who also coaches junior varsity football, often asks me to remain after class. He puts his arm around my shoulder, not sexually but in an avuncular manner. He is fond of me, he says. He cautions me, repeatedly, that it's not good for an attractive girl like me to be such a "brain." He warns me that if I am "too intellectual" I'll have trouble getting a boyfriend. He tells me that I should make more of an effort "to act normal." I take this advice very seriously. I shut up in class; I experiment with lipstick; I read *Seventeen* magazine the way born-again Christians study the Bible. I cannot fathom what it is that "normal" girls know that I do not. I only know that I am doing something terribly wrong; I know I am not normal.

*It is 1980.* I live in Cambridge, Massachusetts, at the dawn of the Reagan era. Seven years have gone by since the day when, in a fit of despair, I enrolled at a state college in New Jersey under open admissions. I had worked as a secretary for five years and felt as if my life were rapidly approaching a dead end. I sailed through a bachelor's degree in three years, with honors, and went on to complete a master's in education at Harvard. Now, loath to leave Cambridge, I'm working as a paraprofessional on the radical fringe of Boston's legal community—buying time, really, before going on with graduate school. My study group is groping toward an understanding of the impact that the turn to the right the nation seems to be taking will have on social movements for liberation. One evening the group meets at my apartment; afterward, a few friends remain to chat informally. We gravitate toward the kitchen, where photographs litter the table, family pictures taken at holiday gatherings in my childhood. A friend shrills, "Beth! You weren't kidding about being working class!" as she riffles through the pile of photos, gazing at some of my uncles in their undershirts, the overflowing ashtrays and quart bottles of Schlitz on my grandmother's kitchen table. I am flabbergasted; I have been trying, to no avail, to get a discussion of class issues on the group's agenda for months. Why would I kid about where I come from? I stare back at my friend in mute wonder. She replies, with a laugh, "I always thought you were born with a silver bookmark in your mouth." Everyone joins the laughter, but somehow I cannot. I do not take the joke; I do not want to. Then or now.

Why tell these tales, why show these snapshots? My purpose here is simple. I want to situate myself—and this project—within the constellation of collective memories, social structures, and institutional contexts where power and privilege take form, find cultural expression, or impact upon our ability to conceptualize "the political." As Marilyn Frye put it, "One cannot create anything new without knowing oneself well as a participant in the political and semantic order one would undermine, abandon, displace, or dismantle."[1] I write as a white, working-class woman who, as bell hooks would put it, "advocates feminism."[2] I also write as an academic who came late to the academy, as a nontraditional student, as one of a small handful of first-generation college graduates in a large extended family, and as the only member of that family to earn advanced degrees. I write as someone who has struggled to hold on to socialist and feminist political ideals over the decade or more when these were hardly in fashion.

Even when I ought, perhaps, to have felt welcome in higher education, even when people and institutions went out of their way to offer friendship or grants and fellowships, an acute sense of not-belonging has always lurked at the edges of my consciousness. Even when I refused to admit it, let alone show it, I have lived with the fear that at some point my unworthiness as an unwelcome other might surface, proving to those who sat in judgment on me or my work that their favorable estimations were misplaced, mistaken, or just plain wrong. I offer this not as special pleading but as testimony to how the question of entitlement, of feeling like *we*, not *they*, is framed in the United States today by a broad spectrum of privilege, particularly with regard to education. I am a survivor, a skilled navigator of this system, but I will never partake fully of the powerful draughts it has to offer.

This knowledge exposes a paradox: On the one hand, education has been looked on by many in the United States as a key to both upward mobility and the creation of civic consciousness, the collective entitlement of a democratic polity. On the other hand, our educational system, with its vast complex of institutions and practices, has often served to circumscribe choice and replicate class distinctions along lines of economic power and privilege. My experiences, subjective as they may have been or remain in the retelling, are hardly unique in this regard. Although I may be luckier than many in some respects, having been able to capitalize on a few intellectual talents and writing skills in ways the meritocracy rewards, I will always be acutely aware of what might have been, or *not* been, had I heeded my high school guidance counselor and history teacher, or had my mother paid attention to the complaints of my classmate's mother so many years ago.

The social and political tensions that surround education form the locus of public knowledge in the context of democracy. Indeed, the past decade has witnessed a series of debates over the form and content of education at all levels, from preschool and primary programs to the nation's elite universities. At stake in all this are issues that strike at the very heart of any democratic politics: equality, freedom, and choice. The complaints levied against schooling in the United States from a variety of ideological and positional perspectives, despite their vast array of difference, share a common concern that, in many respects, our educational system is failing. Schools *can* be places where young people learn to think critically, cooperate with one another, and develop into creative citizens capable of participating in a democratic society. But all too often—especially when the schools in question are urban, public institutions—they are not. The picture that emerges from even the most cursory look at education in this country is at best bleak, if not entirely hopeless.

*Why bother,* one might well wonder. Movements aimed at privatizing public schools or promoting private education through the adoption of state-funded voucher systems of subsidies provide one set of responses. Simply opting out of public schooling is another path taken by those who can afford to do so. Such responses, however, are disturbing demonstrations of the power of private capitalist relations to co-opt democracy and public process. Today, the long-standing American tradition of freely available public education, which is accessible without restriction—however flawed this tradition may have been throughout history and however problematic it may be at the present—is in serious jeopardy. The rhetoric of twelve years of conservative ascendancy during the Reagan and Bush administrations may have dulled somewhat in the wake of the 1992 elections, but the serious structural economic constraints of a decade or more of inertia (described in detail in Chapter 1) still remain. A growing polarization of rich and poor continues to stratify education, from the most elementary levels on up, along racial, ethnic, and economic lines.

In what follows, I argue against "opting out" of public education and for "opting in." The very forms of public knowledge central to democratic politics are only available within a thoroughly public and democratic educational process that is relentlessly egalitarian and universally available. Corollary to this is the concept of the public sphere as a place where the discourse surrounding education and other political issues takes place. A detailed exploration of the concept of public knowledge and its consequences will be undertaken in the first and subsequent chapters of this book; suffice it to say here that public knowledge, broadly construed, entails whatever people need to know in order to exercise their rights fully and fulfill their responsibilities as citizens within a democratic polity.

In exploring the relationship between public knowledge, education, and democracy, I look to the socialist theoretical tradition. This stance is not in fashion at the present—if indeed it ever had much real currency in mainstream political or educational theory and practice in the United States. Certainly, in the wake of recent international events—the breakup of the Soviet Union, the resurgence of nationalist movements in Europe and at home, the emergence of a new world order dominated by multinational corporate interests like Exxon and PepsiCo—it has become more difficult to forward socialist ideas or imagine the implementation of political reforms based on these concepts. However, I will argue that a reorganization of education and reconstruction of public knowledge in accord with the richly democratic heritage of socialist thought would foster both political democracy and enhanced educational possibilities in this country. A fresh look at this neglected heritage is not only necessary today but critical to the success of such a project. I explore these relationships in some detail in Chapter 1, "Education, Democracy, and Public Knowledge: Toward a Socialist Theory of Education."

Although I argue against the nationalist vision throughout this work, contending that any program of study or reform that is restricted to local issues, standards, or history limits freedom's potential precisely to the extent that it denies the cosmopolitan reality of human experience, I realize that any discussion of education must start from some notion of community.[3] The specifically *American* aspects of this project are developed in Chapter 2, "*The Education of Henry Adams* and the Transformation of the Bourgeois Public Sphere: A Case Study." In this chapter, I discuss Adams's autobiography in terms of Jürgen Habermas's analysis of the structural transformation of the bourgeois public sphere in late capitalism.[4]

Adams's *Education* is also an exegesis of the notion of education as a lifelong process of growth, through which individuals learn how to participate in active self-government. The book thus anticipates many of the ideas developed by John Dewey in his work on public philosophy and democratic education.[5] Adams was as pessimistic about the possibility of democracy as Dewey was optimistic. Habermas's category of the public sphere allows us to place both Adams and Dewey in a context of historical and economic development. Adams was unable to consider socialism as a viable alternative to the political corruption he saw around him. I argue, *against* Adams but *with* Habermas, that the democratic possibilities inherent in the socialist tradition open up an emancipatory vision of public knowledge that can serve as the basis for critical analysis—and reform—of educational and political practice.

John Dewey's work is the primary focus of Chapter 3, "A Public Philosophy? Pragmatism and Public Knowledge." Here, I discuss how pragmatism has captured American minds with its appeal to "can-do" spirit and the rhetoric of popular democracy. I will briefly treat Charles Sanders Peirce and Williams James, along with Dewey, in analyzing how pragmatism—which purports to be founded on public knowledge—actually militates against establishing actively democratic discourse in a pluralist society. I will also address the way in which pragmatism, primarily as a result of Dewey's influence, has served as a dominant paradigm in American educational theory throughout the past century.

That pragmatism has influenced American educational thought so deeply for so long is hardly surprising, for this philosophy promotes democracy rhetorically while evading a structural critique of capitalism. The effect of this one-sided approach is to further the economic metaphor's dominion over the body politic. A socialist theory of education will not only incorporate the democratic elements of pragmatism but also surmount its antidemocratic and relativistic tendencies, thus opening up a reconsideration of what is valuable in Dewey's pedagogy and philosophy and the prospects for articulating democracy as a way of life both in and out of school.

Dewey's concern for democracy as a way of life sets the stage for a discussion, in Chapter 4 of "Public Knowledge and the Paradox of Democratic Education." On the one hand, educational institutions play an important part in protecting and maintaining existing cultural arrangements and social hierarchies in modern America. Schools socialize the young; the process generally entails inculcating passive consent to the social, political, and economic structures of late capitalism, many of which are fundamentally antidemocratic. On the other hand, schools have traditionally been among the most democratically permeable of our institutions. More people have access to schools than to any other public institutions; schools thus represent significant spaces where critical thinking can be developed (and where autonomous public spheres may be created or expanded).[6] Schooling in America today encapsulates the fundamental contradictions of capitalist democracy and expresses them in an ongoing struggle between the conservative socialization demands of a capitalist economy and the emancipatory promise of institutionalized access to knowledge, with all its implied power.

Recently, these tensions received nationwide attention when debates over the college curriculum became headline news, with hard lines drawn between those who promote the classics and those who favor including contemporary issues and works challenging the Western tradition. This conflict over the content of higher education summarizes what is at stake in any attempt to reconstitute democracy in the public sphere. In this context, debates about democracy by new communitarians like Benjamin Barber and Michael Walzer, on the one hand, and neo-Kantians like John Rawls and Amy Gutmann, on the other, appear as problematic. Both sides fail to theorize the public as the critical conceptual foundation of democratic theory and education; each assumes that the necessary public spaces *do* or *must* exist, without assessing critical historical developments to the contrary. Unlike either the new communitarian or the neo-Kantian analyses, socialist theory posits a public knowledge grounded in collective history and predicated on the active, critical participation central to democratic practices. It thus opens up the current battles over the canon to criticism and scrutiny from the standpoint of unity expressed in the class ideal of politics.

A new conceptualization of public knowledge founded on informed participation also demands attention to the role of intellectuals in society. In Chapter 5, "Public Intellectuals and Public Knowledge," I will examine the changing role of intellectuals in relation to the public. In response to the dramatic changes of the 1960s this subject has, in recent years, generated narratives of decline that have come from both ends of the political spectrum. Curiously, the proposition that intellectuals no longer exist has become central to arguments on both sides.[7] On the left, one representative obituary is Russell Jacoby's *The Last Intellectuals: American Culture in the Age of Academe*. As one critic put it, Jacoby "condemns ... the left's absorption by academization, specialization, and professionalization, which robs intellectuals of the public role and the oppositional force that had defined them."[8] The grounding of intellectuals in universities is thus seen as a betrayal (at worst) or a compromise (at best) of the intellectual's public autonomy, which, once upon a time, held rich critical and political possibility.

Such narratives of decline have more to do with mythic notions of an intellectual golden age, varying in timing and substance, than they do with historical fact. Universities have, traditionally, been more open to democratic practice than many other institutions of capitalist democracy because they are not directly linked to the profit-based economic structures of capital.[9] They thus represent a public network within which critical discourse may flourish. It has, after all, been within the universities that discussions of leftist theory and practice, feminist issues, and race have flourished in recent years. In addition, the tradition of academic freedom at least nominally ensures spaces within which a genuinely critical discourse can be realized.[10] At the same time, the contemporary debates over the canon would be radically recast along the lines of democratic accountability.

Partisans on either side of these debates rely on a central notion of literacy as the vehicle of empowerment—or privilege. In Chapter 6, "Literacy for What? Critical Literacy and the Power of Public Knowledge," I will examine how changing conceptualizations of literacy have historically been linked to social, economic, and political needs. Contemporary literacy theories have provided very different visions of how this linkage comes about, and equally varied projections for emancipatory outcomes.[11] However, the question that most leave unanswered is "Literacy for what?" This question is central to the discourse of the Critical Pedagogy movement, which represents attempts by educational researchers to theorize and operationalize pedagogical challenges to oppressive social formations.[12]

In Chapter 6, I will argue that literacy is a tool for exposing the speculative or reflexive moment in education. If democratic education is to be founded on the extension of choice, then critical literacy is essential as the *process* of discovering, communicating, and implementing such choices. This involves much more than the discrete tasks of reading comprehension as presently taught or the skills of computer literacy or scientific reasoning. For example, critical literacy calls for a sophisticated understanding and use of reflexivity. If public knowledge is predicated on expanding the emancipatory potential of education, then literacy becomes *the* essential skill by which people gain access to such knowledge.

In Chapter 7, "Framing the Question of Freedom: Public Knowledge in Practice," I will discuss how this concept of critical literacy with a positive intent can be incorporated into a concept of education organized around democratic standards that further the ideals of emancipation and free imagination for all. "Public knowledge" is thus defined as constituting *both* knowledge of historical traditions and the capacity to justify them rationally. This capacity can derive only from concrete experience; for example, high schoolers should study Shakespeare and calculus *alongside* practical trades like plumbing and carpentry. They need not be forced into hopelessly dichotomized academic or vocational tracks where no learning can have much meaning. Critical literacy in this context becomes both a tool for comprehending social reality and a vehicle for protesting stupidity. From this partisan standpoint, it becomes possible to attack the elements of existing culture that inhibit the extension of democracy and to posit new cultural values affirming Enlightenment ideals of freedom, equality, and internationalism within a public sphere of democratic participation.

A socialist theory of education, founded on public knowledge to promote and further the promise of democracy, thus points in the direction of answers to the question Stephen Bronner raised when I began this book. For a number of reasons, I was reluctant to think in terms of the education I should have received, but in the course of thinking and writing about the problems of contemporary education I have come to realize that there is a very simple answer to Bronner's question. The education I should have had, but didn't, would be neither more nor less than the education that ought to be freely and equally available to everyone. It would be one in which class and other ascriptive difference simply would not matter. It would be an education where real choices would be open to all students at all levels. No guidance counselor would advise against high aspirations, and no history teacher would steer a bright young person away from intellectual challenges and appreciation of the life of the mind. In this educational environment, nobody would need to assume that just because a person reads and thinks, or writes and speaks articulately, she must have "been born with a silver bookmark in her mouth." Public knowledge would be a resource to be shared, not a rare commodity to be portioned out to a privileged elite, not a blunt instrument to be wielded by the few against the interests of the many—nationally or globally.

Yes, this is a utopian vision. This much, at least, I share with those old socialists who envisioned a world where needs would be met and abilities rewarded in accord with the betterment of all rather than the enrichment of some. I acknowledge the incipient foolhardiness of such idealism in a cynical, greedy, and violent age. Adrienne Rich's acknowledgment, "Time wears us old utopians," has resonated throughout the several years I have spent with this project.[13] But promises forwarded by ideas like autonomy, liberty, equality, and solidarity have yet to be kept. For those of us who refuse to give up on democracy or education in tough times, public knowledge might serve in some measure to fulfill these unmet, but still worthy, ideals. The stakes are high, but the payoff would be even higher: With meaningful educational reform, Americans—and their children—may yet be able to shake off ignorance, take wing, and fly to heaven.

# 1

## Education, Democracy, and Public Knowledge: Toward a Socialist Theory of Education

It was just a brief segment on the six o'clock news one evening in June—a human interest story, a bit of fluff about kindergarten graduation at a Harlem primary school. The camera played over the scrubbed faces of African American and Hispanic children, all lovingly dressed in their best. The kids were adorable; there was no mistaking the pride on their parents' and teachers' faces. The moment held great hope. With any luck, this would be but the first step on an educational journey leading to the American dream of upward mobility. A good life, yes, with success the fruit of hard work—it could all begin here. When questioned by a reporter, parents echoed these sentiments in a variety of accents. Their children were special; today's kindergartners would become high school graduates in the magical year 2000.

While the camera panned, taking a final shot of the children assembled on stage, a sonorous voice-over noted two alarming facts. At least 30 percent, and up to 50 percent, of these bright-eyed youngsters would *never* graduate from high school. Yet according to projections, by the year 2000 more than 90 percent of jobs open to Americans will require at *least* a high school education. The contrast between education's social promise of upward mobility and the polarization of future job opportunities—with low-paying service positions in fast food and clerical operations at the bottom of the pyramid and high-tech, high-salaried positions open to people with graduate degrees in business and engineering at its apex—could hardly be drawn more acutely. Nor could the basic and long-standing American belief in public education as a vehicle for both supporting and extending democracy have been more strikingly expressed.

From the earliest days of the republic, Americans have taken a great deal of pride in the expression of liberal attitudes toward literacy and education, often with connotations of liberation attached. In 1790, Noah Webster exhorted citizens of the newly created United States to

> unshackle your minds and act like independent beings. You have been children
> long enough, subject to the control and subservient to the interest of a haughty
> parent. You have now an interest of your own to augment and defend: you have
> an empire to raise and support. ... To effect these great objects, it is necessary to
> frame a liberal plan of policy and to build it on a broad system of education.[1]

During the nineteenth century, Americans developed a system of public education common to all, established to disseminate literacy and knowledge and to promote the freedoms upheld in the American Constitution. The process of extending compulsory public schooling was characterized by unevenness and instability, reflecting the fundamental ambivalence of the common school movement, in which conservative motives such as limiting the power of "the mob" and preventing popular anarchy coexisted—and were often confused—with democratic ideals of freedom, equality, and rights.[2] Yet the nineteenth-century movement to establish common schooling and encourage development of broadly based literacy left a profound political legacy, perhaps best summarized by the motto of a stamp the U.S. Postal Service issued a few years ago: "The ability to write. The root of democracy."[3]

The complex set of meanings at work here is, in fact, deeply embedded in the Western cultural tradition. "Knowledge itself is power," philosopher Francis Bacon declared, echoing the biblical proverb, "A wise man is strong; yea, a man of knowledge increaseth strength." Today, these poetic sentiments are often expressed in the pithy statement, "Knowledge is power."[4] Whether knowledge concerns esoteric or arcane wisdom, folk tales, myths, and medicines, practical or highly refined technologies, or merely the hottest new gossip, history and common sense provide infinite examples of how people "in the know" can command powers the ignorant cannot.

Thomas Jefferson's preamble to his "Bill for the More General Diffusion of Knowledge" (1779) eloquently summarizes the critical relationship between education and the power of a citizenry possessed of an acute historical awareness:

> Whereas it appeareth that however certain forms of government are better cal-
> culated than others to protect individuals in the free exercise of their natural
> rights, and are at the same time themselves better guarded against degeneracy,
> yet experience hath shewn, that even under the best forms, those entrusted with
> power have, in time, and by slow operations, perverted it into tyranny; and it is
> believed that the most effectual means of preventing this would be, to illumi-
> nate, as far as practicable, the minds of the people at large, and more especially
> to give them knowledge of those facts, which history exhibiteth, that, possessed
> thereby of the experience of other ages and countries, they may be enabled to

know ambition under all its shapes, and prompt to exert their natural powers to defeat its purposes.[5]

Jefferson's suggestion that knowledge of history enables individuals to not only participate in democracy but also defend against threats to it relies heavily upon the Enlightenment ideals of human possibility enacted through reason, liberty, equality, and communality. It also foreshadows Jürgen Habermas's analysis of how a bourgeois public sphere of rational-critical debate emerged in Europe during a period roughly corresponding to Jefferson's lifetime.[6]

The eighteenth-century philosophers who envisioned an Empire of Reason lived and worked in a world shaped by social forces far removed from those we know today. They stood at the beginning of a process "in which the state-governed public sphere was appropriated by the public of private people making use of their reason and was established as a sphere of criticism of public authority." As Habermas described it, this takeover entailed "functionally converting the public sphere in the world of letters already equipped with institutions of the public and with forums for discussion."[7] Habermas's analysis of how this bourgeois public sphere has collapsed under the structural transformations of late capitalism is central to my argument and will be discussed in detail in Chapter 2. For now, his analysis serves to locate Jefferson's rhetoric in a larger context of history and to call attention to some of the contradictions that emerge from the social relations currently shaping the context of public education in America.

Sheldon Wolin addressed these contradictions in terms of collective American experience. Since the revolutionary movements of the eighteenth century, political theories have referred to "the body politic" as a metaphor for the popular sovereignty that is central to democracy. Wolin suggested that two "bodies politic" have existed throughout much of American political history, each with a distinct conception "of collective identity, of power, and of the terms of power." On the one hand, the traditional body politic comprises politically active citizens who, together, determine democratically the course of national, state, and local governments. On the other hand, the "political economy," essentially and intentionally undemocratic, has all but eclipsed the power and autonomy of the traditional body politic.[8]

Wolin went on to argue that the profoundly participatory, democratic, and egalitarian conception of the body politic was grounded in the philosophy of the Enlightenment, with its political agenda best summarized by the Declaration of Independence. However, the emancipatory goals expressed in that document were severely curtailed by an alternative vision of collectivity and power, which found its expression in the Constitution. The emphasis on representation and a strong centralized government in that document served to depoliticize and formalize democracy. Ultimately, the antidemocratic and antipolitical thrust of the constitutional body politic would mesh with a complex, integrated economy founded on concentrated corporate wealth held by a relatively small number of firms to form today's political economy.[9] Consumer goods and an expanding job market took primacy over political values like equality, participation, and popular sovereignty. People stopped caring about politics and let civic involvements languish to the point that today fewer than half of those eligible to vote in national elections actually do so.[10]

Wolin's descriptions of the body politic and the political economy bear directly upon tensions currently existing between capitalist democracy and public education. Although education is not reducible to politics, in a democracy no political life is possible without a solid theory of education and an abiding commitment to the implementation and maintenance of practices informed by democratic ideals. Sophisticated theoretical arguments are not necessary to show that democracy, which rests on equal political rights and the consent and participation of those governed, *requires* an educated citizenry. Or, as George Washington put it in his Farewell Address: "In proportion as the structure of a government gives force to public opinion, it is essential that public opinion should be enlightened."[11]

But the question of just how enlightened public opinion is, or can be, in late capitalism must be addressed. Men like Washington, who envisioned a republic of educated citizens as the best check on abuses of political power, took the limited democratic impulses of the early bourgeois public sphere for granted. They could hardly have foreseen how historical developments attendant upon industrialization and the global entrenchment of sophisticated forms of capitalist development would impact social and political relationships over the next two hundred years; their eighteenth-century vision excluded consideration of such matters, just as it excluded the propertyless, women, and slaves from democracy. It is as necessary today to address the complex and troubled relationship between capital and democratic enlightenment as it is to consider equally problematic questions of how to extend the democratic promise to previously excluded groups.[12]

The very term "capitalist democracy" is itself fraught with complex meanings. Joshua Cohen and Joel Rogers cautioned against giving undue weight to either component—"capital" *or* "democracy"—by itself. The two complement each other and reflect how privatized labor markets, control of investments, and property coexist uneasily with democratic public institutions such as political parties and regular elections. Thus,

> capitalist democracy is not a system in which a capitalist economy persists alongside a democratic political system, each unaffected by the other. Nor is it a system in which capitalism and democracy are only temporarily joined in an unstable structure of inner antagonism, each striving to forsake the other. Capital-

ist democracy is neither just capitalism, nor just democracy, nor just some combination of the two that does not change its component parts. Indeed even to think of such separate "parts" is to miss the vital integrity of the system.[13]

According to Cohen and Rogers's characterization, capitalist democracy is dynamic and open to change; although each component is vital to the system's integrity, the internal contradictions between them are inextricably linked to current political and educational dilemmas.

The tensions that emerge from structural contradictions between the private property, labor markets, and control of investment decisions basic to capitalist accumulation and the formalized rituals of democratic politics in the United States today are also reflected in the rhetoric surrounding the ongoing education crisis. Here the Left has been very much on the defensive in the wake of Reagan-Bush cutbacks and the anti-intellectual flavor of a new public philosophy articulated by right-wing ideologues.[14] Throughout the past decade, there has been no shortage of rhetoric in the debates over education. As one well-publicized study put it, "Never before in recent history have the public schools been subjected to such savage criticism for failing to meet the nation's educational needs."[15]

Indeed, there is a vocal and growing movement to *privatize* public education in some parts of the country.[16] The dismaying fact is that, especially in the nation's urban areas, public schools are often dreadful places that seem more like prisons than places where young minds can be nurtured and grow. Deteriorating physical plants, dirt, and disrepair; demoralized, underpaid teachers; and pervasive threats and incidents of violence foster a bleak despair that is only occasionally penetrated by dedicated or brilliant individuals.[17] Those parents who can afford to do so quite understandably opt out of such schools for their children, whereas those who cannot are left to suffer the consequences. The situation for those who try to learn or teach effectively in many of the nation's public schools is pretty grim.

Nevertheless, much of the sound and fury emanating from all sides of the current debates simply misses the point. In 1990, conservative political analyst Kevin Phillips made headlines when he documented what critics on the left had been saying for over a decade: Throughout the 1980s and into the 1990s, government policies favoring capital have created an unprecedented level of class polarization in this country, characterized by a widening gap between the elite (where capital, education, and skills are concentrated) and the increasingly impoverished masses.[18] Over the past decade, the middle class has splintered; depending on their jobs, how much (if any) real estate they owned, and their skills or level of education, some people moved up, but many fell into the working poor and suffered from the decimation of social support programs undertaken by the Reagan and Bush administrations. A few statistics make this situation concrete:

By 1986, America's top 420,000 families accounted for almost 27 percent of the nation's wealth. And the top 10 percent of U.S. households controlled 68 percent of the wealth.

In terms of income, the Congressional Budget Office has reported that, from 1977 to 1987, the average family income of the top 10 percent increased from $70,459 to $89,783—up 24.4 percent. The incomes of the top 1.0 percent, which were "only" $174,498 in 1977, grew a whopping 74.2 percent, to $303,900 per year.

Meanwhile, during the same period, the average after-tax family income of the lowest 10 percent of Americans fell some 10.5 percent, from $3,528 a year to $3,157 a year. ... By some calculations, after-tax 1987 median family incomes—around $20,000 (which could hardly be counted as middle-class in a place like Los Angeles), were significantly below those of the late 1970s. For all workers, white- and blue-collar alike, the real average weekly wage—calculated in constant 1977 dollars—fell from $191.41 a week in 1972 to $171.07 in 1986.[19]

The rich got richer and paid less in taxes while the middle class, for the most part, made less money and paid more taxes; as could be expected, the poor got poorer—and their numbers increased. This economic transformation has created a large population of working poor, who struggle to get by on the $5-an-hour service jobs that have replaced $23-an-hour jobs in the manufacturing sector. Nearly 12 million American workers lost their jobs because of plant shutdowns or relocations between 1979 and 1984 alone. Only 60 percent succeeded in finding new jobs, and nearly half of these paid less than the workers' previous jobs. Laid-off steelworkers in Chicago, for example, saw their incomes fall by an average of 50 percent, from $22,000 a year to $12,500 a year, just slightly above the official poverty level.[20]

Class polarization was reflected not only in shrinking pay envelopes but in the voting booths as well. As Jim Hightower, the populist Texas agriculture commissioner, put it in 1988: "The greatest number of electoral drop-outs are people making less than $25,000 a year. It doesn't take a degree in sociology to figure out that these people are telling us they don't see much improvement in their lives from the economic policies of either major party."[21]

Phillips was equally blunt when he referred to the wealthy as "*the* power bloc of the 1980s." Only 53 percent of those eligible to vote did so in 1984; that number shrank to 50 percent four years later, as "the actual lever-pulling electorate" became "disproportionately Buick-owning and Book-of-the-Month Club." Whereas the voting rate was 25 percent in the South Bronx, it was 75 percent in Pacific Palisades.[22] Walter Dean Burnham gave his interpretation of these voting statistics a different twist, remarking that nonvoters had become America's fastest-growing party.[23] Phillips noted the logic—and irony—operating here: "The more politics disillusioned those Americans whose status was in decline (or had never risen), the more they gave up, leaving ballot-box decisions to those profiting from the ongoing rearrangement of American affluence."[24]

These diverse observations—along with the political realities they reflect—provide trenchant commentary on one dimension of the internal contradictions of capitalist democracy. They demonstrate the extent to which private capital has successfully co-opted a putatively public and formally democratic political process. In effect, the past decade has defined American politics as a systematic extension of privilege to those whose interests were already disproportionately advantaged—and a systematic denial of opportunity and choice to everyone else. Economic polarization has been accompanied, of course, by political cynicism or despair.[25]

All of these trends have impacted or been mirrored by corresponding tensions in the educational sphere. Once again, numbers provide a point of entry. Twenty percent of high school students drop out annually—this translates to between 600,000 and 700,000 individuals.[26] For inner-city students, the figure rises to 50 percent.[27] By the year 2000, a third of the jobs available in the United States will require—as they do not at present—a college education. Nearly all jobs will require the high school diploma.[28] Although the good news in this respect is that 91.1 percent of the women and 86.5 percent of the men presently in the U.S. labor force graduated from high school, the bad news is that when college graduation becomes the standard, the percentages of those achieving the standard drop to 26.2 percent and 25.2 percent, respectively.[29]

In the fifteen years between 1975 and 1990, the gap in wages between white-collar professionals and skilled tradespeople rose spectacularly from 2 percent to 37 percent. During the same period, the differential for professionals and clerical workers nearly doubled, rising from 47 percent to 86 percent.[30] By 1987, male high school graduates who had from one to five years of work experience were earning 18 percent less than their counterparts had in 1979.[31] Real wages for young black men declined by 22 percent between 1979 and 1987; for young white men, the rate was 10 percent during the same period.[32] An estimated 27 million Americans lack basic literacy skills, and between 45 and 50 million Americans are functionally illiterate; they cannot read well enough to perform effectively in the workplace.[33]

In the next decade, a third of the currently existing jobs that require the high school diploma will have their minimal requirement shifted up a notch, meaning that applicants will have to possess the bachelor's degree. Yet college costs are rising simultaneously with federal and state cuts in aid to higher education; even the most talented middle-class students are losing the chance to attend private universities. In 1985 for a family with earnings equal to the median national income, keeping a child in a four-year private college or university would have taken 40 percent of that income, up from 30 percent in 1970.[34] At the start of the 1980s, on the average, it cost 2.4 times more to attend a private university than a public university; by 1989, the differential had increased to 2.8.[35] With costs spiraling upward, concurrent reductions in state and federal financial aid for middle-class and poor college students spelled real disaster. At private colleges in 1981, the average aid grant was 33.5 percent of total costs. That figure dropped to 20.9 percent by 1989. This removal of private higher education from the grasp of all but the wealthy threatens cultural unity by polarizing educational possibilities on the basis of social class.[36]

For the United States, with its long-standing tradition of compulsory, freely available public education for all, this situation becomes even more dismal in light of international comparisons. A 1990 study found the United States leading other industrialized nations, with 5.1 percent of its population enrolled in higher education; Sweden (2.6 percent), West Germany (2.5 percent), and Japan (1.9 percent) followed.[37] Another survey, however, found that only 5 percent of U.S. high school graduates were ready for college, whereas between 17 and 24 percent of students who graduated from high school in the United Kingdom, Germany, and France were prepared.[38] Even allowing for different patterns of secondary education, it seems clear that substantial college and university enrollments do not necessarily reflect high educational quality. The distance between the United States and other industrialized countries may also reflect American reluctance to commit economic resources to education. In terms of percentage of gross national product (GNP) expended annually on grades kindergarten through twelve, Sweden is far ahead of the rest, with 7.0 percent, followed by Japan (4.8 percent), West Germany (4.6 percent), and finally the United States, with only 4.1 percent of GNP going for education. Although it is reasonable to suggest that resource commitment alone does not tell the whole story, given the thrust of the data presented in previous paragraphs, it is hard to argue that U.S. schools are doing better with less. On the contrary—given the extent to which the market metaphor dominates social thought, it would appear that Americans are getting what they pay for.

So the situation is as grim with regard to education as it is with regard to economic and political polarization of social classes. In both cases, quantitative measures breathe life into the contradictions articulated by theory. For educational questions, this situation is pernicious. On the one hand, we have a rhetoric that links public education with civic culture and political democracy at the most fundamental levels; on the other hand, the economic and social practices that shape America's educational systems increasingly militate against democratic education and empowerment for the masses while they privilege the elite few. In education as in politics, the internal contradictions of capitalist democracy are played out—daily, repeatedly, and destructively.

As the gulf between rich and poor has widened in American society, our educational system has become increasingly stratified along racial, ethnic, and economic lines. It is possible to distinguish clearly four levels of differen- tiation in education today: first, an underclass whose members have not graduated (or, in many cases, never attended) high school; second, high school graduates—who, as we have seen, find it difficult to acquire and keep jobs in a workplace that increasingly demands the credential of higher edu- cation; then, middle-class graduates of public colleges and universities; and, finally, privileged students from wealthy families, who have been prepared for leadership through an increasingly expensive and exclusive chain of pri- vate boarding schools, colleges, and universities.[39]

If current trends in immigration and birthrates continue as projected over the next decade, the demographics of race and ethnicity will have a dramatic impact upon already existing racial and/or class forms of economic polariza- tion: The Asian population should grow by about 22 percent, the Hispanic by 21 percent, the African American by nearly 12 percent, and the white by only 2 percent.[40] Here the lines will become even more clearly drawn be- tween well-to-do voters who are preponderantly white and poor nonvoters who are preponderantly nonwhite, who need and are entitled to a serious public commitment to education. Consider, for example, the Asian, His- panic, and African American families whose children make up 85 percent of enrollments in the Los Angeles public school system—or recall the Harlem kindergarten students we saw on the six o'clock news. Think of the Class of 2000.

This brief consideration of some of the contradictions endemic to educa- tion in capitalist democracy illuminates the way in which a clear understand- ing of public knowledge and its consequences has been absent from the de- bates over "excellence" in education, curricular reform, multiculturalism, and the like. Public knowledge as a concept central to democratic education has, in fact, received remarkably little attention from theorists of education or democracy. John Dewey hinted at its importance when he suggested, in *The Public and Its Problems,* that the "prime condition of a democratically organized public is a kind of knowledge and insight which does not yet ex- ist." Dewey looked to "the spirit and method of science" as the means by which this public knowledge could be brought to life, stipulating that one "obvious requirement" for its instantiation would be "freedom of social in- quiry and of distribution of its conclusions."[41] Since Dewey wrote, Clarence J. Karier has forwarded a much more positivistic, but equally sketchy, notion of public knowledge as "that knowledge which all men can obtain if they fol- low the same stated canons of inquiry."[42] Both of these attempts to capture the meaning of this very important concept leave a great deal to be desired.

Public knowledge does, indeed, form the basis of social interactions and provide a foundation for political activity. But it represents neither a static body of literature and lore to be mastered, nor a set of skills requiring devel- opment. It subsumes both historical knowledge of collective cultural traditions and the capacity to justify these traditions rationally, providing the very foundation of democratic empowerment and citizenship. Public knowledge is, moreover, firmly grounded in the belief that education is valuable for its own sake and ought not to be considered worth acquiring for utilitarian purposes alone.

The importance of education as an end in itself—especially where groups or individuals who have been denied access to the knowledge/power nexus are concerned—cannot be underestimated. The argument was nicely summarized in 1849 by a forward-looking women's magazine, which urged its readers to consider that "the first reason for the education of every mind should be its own development. We are too much inclined to urge the enlightenment of women, as a sure means of improving man, rather than as in itself an intrinsic experience, with the conviction that every mind should be educated for its own development."[43] Women, along with African Americans ("free" or enslaved), Native Americans, and members of other racial, religious, and ethnic groups, were generally excluded from both the public sphere and political participation when these words were written. Yet throughout the struggle to extend formal suffrage rights (the least common denominator of democratic practice), which has continued for nearly a century and a half, members of disenfranchised or newly enfranchised groups have seldom lost sight of the crucial connections between having access to enlightenment and developing the ability to express themselves or articulate demands in public.[44]

Public knowledge is, therefore, *both* historical and contemporary; it is consensual and critical; it enables individuals to act into and upon the world. As the foundation of democratic citizenship, it is explicitly political, serving as the baseline for expanding and extending opportunity and choice or checking arbitrary power. Public knowledge entails everything people need to know in order to exercise their rights fully and meet their responsibilities. Kant's development of speculative categories that seek to constrain the arbitrary exercise of power is illuminating here: He forwarded universality, cosmopolitanism, individual responsibility, reciprocity, the discursive notion of truth, and commitment to the rule of law. Marx synthesized these concerns when he spoke of emancipation as predicated on "the free development of each [being] the condition for the free development of all."[45] Thus, the extent to which knowledge—or access to knowledge—is privileged is the extent to which it *cannot* be categorized as public.

Public knowledge can be conceptualized only in tandem with the democratic public spaces, or spheres, within which it is articulated and enacted. Without these, democracy becomes reduced to formal ritual, and citizenship to passive consent to bureaucratic practice. The key question, Education for *what?* is central here, for it crystallizes complex issues. Neither practical questions of democratic process nor public political actions have meaning for most individuals today. As Cohen and Rogers made abundantly clear, hopes for short-term gain have largely eclipsed any sense of long-range national goals or principles. It is thus small wonder that no one can agree on how to "fix" systems of public education—which are by their very nature future oriented.[46] After all, these institutions exist to ensure that the next (and all subsequent) generations will inherit both the survival skills of socialization and the cultural traditions handed down as history's legacy. Because public schools play such a central role in maintaining society and culture, they should receive the best in long-range planning and evoke a vision that extends a generation or more into the future of our children and our polity alike. However, the quick fixes promised by a succession of educational fads, summarized by catchphrases like "back to basics" and "cultural literacy," tend to capture—rhetorically if not always substantively—the flag of reform. At the same time, romantic ideals of democracy enacted by an engaged public continue to color much of the discourse about education and politics. In the breach, expedience reigns.

Part of the difficulty here stems from the fact that individualism is deeply entrenched in American social and political culture. Indeed, the moral and political primacy of the individual over the social has often been presented as the foundation of democracy; private happiness, individual initiative, and personal freedom are highly valued aspects of this ideal. This is neither healthy nor desirable. In *Habits of the Heart,* Robert Bellah and his associates noted the underside of the tilt toward individualism. They suggested that Tocqueville "warned that some aspects of our character—what he was one of the first to call 'individualism'—might eventually isolate Americans from one another and thereby undermine the conditions of freedom." Spurred on by the privatized ethos of capital, individualism has generated competitive, egoistic, and atomized social relations, militating against collectivity and rendering emancipatory education for all a massive social fiction.[47]

Elizabeth Cagan cogently suggested that proposals for radical educational reform have often reflected or retained this American individualism. They may appear to promote pedagogical changes aimed at expanding students' empowerment, autonomy, and self-fulfillment. However, close scrutiny reveals that even the most dramatic of these reforms "have paid little attention to the necessity for purposefully fostering social skills and attitudes that lead to altruism, cooperation, and social responsibility."[48] And thus the crisis deepens.

Despite the gravity of the situation, things may not be entirely hopeless. Historically, Americans have placed great faith in the efficacy of public schools as agents of social change.[49] If schools and their curricula can provide an entry point for reconstructing public spheres of rational discourse that lets students and teachers begin to engage a politics of difference and diversity—as I believe they can—then democracy will be ahead of the game. But for this to happen, educational questions must be recast so that problems and solutions are defined in both local and global terms. The corollary of American faith in schools as agents of change has been a long-standing tradition of local autonomy. In recent decades, however, this has fostered an entrenched provincialism of "neighborhoods" that are sharply demarcated by class, racial, or ethnic boundaries. As Jonathan Kozol's *Savage Inequalities* eloquently demonstrates, local autonomy and neighborhood control serve primarily to enforce de facto racial segregation four decades after racially segregated schools were ruled unconstitutional by the Supreme Court in *Brown*.[50] Yet this is not the only direction in which educational vision must be redirected from its present course, for the "public" in "public knowledge" no longer connotes the face-to-face world of the Athenian *polis*, or the comfort Rousseau found in his (real or imaginary) Republic of Geneva, or the direct democratic interplay of a New England town meeting.[51] Today it is simply foolish to imagine any public, whether of a city, state, or nation, as an entity unto itself, in isolation.

Furthermore, the statistics cited earlier in this chapter clearly suggest the need for a *class* perspective on education. They provide an empirical point of reference for progressive social change grounded in socialist theory and practice. Socialist thought, although currently in disrepute, has nevertheless consistently forwarded an ideal of unity based on extending the democratic promises of the bourgeois revolutions to workers and other previously excluded groups. Its democratic heritage locates the individual within a collectivity, where reasoned communication, human freedom, and purposive action form the basis of self-government that is grounded in public authority exercised without qualification.[52]

The socialist tradition has often been brutally suppressed or distorted in American intellectual life and practical politics alike.[53] Yet especially when interpreted critically, it provides a viable alternative perspective for analyzing public knowledge and the public sphere. Whatever their differences, social and political theorists like Barbara Ehrenreich, Erich Fromm, Herbert Marcuse, Michael Harrington, Raymond Williams, Stephen Eric Bronner, and Ellen Meiksins Wood (to name only a few) have worked to keep this tradition alive, insisting that any political project aimed at extending democracy must incorporate those elements of class-based economic and political equity that were integral to socialism even before Marx. This accommodation calls for not merely tolerating but articulating and understanding the many and various forms of difference that have often been elided theoretically by those who pay lip service to socialist and democratic principles. Thus, ascriptive characteristics such as gender, race, ethnicity, or sexual preference must be theorized as integral to class-based analysis if the aims of equity are to realize their full potential.

A socialist politics of education would also entail reformulating Marx's notion of the proletariat's agency as a revolutionary class. Rosa Luxemburg could, for example, confidently proclaim that "Marxist theory gave to the working class of the whole world a compass by which to fix its tactics from hour to hour in its journey towards the one unchanging goal."[54] Indeed, as the nineteenth century drew to its close, socialism was a viable international mass movement led by an industrial working class with a firm political purpose. Its alternative standpoint and teleology were quite clear. Nineteenth- and early twentieth-century socialists shared a commitment to furthering the heritage of the Enlightenment; they took for granted and shared the values of rationalism, democracy, egalitarianism, and internationalism. They pushed for libraries and called for the publication of inexpensive paperback editions of books; they organized study groups for self-education, establishing a proletarian public sphere for the exchange of ideas and information.[55] They presupposed intimate connections between emancipatory education and civic virtue premised on these values. Linked by the movement, convinced that workers could one day overcome their own oppression, they believed in the promise of a better world where the injustices of the present would be eliminated. Among these injustices could be ranked, implicitly, if not always explicitly, the privileging of public knowledge.

The twentieth century, however, has seen institutionalized injustice, violence, and genocide on a grand scale—including the depredations caused by actually existing socialism; complexity and confusion have colored the global spread of capital. Multinational corporations have engaged in an unprecedented internationalization of production as the whole world was becoming a global factory subject to a new international division of labor. At the same time, capitalism has shown itself to be systemically flexible, open to change when pressured from below and remarkably able to co-opt reform. Under the weight of this history, Marx's teleology has collapsed. Ironically, one of the major legacies of the nineteenth-century socialist movement has been, not socialism, but a more humane, rational, and intelligent capitalism, with limited welfare state reforms ameliorating—at least for the time being— the worst depredations of capital throughout the West.

The power of capital depends on the class division of working people; the success of capitalistic power is measured in the extent to which social and political fragmentation presently describe the limits of democratic possibility. Although it is true that throughout the twentieth century, the state has often been a progressive vehicle for social change in this country, it is equally true that the state only responds to power from below. Lacking a point of unity from which to strive for and express political presence, those who benefit least from the present system of privilege (and who are also systematically refused access to public knowledge) will be unable to advance the progressive moment.

Many who claim to be the inheritors of the socialist tradition today seem to have lost sight of the very concepts of radical egalitarianism, democracy, solidarity, and internationalism that formed the core of the early mass movements and shaped their pedagogy of proletarian civic virtue. Michael Harrington drew attention to this state of affairs when he suggested that selective amnesia with regard to the socialist tradition has diluted its meaning and reduced its history to fragments. He condemned not only the way in which Marxist analyses ("often Delphic in their vagueness but always suffused with a sense of history") have often been "turned into historical truths and chiseled in stone" but also their tendency to confuse the antisocialist practices of states that make rhetorical claims to actually existing socialism with the real thing.[56]

Contemporary socialist analysis, however, cannot afford to continue to fall headlong into the futility of an intransigently adversarial stance toward existing institutions. Neither should it lapse into the neo-nihilism of solutions that will only be viable "come the revolution." The question becomes one of utilizing existing social and institutional frameworks to build upon those elements of democratic possibility and hope that already exist—in whatever limited forms—under capital. It is thus simply not enough to *oppose* existing educational institutions; it is necessary to develop, out of the critique, any and all positive moments that may exist within them.[57]

A renewed socialist vision, then, must look both backward to the critical and emancipatory heritage of the nineteenth century and forward to the social, economic, and political realities that will shape the future out of the present day. Freed from the shackles of Marx's teleology, socialism would not only reassert the critical moment but become, to borrow Bronner's term, "unbound." In other words, theory need not necessarily rely on linkages to any specific forms of political organization or constellations of social institutions. It no longer makes sense to theorize the proletariat in terms of class agency and revolutionary change, but it is possible to recast the class interest of workers as an ideal. Thus, an unbound socialism remains premised on the demand that all social, economic, and political issues and contradictions be articulated from the standpoint of the repressed interests of working people.[58] People are enabled to speak and act for freedom from an ethical standpoint of democratic accountability without "the restriction of arbitrary socio-economic or political power."[59]

Within the socialist ethic, everyone must be guaranteed the same formal and substantive chances to pursue individual choice; particular interests neither require that universals be abolished nor demand that the universal and the particular maintain an adversarial relationship. Instead, "It is precisely the commitment to the universal rather than the contingent—the rule of law and civil liberties rather than the immediate habits or customs of a community—which best insures both freedom for the particular and the ability to confront existing prejudices from the perspective of an open future."[60] In other words, individual liberties should, and *can*, be grounded in collectivity through institutional actions to further universal ideals.

The organizing principle here, although stressing unity among those who neither control capital nor facilitate its private appropriation, does not rely on common, empirical interests as the basis of class formation or action. Indeed, it evokes Luxemburg's political and epistemological critique of empiricism: "The ABC's of socialism teach that the socialist order is not some sort of poetic ideal society, thought out in advance, which may be reached by various paths in various more or less imaginative ways. Rather, socialism is simply the historical tendency of the class struggle of the proletariat in the capitalist society against the class rule of the bourgeoisie."[61] Thus, "class" need not describe any aggregate of individuals; for Bronner, it becomes a regulative ideal whose principles—democracy, social equality, and internationalism—are open to discourse and critical scrutiny. The class ideal both incarnates the practical criterion of the socialist project and provides a partisan standpoint from which to establish criteria for judgment.[62] With the articulation of this ideal, teleological certainties are replaced by ethical contingency.

This move is not without some cost; as Bronner indicated, the "socialist ethic cannot offer an infallible way of ensuring a choice for emancipation or practically linking means with ends." There is nothing inevitable about the choices, tactics, and strategies that shape its politics. Since traditional conceptions of the links between theory and practice have been broken, along with the conviction that history was on the side of the working class (and only the working class), it will be impossible to pretend that the socialist ethic can resolve every conceivable problem, whether individual or societal in nature. Socialist democracy here calls, not for a fixed and global set of responses, but merely for the creation of formal and substantive conditions that expand the arena within which people may freely and responsibly make life choices.[63]

Thus, although a socialist ethic should logically insist that educational institutions be open and accessible to all students at all levels, it cannot dictate whether any particular student should attend any particular school or follow any specific course of study. But because the "socialist ethic is ... inherently *public* in character," it would demand the institutional expansion of individual choice and would presuppose that all who participate in education do so out of "the capacity for reflexivity without which critical judgment becomes impossible."[64] Students and teachers alike would be cast as public persons capable of confronting and criticizing their own history. And they would do so by partaking of—and creating—public knowledge.

A socialist theory of education, founded on the premise of public knowledge as an essential component of full and free individual development and democratic politics, would thus represent a significant challenge to the status quo in both arenas. Its *praxis*, defined initially by educational reforms designed to further the creation of autonomous public spheres or to build upon those that may presently exist, calls forth actions that require a great deal of courage and imagination on the part of educators, students, parents—anyone willing to make a commitment to overcoming the limitations of the present.

To say the very least, the task is not an easy one. It demands a vision that steadfastly refuses to lock history into the study of dead yesterdays but links them to the issues raised by contemporary social formations. It requires that constant and careful attention be paid to ideology and human agency as sources of—or impediments to—educational change. And, finally, it calls forth an integration, from many levels, of those specific "voices, desires, events and cultural forms that give meaning and substance to everyday life."[65] In what follows, I will explore some of the dimensions of such a vision and the projects it engenders, focusing on how a socialist reconstruction of public knowledge might expand the horizons of political democracy and educational possibility. I will argue that educational reform is central to any consideration of participatory democracy; only by reconstituting public knowledge as the foundation of expanded educational practices and possibilities for democratic action can we begin to confront the problems of the present day.

# 2

## The Education of Henry Adams
## *and the Transformation of the*
## *Bourgeois Public Sphere:*
## *A Case Study*

"To his life as a whole he was a consenting, contracting party and partner from the moment he was born to the moment he died. Only with that under-standing—as a consciously assenting member in full partnership with the so-ciety of his age—had his education an interest to himself or others." So Henry Adams wrote at the beginning of his autobiography, locating himself firmly within a long-standing Adams family tradition of civic responsibility and public service.[1] From the earliest days of the republic, Adamses had been at the center of democratic politics. Henry's grandfather, John Quincy, and great-grandfather, John, both served as president of the United States. Charles, Henry's father, was elected to the House of Representatives and was Lincoln's appointee as minister to England during the troubled Civil War years.

Henry Adams never held public office; the *Education* may thus be read as documenting his "failure" to uphold a well-established family tradition. On a deeper level, however, the book testifies to the problematic nature of that very tradition in a rapidly changing world. The eighteenth-century ideals of "conscious assent" or "full partnership" in a democratic society had very dif-ferent meanings in his grandfather's day than in the latter half of the nine-teenth century. Adams's autobiography charts the changing shape of public life at the heart of American politics at a time when the democratic principles underlying those politics were being steadily eroded. He bitterly resented and savagely castigated both the politics and the politicians whose actions shaped history during his lifetime.[2]

As Ernest Samuels reminded us in his monumental biography of Adams, the often sardonic exaggerations of the *Education* place it more in the line of

Rousseau's or Augustine's *Confessions* than of factual history.[3] Much as Rousseau retired to tend his garden, Adams, in an age of political corruption, withdrew from the dilemmas of public life to survey the intellectual terrain of the twelfth century in his studies of Mont Saint-Michel and Chartres.[4] His stepping back from his own age, however, does not detract from the *Education*'s value on two important counts. First of all, the book may be read as an exegesis of the notion of education as a life-long process of growth and accommodation to participation in a public sphere of active self-government; it thus provides an excellent introduction to the relationship between education, broadly conceived, and political democracy. In addition, Adams's implicit critique of *capitalist* democracy in the late nineteenth century can serve as the basis for an examination of how the ideals of participatory self-government on which this nation was founded have been limited or contravened in actual political practice.

Adams's critique of capitalism, however, was entirely elitist and negative; he did not follow the path his socialist contemporaries took toward a transformative social vision. He had read Marx extensively. As he put it, however, "Some narrow trait of the New England nature seemed to blight socialism," although "he tried in vain to make himself a convert."[5] Nevertheless, he chronicled how the vital public life of the early republic had degenerated into a ritualized—and very often empty—sort of performance by the scandal-ridden turn of the last century.[6]

Adams described himself as an "eighteenth-century man," who "never could compel himself to care for nineteenth-century style." He had been born to a family whose traditions stressed the power of human reason, exemplifying some of the best of Enlightenment thought: "From cradle to grave this problem of running order through chaos, direction through space, discipline through freedom, unity through multiplicity, has always been, and must always be, the task of education, as it is the moral of religion, philosophy, science, art, politics, and economy."[7] But the world was changing rapidly, almost beyond measure. As a young boy, Adams watched while

> the old universe was thrown into the ash-heap and a new one created. He and his eighteenth-century, troglodytic Boston were suddenly cut apart—separated forever—in act if not in sentiment, by the opening of the Boston and Albany Railroad; the appearance of the first Cunard steamers in the bay; and the telegraphic messages which carried from Baltimore to Washington the news that Henry Clay and James K. Polk were nominated for the Presidency. This was in May, 1844; he was six years old; his new world was ready for use, and only fragments of the old met his eyes.[8]

The shape of political life would also change dramatically during his lifetime. In the face of mounting capitalist consolidation, the public sphere of the "eighteenth-century man" would, by the century's end, be altered almost beyond recognition. Adams limned the relationship between the nascent political economy and the decline of actively democratic discourse. "The work of domestic progress" he ascribed to "masses of mechanical power—steam, electric, furnace, or other." The new machines and the forms of power that ran them could only be controlled by those individuals capable of understanding the technologies involved. This situation had significant political implications, for "internal government" would have to find ways of keeping the newly created technocratic elite, whom Adams described as "socially as remote as heathen gods, alone worth knowing, but never known, and who could tell nothing of political value if one skinned them alive" in line. Otherwise, these new forms of physical energy and the elites who controlled and utilized technologies would entirely prevail, taking over the public sphere, becoming "trustees for the public," since "whenever society assumes the property, it must confer on them that title." For Adams, "Modern politics" would remain, "at bottom, a struggle not of men, but of forces."[9]

Adams analyzed how the decay of domestic politics entailed a shift in the conduct of foreign affairs; American imperialism displayed "the instinct of what might be named McKinleyism; the system of combinations, consolidations, trusts, realized at home and realizable abroad." Here, again, the metaphor is drawn directly from monopoly capital and evokes its alienating power. Confronted with this "system, a student nurtured in ideas of the eighteenth century had nothing to do, and made not the least pretence of meddling."[10] By 1892 the public sphere of democratic discourse had disintegrated. "No one in society seemed to have the ear of anybody in Government. No one in Government knew any reason for consulting any one in society. The world had ceased to be wholly political, but politics had become less social."[11]

Adams responded to this by retreating to the intellectual realm of the Middle Ages. He had no desire either to fight or to join the new forces of industrial capital and technology that were irrevocably altering the political economy. His critique of capital remained implicit; he focused his analysis on the decisive importance of the power of the machine age, best summarized by the image of the giant dynamo exhibited at the World's Columbian Exposition in 1893. Out of this, he believed, the conditions of modernity would be shaped—and not, necessarily, for the better.[12] For all his cavils against Boston's "State Street"—his code words for the worst aspects of bourgeois economism—Adams preferred the individualist worldview of an eighteenth-century mercantilist. Although he had worked as his father's private secretary in London, as a history professor at Harvard, and as a journalist, Henry Adams never needed to earn his living, for both he and his wife, Clover Hooper Adams, enjoyed comfortable private incomes.[13] Thus, he was bound to the values on which his family's fortune had been founded, just as he was bound, in an emotional, if not a practical, sense, to the family tradition of democratic public service. Privatized forms of spectator politics and industrial capital had supplanted both traditions.

Mass media and elites came to dominate what was left of the "public sphere" in this increasingly bureaucratized industrial society. Their effect was detrimental; in the end, Adams could only profess in despair:

> The new forces would educate. History saw few lessons in the past that would be useful for the future; but one, at least, it did see. The attempt of the American of 1800 to educate the American of 1900 had not often been surpassed for folly; and since 1800 the forces and their complications had increased a thousand times or more. The attempt of the American of 1900 to educate the American of 2000, must be even blinder than that of the Congressman of 1800, except so far as he had learned his ignorance.[14]

Adams's *Education* thus represents a significant record of a crucial period of historical change, the issues of which resonate today. His conscious choice of education as the memoir's central metaphor cannot be overemphasized, for it summarizes his struggle to make sense of a world for which he had been utterly unprepared. Simply put, the forms of knowledge necessary to public life in his grandfather's day no longer availed; the "eighteenth-century man" of the republic had no part in "the system of combinations, consolidations, and trusts." Although Adams never used the term, his acute articulation of the shifting nature of what was required for and represented by participation in the public sphere provides an excellent—if implicit—example of what public knowledge is all about.

Adams's treatment of the decay of public life at the center of power in America may be read as a virtual case study of the issues treated by Jürgen Habermas in *The Structural Transformation of the Public Sphere*.[15] In this early (1962) work, Habermas began to address concerns about the future of democracy, which have been central to his thought for three decades, by analyzing the formation and degeneration of the bourgeois public sphere. His model derived from the philosophy and social practice of the Enlightenment, which proceeded unevenly throughout Europe. From the late seventeenth to the early nineteenth century, a public sphere of critical and literary activity constituted itself, distinguished from both the absolutist state and the private realm of nascent bourgeois society. This new public sphere was generated by the specific way in which the *contents* of culture, although not necessarily their distribution, remained apart from the dictates of the marketplace.

In coffeehouses, reading societies, and other public places, people met to discuss the literature and art of the day, articulating a critique of the theory and practice of absolutist domination. Eventually, the expression of public opinion legitimated by rational consensus among relatively equal citizens took on its own political dimension. The bourgeoisie ultimately deployed this new, critical public sphere as a revolutionary instrument of class emancipation. One of its primary goals was to make political and administrative decisions, formerly cloaked in secrecy, open to scrutiny. Another goal of the bourgeoisie was establishment of the rule of law, aimed at promulgating rational and universally binding legal principles. The public sphere, by building opinion in support of such values, served to protect individuals from arbitrary actions on the part of the state, mediating between state and civil society. And the media—newspapers, journals, books—fostered this attitude. New technologies meant that communications were faster, cheaper, and more widely available than ever before, facilitating lively political debate, opposition, and struggle. The bourgeois public sphere may thus be seen as an arena where democratic discourse about common concerns was not only available—at least to a limited extent—but could flourish as well.

Since the late nineteenth century, the initially democratizing aspects of the bourgeois public sphere have been steadily eroding. Around 1870, liberal competitive capitalism began to be eclipsed by the organized monopoly capital of cartels and trusts. At the same time, culture became a commodity consumed as leisure-time entertainment, undermining the rational discourse that had been so important around the turn of the nineteenth century.[16] The state increasingly penetrated the public sphere, "censoring groups and publications that challenged its interests and agenda while operating as an instrument of political indoctrination."[17] This interpretation reflected the growing contradiction between bourgeois political interests and general social interests; social conflict began to be expressed in terms of political demands.

State and society became intermingled as the very foundations of the once relatively autonomous public sphere crumbled. Not only did the state increasingly intervene to resolve social conflicts, but as various "public interest" groups organized to assert their specialized demands and concerns, the function of public opinion as an advocate of the *general* interest disappeared. It was eclipsed by the new advertising industry, which became a central component of mass communication. Advertisers gained an enormous degree of control over the form and content of the media along with manipulative power over a depoliticized public, especially in the wake of the Second World War.[18] With the media increasingly constrained by new restrictions imposed by the state and economic imperatives, the space available to the public sphere became truncated by suburbanization, consumerism, the fascinations of new electronic media, and a decline in book culture. Thus, the public underwent a further transformation as citizens became consumers of media images and events instead of direct participants in political and cultural debates.[19]

Habermas's analysis of the decline and fall of the bourgeois public sphere was not available in English until 1989. Since then, it has been the topic of wide-ranging criticism and debate among social theorists and historians on this side of the Atlantic.[20] A review of the issues raised by critics and defenders of Habermas is beyond the scope of this work, and I do not intend to join the ranks of those who adopt his analysis whole cloth. However, his discussion of the formation of the bourgeois public sphere and its initially democratizing political thrust (which constitutes roughly the first half of *Structural Transformation*) is remarkably illuminating in view of Henry Adams's much earlier autobiographical treatment of American society and politics. Habermas also located the category of the public firmly in the dynamic of history, raising questions of just how, where, and why the public can be theorized today—questions that cannot be answered completely here, but that nonetheless shape my interest in, and account of, public knowledge.

Habermas's account of the transformation of the bourgeois public sphere focused on Germany, France, and England; Adams's *Education* may be read as a first-hand narrative account of how similar patterns emerged from the American experience.[21] It is worth noting that Adams's observations were far from unique. In 1831, for instance, Alexis de Tocqueville described the way in which critical, democratic discourse was shaping public life in the young republic:

> No sooner do you set foot on American soil than you find yourself in a sort of tumult. ... A thousand voices are heard at once. ... One group of citizens assembles for the sole object of announcing that they disapprove of the government's course, while others unite to proclaim that the men in office are the fathers of their country. ...
>
> It is hard to explain the place filled by political concerns in the life of an American. To take a hand in the government of society and to talk about it is his most important business and, so to say, the only pleasure he knows.[22]

But the community of discourse that Tocqueville observed was short-lived—and, in fact, may never have been a factor in the lives of most people who lived and worked in the early republic. It is important to avoid romanticizing such descriptions of American society at a time when citizenship was a category restricted to adult white males and often entailed property or literacy qualifications.[23] Large segments of the population—women from all classes, free or enslaved African Americans, and Native Americans—were categorically excluded from participation until well into the twentieth century, as established power did whatever it could to frustrate any extension of the possibilities that had been opened up but had hardly been made available to all.

Although the instantiation of a bourgeois public sphere made forms of reasoned discourse available to *some* in a manner unknown in feudal or absolutist regimes, new forms and relationships of power came into being.[24] The initial impulses of the struggle for democracy that accompanied the achievement of political freedom were structurally enabled by the bourgeoisie, which then fought tenaciously, especially after 1848, against extending the universalistic claims of the French and American revolutions. Thus, the changes over time that Henry Adams noted in terms of his family's tradition of public service may be read, at least in part, as reflecting the differences between a rising class and one successfully in power.

The common tendency to identify the public with the political has also served to obscure the extent to which public life has been depoliticized in liberal democracies. When ordinary people are routinely denied the chance to take part in articulating and defining issues of importance and concern, apathy and acquiescence become the hallmarks of political stability. So, as Mary O'Brien pointed out, most political questions may well

> appear to the men and women on assembly lines as just as unreal and insignificant as they were for the medieval serf and his family. The impact of the public realm on the lives of the working classes was, for centuries, a reality only when they were called upon to fight and die in the power struggles of their paternalist masters. In the age of democracy, the experienced sense of ordinary people of shaping and forming public affairs is very problematic indeed.[25]

Here, the complex and often unnecessarily mystified relationship between public and private comes directly into play. Hannah Arendt traced the origins of this distinction back to the *polis*, noting the "extraordinary difficulty" of understanding, in this century, "the decisive division between the public and private realms, between the sphere of the *polis* and the sphere of household and family, and, finally, between activities related to a common world and those related to the maintenance of life, a division upon which all ancient political thought rested as self-evident and axiomatic."[26] In the ancient world, the household was the realm of necessity; the sexual division of labor "naturally" prevailed as "the labor of man to provide nourishment and the labor of the woman in giving birth," and both were "subject to the same urgency of life." On the other hand, the *polis* was the realm of freedom, where "to be free meant to be free from the inequality present in rulership and to move in a sphere where neither rule nor being ruled existed."[27] Thus "privacy"

> meant literally a state of being deprived of something, and even of the highest and most human of man's capacities. A man who lived only a private life, who like the slave [or woman] was not permitted to enter the public realm, or like the barbarian had chosen not to establish such a realm, was not fully human. We no longer think primarily of deprivation when we use the word "privacy," and this is partly due to the enormous enrichment of the private sphere through modern individualism.[28]

Arendt blamed the rise of society, or "the collective of families economically organized into the facsimile of one super-human family," for blurring the once clear-cut distinction between these two realms.[29] In the modern world, society has become a third sphere, opposed to both the public and the private. Thus, "modern privacy in its most relevant function, to shelter the intimate [becomes] the opposite not of the political sphere but of the social."[30] Society is monolithic, conformist, and leveling; at its worst,

> with the emergence of mass society, the realm of the social has finally, after several centuries of development, reached the point where it embraces and controls all members of a given community equally and with equal strength. ... The victory of equality in the modern world is only the political and legal recognition of the fact that society has conquered the public realm, and that distinction and difference have become private matters of the individual.[31]

But modern mass society does not merely colonize the public realm; it also invades the sphere of intimacy. Arendt was sharply critical of how this "deprives men not only of their place in the world but of their private home, where they once felt sheltered against the world and where, at any rate, even those excluded from the world could find a substitute in the warmth of the hearth and the limited reality of family life."[32]

Arendt's civic republicanism, perhaps paradoxically, is as heavily gendered as it is overtly disdainful of gender-structured differences. Although vaunting politics as the pursuit of public happiness or the taste of public freedom, her account derogates the household—the "female" sphere of activity—by calling forth a dichotomy between reason and affectivity that has traditionally distinguished the universal, public arena of sovereignty and the state from the private, particular realm of bodily needs and emotional desires. Her transhistorical account is sharply counterpointed by recent feminist reassessments that challenge the equation of the political and the public from a markedly different reference point.

Susan Moller Okin described how conceptual confusion has accompanied the taken-for-granted and transhistorical usage of the public/private dichotomy. Its fundamental ambiguity is highlighted by at least two major conceptual distinctions that generally go unremarked:

> "Public/private" is used to refer both to the distinction between state and society (as in public and private ownership) and to the distinction between non-domestic and domestic life. In both dichotomies, the state is (paradigmatically) public, and the family, domestic and intimate life are (again paradigmatically) private. The crucial difference between the two is that the intermediate socio-economic realm (what Hegel called "civil society") is in the first dichotomy included in the category of "private" but is in the second dichotomy "public."[33]

A further ambiguity, however, colors the public/domestic dichotomy—the sexual division of labor. Men have generally been assumed to be concerned with the sphere of economic and political activity and women with the sphere of domesticity and reproduction.[34] The enduring power of this assumption is, moreover, mirrored in the very etymology of the word "public." The *Oxford English Dictionary* traces how the early Latin *poplicus* (from the feminine *poplus* and later masculine *populus* meaning "people") was superseded by *publicus*, with the shift to *publicus* apparently taking place "under the influence of *pubes* in the sense of 'adult men' or 'male population.'"[35]

It is thus not surprising that in recent years some feminist theories have suggested that the way out of this conceptual dilemma is to scrap the public/private conceptual framework altogether. However, despite the wide range of variety among feminisms, past and present, most, from Mary Wollstonecraft on down, have challenged the traditional dichotomies by demanding that the public sphere incorporate and accommodate gender (along with other) differences. For many contemporary feminists, this challenge has been encapsulated in the popular slogan, "The personal is political." This shorthand reference to the relationship between public and private, or personal and political, viewed through the lens of gender, is far from unproblematic.[36] Yet it does summarize how neither can be conceptualized as a separate entity; the relationship is inevitably one of interpenetration and not strict demarcation. Or, as Anne Phillips put it, "Relations inside family and household are knocked into appropriate shape by a battery of public policies (on housing, for example, social security, education); conversely, relations at the workplace and in politics are moulded by the inequalities of sexual power."[37] It may thus make as little sense to think of personal questions as inevitably removed from politics as it would to conceptualize politics as beyond the reach of private or sexual concerns.

The feminist challenge to traditional views of the public/private dichotomy demands that analysis of the collapse of the public in late capitalism acknowledge the complexities of difference. Although gender-structured meanings have had a powerful hold on theoretical conceptions of the public and the private, gender is by no means the only brake on the exclusionary, homogenizing ideal of the public in modern political thought. Recasting analysis in terms of a heterogeneous public life that is fully accessible to everyone in a complex modern world demands attention to a diverse range of social and political concerns and an openness to the full spectrum of difference. Such an effort precludes articulation of a renewal of public life based on the mere recovery of the Enlightenment ideals that shaped the early bourgeois public sphere or on any simple equation of the public with the political.[38]

What all these comments highlight, of course, is the need for historical specificity, conceptual clarity, and class-based analysis in discussing the public today. Whatever the limitations of Habermas's account of the transformation of the bourgeois public sphere (feminists, for example, claim that his theory is inappropriately gender-blind), it is articulated from the standpoint of a clearly historical dynamic where forms of political and cultural change can be explained in terms of power and domination.[39] Habermas's historical explanation contrasts sharply with Henry Adams's account of the same political and cultural transformations, which he can only perceive in their outward manifestation as symptoms of decline.

Adams flirted with a critique of capitalism but limited his challenge to oblique references to his "inherited quarrel with State Street."[40] Although he eloquently described the symptomatology of social, political, and cultural decay that went hand in glove with the instantiation of industrial capitalism throughout the Gilded Age, he steadfastly refused to challenge the logic of this process and remained locked in the grip of bourgeois individualism. He either had to defend the status quo or mourn the passing of a prior day; there was—as he quite correctly perceived—no positive way out of this dilemma. All of this reflects a contradiction between the ideological individualism that fueled the growth and spread of capital and the democratic impulses of the body politic. On the one hand, Americans have placed great emphasis on the notion that individuals *alone* create "the good life" for themselves and their families. On the other, the ideal of political democracy creates the illusion that all citizens possess the right and duty to self-governance, not as isolated individuals but *as a collectivity.*

The tensions between these two competing visions of the very foundation of social and political organization are profoundly irreconcilable, yet they are often obscured by the ideological force of individualism in the American tradition. A self-centered concept of bourgeois liberty attached to individuals qua individuals perpetually undercuts the possibility of meaningful civic responsibility today just as it did in Henry Adams's time. The consolidation of capitalism in industrialized nations and its globalization have been marked by a tendency of capitalist societies to repudiate the concept of community and increasingly to ground public institutions in the individual. Whereas this is especially true in the United States, the situation here is by no means unique. The extension of suffrage and increasing recognition of individual rights—of married women and of children, for example, with the putative rights of fetuses providing the most extreme instance of this logic—has signaled not just an increased emphasis on individuals per se. It has also marked a continuing process of extending public norms into what was previously seen as the private sphere.[41] All of this is profoundly implicated with public knowledge and educational theory and practice.

For it is *collective* historical memory—what communities believe to be worth saving from the ravages of time—that constitutes the foundation of public knowledge. Hannah Arendt quite correctly described this when she pointed out that the common world is what we enter when we are born and what we leave behind when we die. ... It is what we have in common not only with those who live with us, but also with those who were here before and with those who will come after us. But such a common world can survive the coming and going of the generations only to the extent that it appears in public. It is the publicity of the public realm which can absorb and make shine through the centuries whatever men [and women] may want to save from the natural ruin of time.[42]

It is quite impossible to reduce culture to autobiography or to pretend that individual perception is anything other than a function of collective identity. The post-Freudian obsession with the self has tended to obscure the way in which we can only know ourselves individually through language—through collectivities of expression. And the languages we use to describe ourselves in turn have tremendous influence on how we perceive the very choices and options open to us in life, not vice versa.[43] All of this suggests that, as Henry Adams implied in his *Education, public knowledge,* founded upon the active, critical, and ongoing engagement of individuals with society, is central to any democratic project and subject to the same sorts of deformation as the public sphere.

The same cautions that apply to analysis of "the public" or to demarcations of "the public sphere" are thus applicable to public knowledge. Unless it is conceptualized in terms of a public philosophy founded in an as yet unrealized vision of the good society, grounded in history and change and predicated on challenges to existing power relationships in society, public knowledge will be locked into a static, positivistic study and preservation of past and present alike. Furthermore, as I argued in Chapter 1, the extent to which knowledge—or access to knowledge—is privileged is precisely the extent to which it cannot be characterized as public. This presents a significant challenge to much of the prevailing American educational theory and practice. Although perhaps most obviously apparent in the marked disparities of resources available to wealthy and poor public school districts, the privileging of knowledge is also central to the maintenance of public/private hierarchies across the entire spectrum of education in America today.

The story, by now, is familiar; the "failure" of American public schooling has made good press throughout the past decade. The dire predictions and apocalyptic rhetoric of the National Commission on Excellence in Education's *Nation at Risk* report were widely publicized in 1983, and heated debates over educational reform have continued to this day. Deborah W. Meier called attention to how all too often the focus of these debates has been some mythic golden age in the past, when America's public schools did a better job of educating students than they do today. A closer check shows that it is only since the end of the Second World War that most average Americans have graduated from high school, for example, and that the much-vaunted "ignorance" of seventeen-year-olds today with regard to things like the names of presidents, scientific laws, historical dates, and other basic information really represents nothing new but simply the continuation of a trend that has been in place for fifty years. Perhaps more important, Meier reminded the reader, "the students tested in those earlier years were overall a far more elite group than today's general student body."[44] Given all the sound and fury that has been attached to debates over the state of the nation's public schools, it is important to see clearly that the problem is not merely how to recapture or reconstruct a lost era of success in educational achievement. The real question for public education today is how to invent a totally new system that will substantively fulfill the nation's obligation—legally in place at least since the *Brown* decision almost forty years ago—to educate all students equally.

That this obligation remains shamefully unmet is almost beyond debate. The grotesque inequities that continue to exist in America's public schools were powerfully documented in Jonathan Kozol's recent *Savage Inequalities*, but here again the story is familiar. Wealthy (read "white, suburban") school districts can afford state-of-the-art buildings, equipment, textbooks, and technology. They pay and treat their teachers well. The school buildings themselves are clean, pleasant places that reflect care and concern for future generations; they are full of hope. Poor (read African American, Hispanic, "minority," and rural or urban) school districts can afford none-of-the-above and are often dilapidated, ramshackle structures that, especially in the cities, look a lot like prisons. Not surprisingly, in such places, hopelessness is the best lesson learned, by students and teachers alike.

The brutality of public schooling in America today is perhaps best expressed by the fact that wealthy districts and poor districts may be separated by only a few blocks or a couple of miles. Cherry Hill High, one of the best in the state of New Jersey, is located just a few minutes' drive away from Camden High, one of the worst. At Cherry Hill, students learn and work in rooms packed with new computers; at Camden High, they practice "word processing" on cardboard replicas of computer keyboards. Cherry Hill is preponderantly white; Camden is almost exclusively African American and Hispanic.[45] Racial segregation, officially outlawed by the Supreme Court before some of today's high school students' parents were born, is de facto the rule, not only in New Jersey but also across America. And other forms of segregation—based not so much on racial or ethnic characteristics as on class-based criteria such as family wealth or social status—prevail as well. The extent to which these structural inequities must be viewed as representing not merely entrenched historical tradition but contemporary voter *preferences* is seen in the response of New Jerseyans to the efforts of a governor to equalize funding across districts on a statewide basis. Within weeks of the proposal, "Impeach Florio" bumperstickers appeared on cars in suburban locations, and a grass-roots movement was organizing and calling for the governor's removal from office.

Traditions of neighborhood-based "local autonomy," however, although they have certainly contributed to racially segregated public schools (particularly in urban areas), do not tell the whole story with regard to the privileging of public knowledge. Complementary to disparities between rich and poor districts—often, and mythically discounted as accidents of geography—is the ideology of meritocracy, which has been central to public education in America since the early days of the common school movement. This is best expressed in Horace Mann's famous description of public schooling as "the great equalizer."[46] Indeed, Americans have long believed in education as both a right and a ladder to the dream of a better life. Ralph Waldo Emerson, writing in 1884, eloquently captured this belief:

> We have already taken, at the planting of the Colonies ... the initial step, which for its importance might have been resisted as the most radical of revolutions, thus deciding at the start the destiny of this country—this, namely, that the poor man, whom the law does not allow to take an ear of corn when starving, nor a pair of shoes for his freezing feet, is allowed to put his hand into the pocket of the rich, and say, You shall educate me, not as you will, but as I will: not alone in the elements, but, by further provision, in the languages, in sciences, in the useful and in elegant arts. The child shall be taken up by the State, and taught, at the public cost, the rudiments of knowledge, and, at last, the ripest results of art and science.[47]

This meritocratic perspective masks class privilege. It militates against linking educational questions to other social problems and stipulates that the knowledge offered by public schooling is simply there for the taking. Anyone who wants to work hard in school will have free and equal access to that knowledge. So if a student fails to learn, it is because she is lazy, or culturally deficient, or perhaps has a learning disability of some sort. Individual characteristics are the source of success and failure alike—which makes it easy to blame the victims who fail and extremely difficult to articulate the social dimensions of the educational problems. It is a reminder that, whereas capitalist democracy is premised on *formal* guarantees of equality under the law, it has never promoted or guaranteed *substantive* equality.

Perhaps paradoxically, however, most Americans feel distaste for overt methods of sorting and segregating students *within* public schools on the basis of ascribed characteristics like class or race. Thus, throughout this century, educators (and, often, parents) have shown great enthusiasm for objective measures of aptitude and potential that claim to provide unbiased assessments of students' ability and progress. But as Jennie Oakes showed, these measures are never so value-free as they pretend to be and often result

in a selection process within schools that "may in part be very much class related, with the screening devices that appear to be objective having much the
same results as if we sorted directly on background characteristics."[48] In
practice, this means that students who start out "at the bottom of the social
and economic ladder" often struggle along in "the great equalizer" for
twelve years or so, only to "end up still on the bottom rung."[49]

Far from being places where people can, on a meritocratic basis, find
routes to upward mobility or success in adult life, public schools often serve
to reproduce existing social, economic, and political inequalities. This idea
has driven the analyses of reproduction theorists—scholars who see schools
as places where knowledge and access are privileged on the basis of class and
race.[50] This literature directly challenges claims that the meritocratic vision
of public schools as great equalizers, where the best and brightest may rise to
the top regardless of racial, class, ethnic, or gender distinctions. It focuses on
the question of equality and how best to achieve it and on the often dispro-
portionate distribution of knowledge within public schools.

A comprehensive summary of the vast literature on social reproduction is
beyond the scope of this chapter, but a few highlights can suffice to show
how its instrumental brushstrokes offer a bleak vision of educational possibility. Samuel Bowles and Herbert Gintis argued that schools serve less to educate for knowledge than to turn students into adults who will accept the
terms of the capitalist workplace. This is not so much the result of conscious
decision making on the part of educators as it is the side effect of a structural
correspondence between public schools and the workplace. Bureaucratically
organized and often employing assembly-line methods, these institutions effectively replicate existing class stratification. Different behaviors, capabilities, and attitudes are both required and rewarded depending on where students start out in life and what will be expected of them as adults. In other
words, working-class children become adults who are acculturated to subordinate themselves, readily, to various forms of external control. They may
grumble and express different aspects of alienation, but they remain in the
long run quite willing to conform to the demands of the workplace.[51] Paul
Willis elaborated on this phenomenon in the British case, showing how differential treatment and student resistance interact as class reproduction takes
place in schools, producing students who are "learning to labor."[52]

Class stratification or standing is not the only thing reproduced in schools,
however; knowledge itself may be privileged in the process. Michael Apple
suggested that "high-status" knowledge becomes a scarce commodity closely
linked to power through an institutional process whereby cultural resources
are both legitimated and differentially distributed in schooling. This distribution reflects the economic inequalities and values of corporate capitalism;
in a world of increasingly sophisticated technology, "high-status" knowledge reflects the forms of know-how that are necessary to keep the economy

operating efficiently. Most of the generation or preservation of the high-status knowledge applicable to the real world today takes place in universities. But in elementary and secondary schools, high-status knowledge is important because it is the avenue leading to university access. For example, it is one thing to learn keyboard skills and be able to operate word processing programs on a personal computer and quite another to understand the mathematics and computer languages necessary to develop sophisticated programs independently. So the process of tracking students into either secretarial training programs or highly academic college preparatory courses and competitive preparatory schools not only relies on the fact that high-status knowledge is a limited commodity but also uses this fact quite effectively to limit the extent to which different students will be able to access various educational or employment options in the future.[53]

Bourdieu and Passeron used the concept of "cultural capital" to amplify Apple's work. They suggested that this sort of high-status knowledge becomes a mechanism for sorting students and keeping them in stratified social and economic groups. The extent to which a person can access high-status, university-based knowledge is the extent to which he or she possesses the cultural capital necessary to succeed at the top echelons of society. This knowledge may be characterized in Apple's terms as a limited commodity in and of itself, or it may be considered the exclusive property of the bourgeoisie. In either case the consequences are the same; existing social relations will be reproduced to the extent that knowledge is privileged and cultural capital accrued in schools.[54]

If privilege accrues in the public schools, what of the *private* sector? Most studies of schooling focus on public systems of primary and secondary education, which serve the vast majority of American children. Only recently has any attention been focused on the systems of Catholic parochial schools, which, especially in urban areas, are often seen by parents as a desirable alternative to public schooling. Very little systematic research has been done on the elite boarding schools, whose students are drawn from a small but disproportionately privileged segment of the population.[55] The number of students who attend prep schools may be small, but their impact upon American society and politics is not. David Halberstam's description of McGeorge Bundy makes abundantly clear the relationship between these institutions and elitist echelons of power:

> He attended Groton, the greatest "Prep" school in the nation, where the American upper class sends its sons to instill the classic values: discipline, honor, a belief in the existing values and the rightness of them. Coincidentally, it's at Groton that one starts to meet the right people, and where connections which will serve well later on—be it at Wall Street or Washington—are first forged;

one learns, at Groton, above all, the rules of the Game and even a special language: what washes and does not wash.[56]

C. Wright Mills's interest in the "power elite" drew him to conclude that prep schools were essential to the preservation of class privilege in American society:

> As a selection and training place of the upper classes, both old and new, the private school is a unifying influence, a force for the nationalization of the upper classes. The less important the pedigreed family becomes in the careful transmission of moral and cultural traits, the more important the private school. The school—rather than the upper-class family—is the most important agency for transmitting the traditions of the upper social classes, and regulating the admission of new wealth and talent. It is the characterizing point in the upper-class experience.[57]

Perhaps not surprisingly, given the inherently conservative nature of these elitist institutions, Peter W. Cookson and Caroline Hodges Persell's 1985 study of prep schools and their students, *Preparing for Power,* demonstrated repeatedly that little had changed in the decades since Mills wrote.

It is in the nation's elite boarding schools that the notion of cultural capital becomes concrete. Cultural capital is, of course, a social creation. It reflects a set of deeply embedded cultural, economic, and political values that are assumed—for well or ill—to be universal. The curricula of such schools thus represent and synthesize "high culture," at least in embryonic form. Although Latin and Greek—once prime signifiers of a high degree of cultural capital—are no longer required subjects, a broad and demanding range of intellectual disciplines is offered. To take a typical example:

> The Groton curriculum is predicated on the belief that certain qualities of mind are of major importance: precise and articulate communication; the ability to compute accurately and to reason quantitatively; a grasp of scientific approaches to problem-solving; an understanding of the cultural, social, scientific, and political background of Western civilization; and the ability to reason carefully and logically and to think imaginatively and sensitively. Consequently the School puts considerable emphasis on language, mathematics, science, history, and the arts.[58]

Course descriptions in most prep school catalogues are designed "to whet the intellectual appetite," with provocative titles like "Varieties of the Poetic Experience," "Effecting Political Change," "Rendezvous with Armageddon," and "Mammalian Anatomy and Physiology." Deep and wide reading is emphasized; a term of American literature might include as many as ten authors' works, ranging from William Faulkner to Jack Kerouac, and it is not unusual for a Shakespeare course to require six or seven plays in a semester. At one school, a course on the presidency included the following requirements: Clinton Rossiter, *The American Presidency;* Richard Hofstadter, *The American Political Tradition;* Erwin C. Hargrove, *Presidential Leadership;* Arthur Schlesinger, Jr., *A Thousand Days;* Doris Kearns, *Lyndon Johnson and the American Dream;* and Theodore H. White, *Breach of Faith.*[59]

In marked contrast to the public school students described by Bowles and Gintis, who were bound for boring and repetitive jobs in industry, the elite students studied by Cookson and Persell were "part of a world where success is expected, and celebrity and power are part of the unfolding of life. ... Nowhere is the drive for athletic, cultural, and academic excellence more apparent than in the awards, honors, and prizes that are given to outstanding teams or students at the end of each year."[60] Despite their relatively small numbers, prep school students and their differentially structured educational experiences crystallize the issues surrounding public knowledge and its deformation in America today. This truth is borne out in the choices these privileged students make with regard to higher education. Nationally, close to 80 percent of college students attend public institutions. Only about 60 percent of prep school students even apply to public colleges and universities, however. The most selective schools serve only about 2 percent of the nation's college population, yet over 80 percent of prep school students apply to these schools. And then there are the Ivy League colleges, which account for 1 percent of all college enrollments; almost half of all prep school students apply to one or more of these eight colleges.[61] Here, the consequences of educational stratification and the privileging of knowledge stand out in particularly sharp relief. Young men and women whose elitist secondary education has prepared them to expect success, celebrity, and power disproportionately prefer to attend a few equally elitist, private postsecondary institutions. Thus, the cycle of privilege continues—with ever greater assurance that the undemocratic distribution of purportedly public knowledge will continue undisturbed.

At stake here is the question of whether, and to what extent, public knowledge and its articulation can be democratized. It is hard to argue that the American educational system—of public and private schools—does not, at present, privilege knowledge and its distribution. The issue is really quite simple: *who* has the right to know *what?* In other words, who deserves to have access to highly valued forms of cultural capital, and according to whose plan? If a democracy takes equality seriously, the answer to this question is simple—knowledge can never be privileged; it is a right accorded everyone without distinction. Although Americans have long believed in education as a right and as a ladder to their dreams, the profoundly radical foundations of this belief have seldom been part of the discourse on education.

The history of education in America has shown, over and over, how the most exploited and oppressed have avidly sought literacy and learning, often inventing their own means by which to attain an education after having been denied access to established institutions. Herbert Gutman, for instance, detailed how newly freed slaves "voluntarily paid school tuition, purchased schoolbooks, hired, fed, boarded, and protected teachers, constructed and maintained school buildings, and engaged in other costly (and sometimes dangerous) activities to provide education for their children."[62] Historian Theodora Penny Martin told of how middle-class women formed study clubs throughout the decades following the Civil War. Denied access to higher education, yet determined to learn about the world beyond their parlors and participate in "culture," they organized in small groups and met regularly at each other's homes to study and discuss art, music, history, geography, and literature. One of these women wrote a memoir of her experiences, in which she referred to herself and other clubwomen as "Light Seekers." It would be difficult to find a phrase more evocative of Kant's famous definition of enlightenment as emergence from self-incurred immaturity.[63]

These are two brief examples from the many that could be drawn to substantiate the extent to which Americans have believed in education's emancipatory prospect. They also show how important it is to resist falling under the spell of a totalizing instrumentalism, which collapses all possibilities within a single deterministic framework, when discussing public knowledge and education. Although the reproduction theories discussed above shed valuable light on the complex ways in which the contradictions of capitalist democracy have been enacted in schooling through the privileging of public knowledge, they tend to focus rather exclusively on the more negative aspects of the role of schooling in contemporary society.

Such one-sided approaches distort the truth; there is another, positive dimension to education that cannot be reduced to functionalist outcomes of sorting or social reproduction. As I will argue in subsequent chapters, it is possible to identify and articulate these emancipatory aspects of education without falling into the complacency that is a corollary of "great equalizer" ideology and meritocratic approaches to the problems of democratic education. Thus, it is as important to remember the promise and hope inherent in education for public knowledge as it is to articulate a critique of its deformation and limitations under present conditions. Given the intensity of right-wing rhetoric connecting the perceived failure of public education to economic decline, it is equally necessary to remember that just as the public cannot be reduced to the political, neither can educational empowerment be considered synonymous with employment.

All of these concerns, of course, tie the question of public knowledge to the larger question of the public sphere in late capitalism. They serve to make the differences between Henry Adams's vision, which limited him to a narrative of public decline, and the socialist perspective, which opens up an array of new alternatives, all the more clear. Adams closed the circle of public knowledge by beating a personal retreat into medieval history. American democracy in decline held no prospect for the "eighteenth-century man," nor could he afford an element of hope for a better future. There are many who would agree that little has changed in the century since and that what has changed has been for the worse. Although it is certainly clear that public life and political democracy have taken a beating, Habermas suggested (and so, interestingly enough, have several of his critics) that it would be premature to sound their death knell altogether. With these thinkers, I will argue against static narratives of decline and for a new conceptualization of the public sphere and public knowledge. The articulation and implemention of this new vision would initially depend upon the existing institutional framework of public schooling in America, but it is important not to lose sight of its broader implications, which signal a revitalization of democracy across the social and political spectrum.

# 3

## A Public Philosophy?
## Pragmatism and Public Knowledge

"We have frequently printed the word Democracy," Walt Whitman wrote in "Democratic Vistas," "yet I cannot too often repeat that it is a word the real gift of which still sleeps, quite unawakened, notwithstanding the resonance and the many angry tempests out of which its syllables have come, from pen or tongue." He went on to suggest that the history of democracy "remains unwritten, because that history has yet to be enacted"—even in the United States. Perhaps no single person has better exemplified, in life or work, the experimental vision Whitman summarized with these words than the philosopher John Dewey, who, like the poet, believed in "democracy as a way of life." Over sixty years ago, in *The Public and Its Problems*, John Dewey articulated a general narrative of decline in American political life, which in many respects, evokes Henry Adams's *Education*. But whereas the *Education* is a literary and historical memoir, Dewey's analysis of the public sphere is grounded in the "new American philosophy" of pragmatism.[1]

Dewey believed that the "American democratic polity was developed out of a genuine community life" on the model of New England villages, "where industry was mainly agricultural and where production was carried on mainly with hand tools."[2] The frontier societies of these early days "put a high premium upon personal work, skill, ingenuity, initiative and adaptability, and upon neighborly sociability."[3] These communities were cohesive public spheres. Through political institutions like the electoral college, which "assumed that citizens would choose men locally known for their high standing," the nation's highest authority would be founded on public gatherings, where, in consultation, electors would "name some one known to them for his probity and public spirit and knowledge."[4] But Dewey also noted "the rapidity with which the scheme fell into disuse" as, with the spread of modernity, the active public sphere of the early republic declined. Indeed, he felt that "the machine age" had "formed such immense and consolidated" social institutions "on an impersonal rather than a community basis, that the resultant public" could neither "identify" nor "distinguish itself."[5]

In a manner similar to Adams, Dewey hinted at the social and economic aspects of this decline but shied away from analyzing them critically, refusing, as Adams did, to confront directly the capitalist system that fueled both the machine age and the formal institutions of liberal democracy. Instead, he shifted the terms of discussion to questions of scale and definition: "There are too many publics and too much of public concern for our existing resources to cope with. The problem of a democratically organized public is primarily an intellectual problem, in a degree to which the political affairs of prior ages offer no parallel."[6]

This passage both illuminates continuities between Adams and Dewey and places them in a setting that foregrounds issues Jürgen Habermas would later explore in detail—especially in terms of the difficulty of defining a "public" in late capitalism and constituting discursive action founded on human reason. Indeed, besides articulating a concept of public knowledge and emphasizing the importance of the public sphere, Dewey also anticipated Habermas's theory of communicative action.[7] In a 1986 interview, Habermas noted that from early in his own career he "viewed American pragmatism as the third productive reply to Hegel, after Marx and Kierkegaard, as the radical-democratic branch of Young Hegelianism, so to speak." Ever since, he has "relied on this American version of the philosophy of praxis when the problem arises of compensating for the weaknesses of Marxism with respect to democratic theory."[8]

Pragmatism appealed to educational reformers in the first few decades of this century because it signaled a break with the past and offered a progressive vision of the future. Calling upon the popular rhetoric of democratic citizenship, it evoked the traditions of the "body politic" by celebrating experience and activity while accepting ordinary common sense as the ultimate source and test of all knowledge and value. It located potential solutions to the problems presented by increasing social and technological interdependence within the institutional context of American schools. As a representative textbook on educational philosophy put it at mid-century: "Pragmatism has become a leading educational philosophy in America. Without embarrassment of any kind, it has given education a primary and central place among social institutions. Whereas it has not been uncommon for other philosophers to give educational considerations a menial place, this has never been the case with the pragmatists."[9]

Indeed, Dewey's pedagogy represented a continuous attempt to suggest the kinds of reforms that would help bring a "Great Community" of active citizens into being. In accord with his contention that philosophy should be based on active experimentalism, his psychology emphasized continuous growth and development on the organic model. Just as he saw the political life of a community, not as a process that could be preordained, but rather as necessarily resulting from the constant interaction of human beings with each other in day-to-day life, so too did he believe in education as a continuous process of development, which unfolded as the individual grew into the world, learning how to *be* part of a particular community. His pedagogy was thus child centered and community based. It was founded on a notion of human development as a continuous, permanent, and absolutely open-ended process.

In a famous passage from *Democracy and Education,* Dewey summed up his view of the proper relationship between human growth and education:

> Our net conclusion is that life is development, and that developing, growing, is life. Translated into its educational equivalents, this means (i) that the educational process has no end beyond itself; it is its own end; and that (ii) the educational process is one of continual reorganizing, reconstructing, transforming. ...
>
> Since growth is the characteristic of life, education is all one with growing; it has no end beyond itself. The criterion of the value of school education is the extent in which it creates a desire for continued growth and supplies the means for making the desire effective in fact.

Here, Dewey was not speaking metaphorically. He was asserting, quite simply, that education *is* growth; life *is* development. Any attempt to define the ends of education will thus be futile. There simply can be no further end to the process than more education: "The aim of education is to enable individuals to continue their education."[10]

In fairness, it must be acknowledged that Dewey never argued for utterly *directionless* education and indeed went to great pains to distance himself from those of his disciples who did so. However, his central tenet of education as growth (and vice versa) utterly obviates the formulation of any criteria by which schools—with teachers as agents—could or should guide and direct children toward the acquisition of that same "social knowledge." Dewey put this explicitly and approvingly: "It is as absurd for [an educator] to set up his 'own' aims as the proper objects of the growth of the children as it would be for the farmer to set up an ideal of farming irrespective of conditions."[11]

Dewey even articulated a concept of public knowledge as an integral part of the process of human development within his "Great Community":

> The prime condition of a democratically organized public is a kind of knowledge and insight which does not yet exist. In its absence, it would be the height of absurdity to try to tell what it would be like if it existed. But some of the conditions which must be fulfilled if it is to exist can be indicated. We can borrow that much from the spirit and method of science. ... An obvious requirement is freedom of social inquiry and of distribution of its conclusions.[12]

Furthermore, there "can be no public without full publicity in respect to all consequences which concern it. ... Without freedom of expression, not even methods of social inquiry can be developed."[13] This passage is key to understanding the appeal and influence of pragmatism in general and of Dewey's thought in particular. He cited an as yet unrealized public knowledge as one of the essential components of a radically democratized modern society and evoked the Enlightenment ideal of freedom of expression in conjunction with the scientific method. This appealed to the American tradition of "can-do" spirit while forwarding putatively critical forms of knowledge as the basis for democratic participation in the "Great Community." The question I will address here, however, is whether this promise can be fulfilled. In other words, within pragmatism, is it possible to develop standards and criteria for articulating or implementing a politics of public knowledge?

Although Dewey's influence on American education (whether along lines Dewey himself intended or not) has been more pervasive than any other, it is impossible to discuss his ideas outside of the historical development of pragmatism, which was also shaped by Charles Sanders Peirce and William James.[14] It was Peirce who originated the root idea of pragmatism. He systematically and rigorously developed a logical understanding of the nature of action and conduct, but it was James who popularized pragmatism. Lifelong friends, these two men had little in common intellectually or theoretically. As Ralph Barton Perry suggested, it is probably "correct, and just to all parties, to say that the modern movement known as pragmatism is largely the result of James's misunderstanding of Peirce."[15]

In a series of lectures at the University of California in 1898, James introduced the term "pragmatism" to American audiences, attributing it to Peirce—who quickly disavowed the attribution, believing that James had distorted the meaning of his (Peirce's) original ideas beyond recognition. From then on, Peirce took pains to refer to *his* philosophy as "pragmaticism," which, he felt, was a label "ugly enough to be safe from kidnappers."[16] The two men's thinking proceeded from diametrically opposed positions. Peirce emphasized the social character of the individual and saw pragmatism as a method for clarifying the meaning of ideas in a process of discovering general truths.[17] James, in contrast, began with the individual; his interpretation of meaning and truth was based on the immediate sensation of personal experience.[18]

This element of subjectivity colored James's pragmatism with elements of spirituality and eroticism that were not shared by either Peirce or Dewey. The latter two thinkers were far more concerned with public knowledge than was James; as a consequence, their thought reflects a certain bloodlessness that mirrors the common notion that the public sphere is, or ought to be, devoid of intimacy. Richard Bernstein described this relationship a bit differently, suggesting that whereas "Peirce supplied the intellectual backbone of pragmatism," Dewey "perceived the ways in which Peirce's ideal of a self-critical community of inquirers had important consequences for education, social reconstruction, and a revitalization of democracy."[19] It is thus perhaps more productive to think of pragmatism in terms of Cornel West's notion of "a diverse and heterogenous tradition" whose "common denominator consists of a future-oriented instrumentalism that tries to deploy thought as a weapon to enable more effective action" than to try to define it as a coherent philosophical system or method.[20] Even so, it is possible to begin with what James, Peirce, and Dewey share.

A consequentialist approach to meaning is central to pragmatism; the notion that the meaning of any idea can be found by putting all of its conceivable consequences to an active test underlies definitions of truth in Peirce, James, and Dewey alike. All rely on the application of science—primarily through the scientific method of objective investigation of facts—to human affairs. Each sees the universe as fluid and open-ended; life is characterized by chance; there are no absolutes. As a result, all three philosophers view human growth as a process of evolutionary change. Following upon the notion of evolution, they always define "human nature" as something plastic, or malleable. And all three would agree that the best society is one that maximizes human freedom.[21]

Echoes of the Enlightenment are particularly strong in Peirce and Dewey, less so in James. Peirce, especially, was concerned with finding an objective basis for meaning and knowledge; he sought to bridge the Kantian chasm between the mind's subjective processes and the world's objective realities. As Habermas put it: "The methodologically secured progress of natural-scientific knowledge had given Kant occasion to investigate the transcendental conditions of knowledge as such; it had led Comte and the positivists to identify all of knowledge with science. Peirce was the first to gain clarity about the systematic meaning of this experience."[22]

For Peirce, the principle of pragmatism was a process of giving meaning to the world. Extrapolating from individual cognition to collective, species-based knowledge and relying uncritically on the assumption that the scientific method would guarantee a certain lawlike progress to any inquiry, he emphasized that meaning could be discovered through insistence on uncompelled, permanent consensus: "Investigation differs entirely from these methods in that the nature of the final conclusion to which it leads is in every case destined from the beginning, without reference to the initial state of belief. Let any two minds investigate any question independently and if they carry the process far enough they will come to an agreement which no further investigation will disturb."[23] Peirce's analysis of the meaning of concepts such as "reality" and "truth" was thus utilitarian. It entailed, however, a self-regulating, cumulative learning process: "This great hope is embodied in the conception of truth and reality. The opinion which is fated to be ultimately agreed to by all who investigate, is what we mean by truth, and the object represented in this opinion is the real. That is the way I would explain reality."[24]

Although he emphasized the consensual, social construction of reality and relied on the educative capacities of human beings, Peirce's application of the scientific method of investigation to questions of truth was based on a deceptively simple criterion: "In order to ascertain the meaning of an intellectual conception one should consider what practical consequences might conceivably result by necessity from the truth of that conception: and the sum of these consequences will constitute the entire meaning of the conception."[25] This approach would appear to promise a great deal for any project of framing the critical, positive public knowledge essential to democracy. Under Peirce's criterion, truth is inherently public; nothing that holds only in private for an individual subject can reference reality. Those beliefs that can be arrived at mutually, independently of personal preferences or idiosyncrasies, and that can be affirmed intersubjectively in the face of infinitely expressible doubts, and *only those beliefs* can represent matters of fact.[26] Thus we have in place a framework for public knowledge located in the lived realities of people's everyday experience. On the face of it, we find a progressive moment of democratic theory and practice.

Although Peirce made a compelling argument for public knowledge, his criterion, as Habermas pointed out, was founded on a tautology: "If we assume that reality is not constituted independently of the rules to which the process of inquiry is subject, we cannot refer to this reality to justify the validity of the rules of the process of inquiry."[27] Peirce here "accedes to a concealed positivism and treats the pragmatist criterion of meaning in such an absolutistic manner that it destroys the foundation of pragmatism itself."[28]

This collapse has serious implications with regard to the relevance of pragmatism for a theory of public knowledge—all the more so because Peirce was arguably the most philosophically sophisticated of his colleagues. What it points toward is the necessity of incorporating an element of self-reflection within any conceptualization of public knowledge. In other words, since public knowledge relies on open communication, it "requires the use of language that is not confined to the limits of technical control over objectified natural processes" but "arises from symbolic action between societal subjects who reciprocally know and recognize each other as unmistakable individuals."[29] If, as Habermas suggested, such self-reflection is simply beyond the scope of pragmatism, why bother to explore articulations of this theory any further?

The work of James and Dewey bears exploration and close scrutiny here because their interpretations of pragmatic philosophy have had the most far-reaching effects on American educational theory and practice—intended or otherwise. Peirce's writings went virtually unpublished during his lifetime, and his academic career was limited to a five-year stint at Johns Hopkins University.[30] Although his two colleagues enjoyed substantial popular and academic audiences, Peirce's work has been largely marginalized even within intellectual circles.[31] Furthermore, he paid scant attention to pedagogy or educational theory, although he approached both indirectly by insisting on the social construction of knowledge and meaning. This in no way, however, even begins to approximate the extent to which the works of James and Dewey influenced American educational theory and practice.

William James may have had more immediate influence on education as a psychologist than he had as a philosopher. As Merle Curti pointed out, it "has been estimated that nine tenths of the teachers who studied any psychology at all in the years between 1890 and 1910 read James."[32] His landmark *Principles of Psychology*, first published in 1890, was followed by *Psychology: Briefer Course* and *Talks to Teachers,* both of which were attempts to make the sophisticated concepts of *Principles* more readily accessible to teachers and students.[33] Clark Kerr, however, found James's philosophy instructive and expressed regret that he had not incorporated James into his argument in *The Uses of the University:*

> I wish I had then [1963] read William James on the "multiverse." It would have given me a good footnote to employ in lectures ... and helped me to clarify my ideas. ... The multiversity can be compared, as James compared the multiverse, to a "federal republic" as against a "kingdom," a federal republic where attention should be paid to "each form" by itself, rather than only to "all forms" together.[34]

Although James spent virtually his whole career as a Harvard professor, he popularized philosophy, making it accessible and available to common readers by writing and lecturing in a clear, colloquial style. His main work on education, *Talks to Teachers* (a collection of lectures addressed to public school teachers in Cambridge, Massachusetts, in 1892), predated his work in pragmatism, but it exemplified his talent for translating "analytically technical" ideas into everyday language. This effort to make his work available to people outside the universities was itself pedagogical and reflected James's commitment to forging links between his biologically based psychology, philosophy, and pedagogy. There are strong continuities between these aspects of James's thought, and all proceed from the same radical individualism. This point of view sharply demarcates him from both Peirce, who found James's reliance on privatized experience repugnant, and Dewey, in whose opinion "Peirce [was] more of a pragmatist than James."[35]

James simply had no sense of the social foundations of education. As Curti summed up the problem:

Nowhere in *Talks to Teachers* does he speak of education as a social function. Maintaining that the basis of all education is the fund of native reactions with which the child is endowed, emphasizing interest as the motive power of all educational progress, and instinct as the beginning of interest, James conceived of education as the organization of acquired habits on the part of the individual in such a way as to promote his personal well-being.[36]

This stance shows an "elective affinity" (Max Weber) with his background and political convictions. James had been born into a wealthy family and lived most of his life in the shadow of Harvard Yard. He was a dedicated humanist but also very much a social conservative who believed that class stratification was part of the natural order of things. He celebrated private property as an inherently instinctive individual endowment. The aim of education, therefore, was the development of proper habits, which alone, as the "fly-wheel of society," could save "the children of fortune from the envious uprisings of the poor."[37] To this end, he suggested, teachers should "conceive, and, if possible, reproduce sympathetically in their imagination the mental life of their pupil *as the sort of active unity which he himself feels it to be*" (emphasis added).[38]

This outlook colored James's pragmatism, which combined individualism with radical empiricism. He took Peirce's belief that an empirical method of experimental inquiry could provide an objective foundation for articulating meaning and gave it a spectacularly subjective twist. For James, pragmatism was a theory of truth in action, founded on the notion of "what works." He did not attempt to interpret or constitute meaning socially. He defined his project by saying, simply, that "the pivotal part of my book named *Pragmatism* is its account of the relation called 'truth' which may obtain between an idea (opinion, belief, statement or what not) and its object."[39]

Furthermore, James believed that truth would be derived, not from the exercise of pure reason or the scientific observation of the natural world, but from individual experience: "The truth of an idea is not a stagnant property inherent in it. Truth *happens* to an idea. It *becomes* true, is *made* true by events: its verity *is* in fact an event, a process: the process namely of its verifying itself, its veri-fication. ... The true is the name of whatever proves itself to be good in the way of belief, and good, too, for definite assignable reasons."[40] In short, "the true is only the expedient in the way of our thinking, just as 'the right' is only the expedient of our behaving." Truth thus becomes both contingent and flexible; it can accommodate any situation because it has, according to James, "no doctrines save its method."[41]

If truth is contingent, by what standards ought we—in James's own terms—to "assimilate, validate, corroborate, and verify" ideas?[42] Precisely because there is no way to link the notion of a flexible, mutable truth founded in ever changing reality to the concrete, historical conditions of social experience, the pragmatic method for arriving at such truth can only justify an ethic of particular interest on the abstract terrain of individual subjectivity. Although it is true that a specific *individual* may perceive the worthiness of, for instance, Kant's Enlightenment values and then act in such a way as to extend democracy and choice, it is not possible to say that others should do the same or to articulate *why* universal extension of those values might be desirable. There is, simply, no way to judge the consequences of any choice—outside of the question What benefits *me?* James's pragmatism here thrusts toward a dangerous relativism, which makes it impossible to determine whether one perception, one judgment, one behavior, or one theory should be valued over any other. At the very least, this relativism obviates any efforts to discover or articulate standards for critical, dynamic public knowledge. Taken to the other extreme, it opens the door to fascism (a variant of decisionism); in fact, Mussolini acknowledged having read and admired James's philosophy: "The pragmatism of William James was of great use to me in my political career. James taught me that an action should be judged rather by its results than by its doctrinary basis. I learnt of James that faith in action, that ardent will to live and fight, to which Fascism owes a great part of its success. ... For me the essential was to act."[43]

By celebrating the perceptions of the average person, James made philosophy an instrument and any individual a philosopher. He stressed that it was "only the minds debauched of learning who have ever suspected common sense of not being absolutely true."[44] Here, his notion of putting ideas "to work" and judging them by their results—but offering no criteria by which standards for such judgment could be developed—must be seen as particularly suspect. Ultimately, his theory, despite progressive pretensions, cannot provide any critical standpoint. We may be able to respond to the question Does it work? with a simple yes or no. (We may not even be able to make this response, of course.) But whether "it" works *well* (or not) simply cannot be ascertained, for in extending James's logic we can get no further than the common wisdom that tells us "if it ain't broke, don't fix it." Here we can only contemplate the status quo.

The problem, with regard to public knowledge, is twofold: On the one hand, it is impossible to get past individual subjectivity to a critical standpoint grounded in commonality, and on the other, it is equally impossible to situate communication—or, for that matter, education—in any social context. Public knowledge would here reduce to a cacophony of private subjectivities—the Tower of Babel writ large—all celebrating, in their own way, what *is*. No means of speculating on what *might be* or of sharing subjectivity avails. In such a situation, a politics of public knowledge must inevitably reduce to a politics of individual advantage, something to be continually bargained for within a fragmented, parochial social framework that looks a lot like Sarajevo—or South Central Los Angeles.

From this perspective, Dewey's thought is also problematic, although less acutely so than James's. Far more than either Peirce or James, Dewey focused on reconstructing philosophy and pedagogy in the context of publicly enacted human experience. Unlike Marx, Dewey felt no need to abandon or go beyond philosophy; rather, his aim was to recast theory so that it could become a guide to enlightened *praxis*.[45] Dewey's social and educational philosophy was founded on his belief that human beings are interdependent, with the welfare of any one individual linked to that of any other, and with each member of society obligated to maintain the system of relationships and activities by which particular interests can be met. He believed passionately in democracy as a way of life, taking as his model the face-to-face politics of a New England town meeting in the early days of the republic. Indeed, he located the historical roots of his philosophy in the eighteenth century: "If I were asked to give an historical parallel to this movement in American thought, I would remind my reader of the French philosophy of the Enlightenment."[46] He wanted to make Enlightenment ideals meaningful in the everyday experiences of ordinary people: "Fraternity, liberty, and equality isolated from communal life are hopeless abstractions. Their separate assertion leads to mushy sentimentalism or else to extravagant and fanatical violence which in the end defeats its own aims."[47] Experience, inquiry, and education shaped his vision of democracy as a form of faith; he believed that "every way of life that fails in its democracy limits the contacts, the exchanges, the communications, the interactions by which experience is steadied while it is also enlarged and enriched." Democracy, however, is no easy walk to freedom; it is an unending series of hard tasks and questions which must be faced day to day. Ultimately, "the task of democracy is forever that of the creation of a freer and more human experience in which all share and to which all contribute."[48]

In the context of such faith in democratic practice as a way of life, Dewey's concern for the public and the articulation of a form of public knowledge were all but inevitably linked to his insistence on free and open communication and on the importance of education. As the means by which individuals who are capable of meeting the challenges of democracy can be developed and nurtured, education is central to Dewey's social and political thought. Indeed, he suggested that philosophy and education were virtually synonymous: "If we are willing to conceive education as the process of forming fundamental dispositions, intellectual and emotional, toward nature and fellow men, philosophy may even be defined as *the general theory of education*."[49]

Dewey's critique of modernity proceeded from his notion that "man has suffered the impact of an enormously enlarged control of physical energies without any corresponding ability to control himself and his own affairs."[50] In response to the problems of social and intellectual fragmentation and worn-out institutional forms, he set out to discover "the means by which a scattered, mobile, and manifold public may so recognize itself as to define and express its interests," believing that this task was "in the first instance an intellectual problem: the search for conditions under which the Great Society may become the Great Community."[51] Conditions had changed so profoundly that it would be necessary in the modern world "to re-create by deliberate and determined endeavor the kind of democracy which in its origin one hundred and fifty years ago was largely the product of a fortunate combination of men and circumstances."[52]

Dewey set his prescriptions for social reform squarely within "the corporate and industrial world in which we live, and by thus fulfilling the preconditions for interaction with it, we ... create ourselves as we create an unknown future."[53] Here, as elsewhere, he appears to flirt with the Marxian notion that people create history through their interactions with nature and with each other. But because he took these interactions as given rather than as socially constructed, he believed that it is difficult either to posit or to enact social and political reforms by any means other than moral exhortation. His technological focus on problems of public life and education often failed to acknowledge the vital political issues of power, ethnicity, social class, and racism that colored public life at the turn of the century just as they do today.

In narrating "the eclipse of the public," for example, Dewey hinted that the "the machine age" might be somehow involved, but he avoided a critical confrontation with the economic and social structures of capitalism. Instead, he characterized the decay of the public sphere as a "failure of intelligence." Or, as he put it in a key passage of *Liberalism and Social Action:* "Every problem that arises, personal or collective, simple or complex, is solved only by selecting material from the store of knowledge amassed in past experience and by bringing into play habits already formed. But the knowledge and the habits must be modified to meet the new conditions that have arisen."[54] Social breakdowns thus become translated into collective misunderstandings; if people could just find better ways of adapting themselves to these new conditions, many, if not most, problems would be solved. Although the emphasis on public knowledge as intrinsic to the historical dynamic is laudable, this sort of analysis is really a two-edged sword. To the same degree that it forwards a progressive notion of public knowledge, it implicitly blames the victims, whose ability to conceptualize and utilize new forms of public knowledge may well be impeded by the very structural conditions through which power and domination are socially instantiated, conditions that Dewey's experimental method does not necessarily challenge.

Dewey's democratic faith was premised on "the capacity of the intelligence of the common man to respond with common sense to the free play of facts and ideas which are secured by effective guarantees of free inquiry, free assembly, and free communication."[55] However, by virtually reducing the problems of democracy to a collective misunderstanding of modernity, he all but contradicted his emphasis on "common sense" as a vehicle for transcending these difficulties. On the one hand, he wanted to comprehend structural problems of inequity as "misunderstandings"; on the other, he wanted to assert that the common man had the common sense to respond effectively to the world. If common sense is, in fact, a viable means for effecting social change, how does it misunderstand modernity? The contradiction here is significant: You simply cannot have it both ways. Either common sense avails or a failure of intelligence limits progressive vision—but the two cannot pertain simultaneously.

This contradiction is especially disturbing because Dewey was well aware that the structural conditions of capitalism would inevitably circumscribe democratic practices in everyday life—in his day, as in ours. In an early (1888) essay entitled "The Ethics of Democracy," he suggested that "there is no need to beat about the bush in saying that democracy is not in reality what it is in name until it is industrial, as well as civil and political," although he failed to specify precisely what he meant by "industrial democracy."[56] Perhaps, as Robert Westbrook suggested, this was a politic move on Dewey's part after a close friend and colleague at the University of Michigan had experienced difficulty on the academic job market when he publicly defended the Knights of Labor and social democracy. Whatever his motives for pulling back from a direct confrontation, Dewey had both articulated (and evaded) his awareness of the links between political and economic democracy, setting up a pattern that would recur throughout his career.[57]

In "The School as Social Centre," an address delivered before the National Council of Education in 1902, Dewey insisted that all citizens should be equally entitled to an education geared toward making everyone a full participant in the democratic process:

> Men will long dispute about material socialism, about socialism considered as a matter of distribution of the material resources of the community; but there is a socialism regarding which there can be no such dispute—a socialism of the intelligence and of the spirit. To extend the range and the fullness of sharing in the intellectual and spiritual resources of the community is the very meaning of the community."[58]

In other words, children should be equally empowered to become both self- and other-directing individuals, leaders as well as followers, citizens, and workers. In a rapidly changing world, no child could be educated for a "fixed station in life"; rather, schooling would have to provide children with training that would "give [them] such possessions of [themselves] that [they] may take charge of [themselves]; may not only adapt [themselves] to the changes which are going on, but have power to shape and direct those changes."[59] Indeed, the concept of forming a democratic character through radically egalitarian education was at the heart of Dewey's philosophy of education. However, the political question of how to implement this egalitarianism—whether in schools or in society—received short shrift from him.

In his classic *Democracy and Education,* Dewey suggested that the primary obstacle to egalitarian educational practice was the tendency, from Plato through the present day, for educational thought to form an unholy alliance with class privilege, drawing sharp demarcations between mind and body, theory and practice, culture and utility. Thus, much educational practice represented the institutionalization of profoundly antidemocratic ideas; especially threatening to public knowledge was the split between culture and utility, "itself imbedded in a social dualism: the distinction between the working class and the leisure class." Two separate forms of education emerged from this distinction: one for those who worked with their hands and the other for those who worked with their minds (or not at all). The alliance of privilege and philosophy equating "the educated class and the ruling class" meant that democrats would have to acknowledge that "the reconstruction of philosophy, of education, and of social ideas and methods thus go hand in hand."[60] This kind of remodeling would entail, he further suggested, removing democracy from the formal plane of the voting booth and taking it into the workplace. "What does democracy mean," Dewey asked, "save that the individual is to have a share in determining the conditions and aims of his own work; and that, upon the whole, through the free and mutual harmonizing of different individuals, the work of the world is better done than when planned, arranged, and directed by a few, no matter how wise or of how good intent that few?"[61]

The truly radical element of Dewey's educational thought here collides with his reliance on "intelligence as method" in enacting social or educational reforms. On the one hand, he seems to have argued that prospects for radically democratic education would be blocked by the capitalist division of labor, but, on the other, he seems to have conceived of the exercise of class interests as a failure of insight or communication that could be overcome by moral exhortation in lieu of more basic, structural reforms. Here his thought accommodated the particularist ideology of capitalist democracy, which, as we have seen, rests on a division between a formal commitment to egalitarian rights and ideals and a fundamentally inegalitarian set of economic and social practices. On this point, Antonio Gramsci's analysis of how ideology permeates everyday forms of social relations is particularly instructive. Gramsci's insight was that the habitualized ideas and practices that make up common sense can never be taken for granted. They are neither inevitable nor simply "how things happen to be." Rather, our ideas are socially constructed; they are the product of our interactions with each other and with the natural world.[62]

The real problem with Dewey's pragmatism, however, is neither its questionable ideological content nor its tendency toward acceptance of the common sense of capitalist hegemony. Dewey's argument for democracy founders on his inability to articulate a democratic ideal that can be immanently related to a political strategy for redistributing power and resources—or to instantiating public knowledge along democratic lines. He quite cogently argued against Taylorism and Fordism, pointing out that a "great majority of workers have no insight into the social aims of their pursuits and no direct personal interest in them" and realize "not the ends of *their* actions but only of their employers." He acknowledged that work cannot be "free" until workers gain "direct participation in control."[63] However, although his thought opened up the prospect of democratic public knowledge, it failed to articulate a politics commensurate with this radical vision. The fall-back position, unfortunately, is acceptance of the formalized conditions and mechanisms of purely political democracy as the means by which "effective guarantees of free inquiry, free assembly, and free communication" are to be secured.

The sincerity of Dewey's commitment to democracy is beyond dispute, but it is undercut by his tendency to avoid confronting the structural constraints that limit people's capacity to respond "with common sense to the free play of facts and ideas." In Chapters 1 and 2, I discussed some of the complex ways in which these constraints impede the realization of democracy in politics and in education. In the bleakest scenario, a depoliticized citizenry, intellectually stunted by the privileging of so-called public knowledge available within the stratified educational system, numbly switches channels in its quest for the lowest common denominator of "entertainment" offered by the culture industry. The question that must be addressed if the contradictions of the present are ever to be overcome is how to create conditions that would guarantee all persons an equal chance, first to acquire public knowledge, which is the "common sense" of freedom, and then to enter the discourse, or "free play of facts and ideas," where public choices are pursued.

Clearly, even formalized democracy is better than no democracy at all—but reliance on the assumed benevolence or neutrality of established institutions ultimately reduces to a position that is antipragmatic. By falling back on formal conditions of democracy, Dewey ironically denied his own emphasis on people's experience as the basis of politics—experience that might otherwise provide the basis for the kind of substantively democratic practices that putatively remained his goal. Although political democracy is certainly a precondition for economic democracy, it is—as the endurance and resilience of capitalist democracy have demonstrated—hardly a sufficient condition for the substantiation of practices extending the promise of political democracy to aspects of everyday life.

Thus, it can never suffice simply to assume (implicitly or explicitly) that formally democratic principles, however reconstructed, can in themselves provide the necessary guarantees of freedom—or that proclaiming a particular project socialist or democratic automatically guarantees reflexivity. The objective conditions standing between the formal, political, and juridical concept of bourgeois democracy and the substantive, economic, and practical instantiation of freedom must be articulated and challenged in theory and in practice if reflexivity is to prevail and substantive democracy be won. The political democracy that Marx defined in *On the Jewish Question* as "the final form of emancipation within the framework of the prevailing social order" cannot be conflated with either the *idea* of democracy or its yet to be realized potential.[64] If what is at stake here is the ability to develop standards for public knowledge that critically confront the worst values and norms of capitalist democracy, Dewey's pragmatism is problematic at best. The fallback position of formal, political democracy in the end limits this theory to articulation of "the limits of technical control over objectified natural processes."[65] Indeed, on at least one occasion Dewey admitted to taking the conditions of the present entirely for granted: "We cannot set up, out of our heads, something we regard as an ideal society. We must base our conception upon societies which actually exist."[66]

Such a circular vision, in the end, precludes the transformative possibilities of democratic public knowledge—ironically, since it is pragmatism that opens the door to these possibilities in the first place. Although putatively founded on the concept of democratically conceived and enacted public knowledge, pragmatism tends to further a limited, privileged, and ultimately potentially oppressive set of social and political ideals. Although Dewey's emphasis on "democracy as a way of life" may seem far removed from James's radically individualist subjectivity, there is no necessary disjuncture between the two in terms of outcomes; from the pragmatic position, however articulated, public knowledge can only celebrate things as they are and recapitulate existing privileging of knowledge within the American educational system.

Within a pragmatic paradigm, it is easy for educators with the best of intentions to fall into the delusion of thinking that they are furthering democratic goals when they are, in fact, merely inculcating consent to a set of social institutions that reflect and reproduce the hegemony of capital. Neither pragmatism's democratic social promises nor its innovative pedagogical imperatives can be fulfilled in the context of late capitalism. In an ultimate twist of irony, the pragmatic paradigm's failure to confront the ethic of capital on its own terrain and to forward a politics of authentic public knowledge has both ensured its enduring influence on American educational thought and guaranteed that the bright promises of social and educational reform will remain perpetually unmet.

# Public Knowledge and the Paradox of Democratic Education

In 1880, New York publisher Henry Holt brought out an anonymously writ-ten political satire entitled *Democracy: An American Novel*, which became an overnight sensation and bestseller. The book's mysterious provenance sparked a national guessing game, with newspapers and magazines fueling speculation about the author's real identity. No one imagined that it was Henry Adams; this closely held secret was only publicly revealed after Adams's death in 1918.[1] The novel's protagonist, Mrs. Lightfoot Lee, is a wealthy young widow who forsakes the high society of New York for Wash-ington, D.C. Obsessed with a desire to understand power and politics, she is "bent upon getting to the heart of the great American mystery of democracy and government."[2] She rents a house on Lafayette Square and plunges into her studies, attending sessions of the Senate, reading the *Congressional Rec-ord,* and surrounding herself with the politicos, diplomats, and hangers-on who enjoy her Sunday evening salons.

Mrs. Lee's principal object of study quickly becomes Senator Silas Ratcliffe, of Peonia, Illinois.[3] He is a strikingly handsome man, whose silver tongue and hair are equally affecting. Having barely lost his party's nomina-tion as candidate for president in the last election, he now promises to be "the stumbling block of the new President, who is to be allowed no peace until he makes terms with Ratcliffe." A Cabinet post may be in the offing: "Everyone thinks that the Prairie Giant of Peonia will have the choice of the State or Treasury Department. If he takes either it will be the Treasury, for he is a des-perate political manager, and will want the patronage for the next national convention."[4]

Madeline Lee is eager to learn, and she finds Ratcliffe an obliging tutor in the ways of the Capitol. He lectures her on the dissonance between demo-cratic theory and practice, explaining that "no representative government can long be much better or much worse than the society it represents. Purify

society and you purify the government. But try to purify the government arti-
ficially and you only aggravate failure."[5] Madeline's lessons demonstrate
over and over how deeply cynicism and corruption pervade American politics. Shaken, she wonders where her pristine democratic ideals fit in "this
wilderness of stunted natures where no straight road was to be found, but
only the tortuous and aimless tracks of beasts and things that crawl."[6]

Desperately hoping for some affirmation of her democratic faith, one Sunday evening Mrs. Lee confronts Nathan Gore, who, like Adams, is a New
England Yankee, erstwhile diplomat, and historian. Gore is newly returned
to Washington and "willing to be restored to his old mission."[7] He has hopes
of an appointment with the new administration. Lee demands that he tell her
"whether America is right or wrong." Is, she asks, "democracy the best government, and universal suffrage a success?"[8]

Gore's reply is interesting in that it anticipates Dewey's democratic credo
and is, at the same time, pure Henry Adams. "I believe in democracy," he
tells Lee, because

> democracy asserts the fact that the masses are now raised to higher intelligence
> than formerly. All our civilization aims at this mark. ... I grant that it is an ex-
> periment, but it is the only direction society can take that is worth its taking; the
> only conception of its duty large enough to satisfy its instincts. ... Every other
> possible step is backward, and I do not care to repeat the past.[9]

For Adams, this was optimism. Although he had failed in public life and re-
treated from direct involvement in politics, as a historian he tried to show
where America had gone wrong. Here, his outlook is sharply demarcated
from Dewey's buoyant optimism regarding the promise of democracy. Adams was ambivalent about whether democratic politics could ever be "put
right" in America. This ambivalence—which at times slides into pessimism—permeates the *Education*; it also shapes the novel's denouement.

Mrs. Lee hopes to reform Ratcliffe by marrying him—assuming that afterward, under her influence, he will reform democracy. But she calls off the
wedding in distress after discovering that the senator's vote can be readily
purchased. Neither Silas Ratcliffe nor the system he represents could ever be
shaped to fit with Madeline's high standards. She is left with no choice but to
follow Adams's example and remove herself from the public fray. She an-
nounces that she will make an expedition to Egypt: "Democracy has shaken
my nerves to pieces. Oh, what a rest it would be to live in the Great Pyramid
and look out for ever at the polar star!"[10]

For Madeline Lee, as for Henry Adams, democracy had become simultaneously a best hope and a worst enemy. This paradox is not surprising, for
the concept of democracy is very old and complex; the term has multiple
meanings.[11] As Ellen Meiksins Wood stressed, following Kant, Luxemburg,

and others, "The very diversity of meanings of the concept of democracy highlights the differences between bourgeois democracy and other forms; and it is precisely the conflation of these meanings that has supported the capitalist claim to exclusive ownership of democracy, encouraging us to identify democracy as such with its bourgeois-parliamentary forms."[12] This identification of democracy with one particular historical manifestation of the concept was at the heart of Adams's ambivalence—and, as was discussed in Chapter 3, also proved problematic in Dewey's thought.

The ideology of capitalist democracy relies on a strict demarcation between politics, on the one hand, and economic and social questions, on the other. For all practical purposes, democracy is restricted to a formal realm predicated on the rule of law, individual liberty, and free elections—and firmly excluded from the substance of social relations. The hegemony of capital depends upon strict separation of the principles of citizenship from the rules that apply in nonpolitical arenas and on maintaining that separation. In the process, these principles become ever more formalized and distanced from the everyday lives of ordinary people. Here, Dewey's famous concept of "democracy as lived experience" has little, if any, resonance.

A commitment to democratic education and public knowledge demands a commitment to children—indeed, to all people—founded on equality and human dignity. The seeds of this obligation are found in the Declaration of Independence: "We hold these truths to be self-evident, that all men are created equal, that they are endowed by their Creator with certain unalienable Rights, that among these are Life, Liberty, and the pursuit of Happiness." All too often, arguments for educational equity are dismissed as counterfactual; since individuals vary widely with regard to physical and intellectual aptitudes, talents, and abilities, claims for "equal creation" are a priori invalid. But as Howard Zinn pointed out, there is no period after the word "equal" in Jefferson's sentence, only a comma. The full meaning of the phrase turns on the notion that people are equal, not in terms of their natural capabilities, but in terms of their rights.[13] Yet, what Jefferson believed to be self-evident two centuries ago is hardly so today, especially where questions of public education are concerned.

For decades, policy makers and public educators have confused rhetoric and action. Americans have a long-standing rhetorical commitment to the idea that one primary purpose of politics is building better lives for their children and grandchildren. This commitment has served to mask a reluctance to take actions that might substantively improve the lives of real children who have real needs. Where children are concerned, Americans have been remarkably slow to act for the public good. The decades-long debates over federal aid to education, in which racism stymied efforts to improve the nation's public schools, are just one example.[14] The reluctance to translate rhetoric into action where children are concerned is logical; there is no public profit to be derived directly from such action—the cynic would add here, more-over, that children cannot vote.

Beginning in 1980, social programs of all kinds were steadily gutted in the United States at federal and state levels. At the same time, it was fashionable in right-wing circles to announce that our educational failures placed na-tional security in jeopardy.[15] Yet, there are other, more productive ways of addressing the problem of public education. Marian Wright Edelman of-fered an alternative view along with some chilling statistics:

> Our national security is at imminent risk because of the current living conditions for children in the United States:
>
> - Every eight seconds of the school day, a child drops out (552,000 during the 1987-1988 school year).
> - Every 26 seconds of each day, a child runs away from home (1.2 million a year).
> - Every 67 seconds, a teenager has a baby (472,623 in 1987).
> - Every 7 minutes, a child is arrested for a drug offense (76,986 a year).
> - Every day, 100,000 children are homeless.
> - Every school day, 135,000 children bring guns to school. A child is safer in Northern Ireland than on the streets of this country.
> - Every 53 minutes, a child dies due to poverty (10,000 a year).[16]

Year after year, economic insecurities have been mounting—and the conse-quences are far greater than the simple sums of money involved. Consider some further facts:

- In 1960, corporate CEOs made 41 times what factory workers earned. By 1988, CEOs were earning 93 times the average factory worker's salary; this means that almost twice a week, the CEO re-ceived a check equal to the factory worker's *annual* salary.
- In the same period, CEO salaries went from 38 times to 72 times the salary of the average schoolteacher.
- Between 1982 and 1989, the number of billionaires in the U.S. quintu-pled.
- In the same period, the number of children living in poverty in-creased by 2.1 million.
- In 1990, Head Start programs served only 27 percent of those chil-dren eligible.[17]

What these facts suggest is that much of the discomfort Americans feel about educational questions today stems from a sense that deep-seated inequities exist. Unless and until national priorities change dramatically, un-less and until human lives become as valuable as high-tech weaponry, it will remain impossible to postulate suggestions for meaningful reforms in public education. There is nothing in the capitalist ethic, which places profits over people, to mandate such a shift. However, a socialist ethic of democracy would immediately demand a realignment of priorities to bring national practices in line with what is at present the empty rhetoric of democratic political culture. This realignment is just one of many preconditions for democratic education. Others emerge from the dialectical nature of public schooling in contemporary capitalist democracy.

On the one hand, schools—whether public or private—are intrinsically conservative cultural institutions, entrusted in large measure with the task of social reproduction. Because they socialize huge masses of young people by inculcating and replicating the behaviors, habits, and hierarchies central to the maintenance of consent, these institutions serve as agencies of capitalist cultural and social hegemony.[18] Yet, on the other hand, schools are also places where students gain access to the tools of literacy, criticism, and reason; as such, they have tremendous emancipatory potential. Schools must thus be seen as something other than mere instruments of domination, because counterhegemonic ideas, questions, and possibilities are always present, no matter how strong the apparent edifice of consent.[19] As Martin Carnoy and Henry M. Levin suggested, this contradiction is firmly rooted in the context of capitalist social reproduction: "Public education is both a subsidy to employers and a way for workers to gain social mobility; it trains young people to be good workers and good democrats, reproducing a class structured labor force to fit into a historically defined division of labor, but also inculcating aspirations about the nature of work in a democratic society."[20] Education thus mirrors the tensions between universal and particular interests that shape capitalist social relations and relegate democratic practice to the formal rituals of a politics that is removed from everyday life.

Although, to be sure, representative political institutions that guarantee formal rights do not preclude expression of the substantive concerns of working people, they do not provide any incentives for such expression either. It is not the institutional forms of parliamentary democracy that are in question but the denial of popular power entailed when political rights are permanently detached from social and economic questions. Indeed, this split undergirds the privileging of private property under capitalism. Other exploitative forms of property rely on linkages between political and economic power, which assure that political rights remain exclusive to specific individuals or groups. Within capitalism, however, it is at least theoretically possible to extend formal political rights without limit, without in any way altering the exploitation central to maintaining the economic system. This structural characteristic of capitalist democracy renders any effort to unify political, economic, and social rights or power extremely difficult, for class barriers stand sentinel over any challenges to the property rights of capital.[21]

Thus, the goals of expanding choice and extending participation must be conceptualized in both quantitative and qualitative terms that take class seriously. This is true for politics and education alike. Here, the socialist project of making the *formal* promises of democratic politics *substantively* available to all, not just on the terrain of rights and liberties, but in everyday life as well, illumines present difficulties with regard to democratic theory and democratic education.

The national furor provoked by discussion of "political correctness" and "the canon" in higher education serves as a sad reflection of how barren public discourse really is at present—even, or perhaps especially, in the academy. These conflicts clarify what is at stake in attempts to reconstitute a democratic public sphere, and the clarification in turn provides a context for assessing contemporary debates over democratic theory among new communitarians and neo-Kantians. Both sides mistakenly assume that public spaces for democratic deliberation do or must exist; they virtually ignore the history that suggests otherwise. This misconception becomes especially problematic in light of the way that both camps have either addressed or influenced questions of democratic education.

Although new communitarians like Michael Walzer and Benjamin Barber attempted to derive prescriptions for practice from the habits and mores of a particular society, they justified existing customs simply because they are already in place. As Walzer put it in a typical passage: "The political community is probably the closest we can come to a world of common meanings. Language, history, and culture come together ... to produce a collective consciousness. National character conceived as a fixed and permanent mental set, is obviously a myth, but the sharing of sensibilities and intuitions among the members of a historical community is a fact of life."[22] Barber also emphasized such cultural and civic ties when he defined "citizens" as "neighbors bound together neither by blood nor by contract but by their common concerns and common participation in the search for common solutions to common conflicts."[23] "A community of citizens thus cannot be treated as a mere aggregation of individuals."[24] The whole, it seems, is something quite different from the sum of its parts.

Locating citizenship and democratic deliberation within the context of community is certainly an improvement on the individualistic premise of classical liberalism. The suggestion that there is something in the collective life of the group beyond mere accidents of locale or birth militates against the myth of rugged individualism that has shaped so much in American culture. The notion that people might be bonded by the struggle to solve problems or settle conflicts and, in the process, become something quite different as a group than they might have been as a mere aggregate of disparate individuals is central to the concept of democracy as a process. Yet the communitarian standpoint still leaves a great deal to be desired. How, in a world characterized by complexity if nothing else, are we to decide on what constitutes common culture?

A given society is more than just the sum of its cultural habits and concerns. Especially (but not exclusively) in modern industrial societies, multivariant economic, social, and political structures shape the historical communities within which human beings produce and reproduce themselves and their cultural forms. How to winnow out any single set of traditions on which to ground choice and guide democracy is the question that communitarians cannot answer. If, in today's complex world, multiple options and traditions coexist within particular communities—peacefully or otherwise—where should we begin to stipulate the collective consciousness that will shape and articulate political culture?

Communitarians mistakenly assume common culture as their starting point, taking it as a fact of life. They thus cannot respond reflexively to the structures within which history manifests itself. Furthermore, if mutually exclusive traditions exist within a given community, it will be utterly impossible to determine which standards should apply as the basis for judgment. The very shape of everyday life is circumscribed by such cultural givens; communitarians can neither justify the present nor speculate about the future without falling back upon inherently circular logic.

The circularity of the communitarian approach to democratic theory becomes especially problematic when that approach is contrasted to Habermas's category of the public sphere, which links the concept of the public to the transition to modern capitalism made by eighteenth and nineteenth century liberal democratic societies.[25] This analysis incorporates a theory of cultural change and transmission, accommodating structures of social reproduction in historical process. Communitarian theories of democracy, however, rely heavily on a transhistorical notion of the public. They thus can neither explain how publics may be manifest variously in different times and places nor specify how the very meaning of "the public" might change over time.

Barber, for example, hinted at the need for actively critical public knowledge as the cornerstone of his "strong democracy." Although he did not develop an explicit concept of public knowledge per se, he contended that "only direct political participation—activity that is explicitly public—is a completely successful form of civic education for democracy," explaining that the "politically edifying influence of participation has been noted a thousand times since first Rousseau and then Mill and de Tocqueville suggested that democracy was best taught by practicing it."[26] Barber also stressed the linkages between public participation and civic education in *An Aristocracy of Everyone,* his recent defense of public schooling.[27] However, because he consistently treated cultural meanings as given rather than as the terrain of struggle and disputation, Barber was not able to provide a critical perspective from which to assess whether any particular project or activity—however explicitly public—might be emancipatory. Thus, it is impossible to distinguish how or why Shakespeare, for instance, should be taught in high schools in urban ghettos or even how the kind of community service that Barber believed should be part of the college curriculum would further democratic ends. Moreover, Barber omitted any consideration of the many different kinds of civic pedagogy—for example, Tocqueville's view of participation rooted originally in interest or necessity—that suggest alternatives to the schemes he proposed.

Communitarian theories of democracy are also incapable of positing criteria for assessing public actions in terms of a democratic ideal; indeed, they cannot even recognize that the need for such criteria exists. The abstract notion of community at the heart of this theoretical stance thus assumes an ironically utopian mantle. "The public" may mean anything, or everything, or nothing; along with the very notion of community, it is simply something to celebrate. At the surface level, this aspect of communitarian thought has great appeal, for it offers a line of putative defense against the centrifugal forces of modernity. "Putative" is the key word here, however; celebrating the public or community without at the same time stipulating substance and standards simply serves to mask the root causes of modern social conditions. From the communitarian standpoint, it is impossible to confront the structural contradictions of late capitalism critically; it is equally impossible to suggest insights on how to overcome these problems. The metaphorical content of such theorizing emerges clearly: "community" represents a value-neutral substitute for the value-laden social bonds—continuity, affinity, family, loyalty—that the capitalist marketplace continues to erode.[28] Attempts to posit reform that would lead to expanded literacy, class access, and equality in education—or contest the privileging of knowledge through privatized forms of elite education—will be caught in the same circular logic as inheres in the pragmatist paradigm discussed in Chapter 3.

Neo-Kantian theories of democracy and democratic education, such as those put forward by John Rawls and Amy Gutmann, attempt to provide sets of a priori principles that can inform democratic social and political practice. Whereas communitarians fail to distance themselves reflexively from cultural givens, the neorationalists successfully release their thought from the bonds of immediacy. They do so, however, only at a price. By removing individuals from any and all contingent sociohistorical and political circumstances, the neorationalists sacrifice contextual and contingent concerns. This "take" on democratic thought is thus no better equipped to accommodate concrete social, economic, and political relationships within a dynamic of change than the communitarian stance that it opposes.

Rawls, of course, developed a criterion of judgment along with a commitment to positive values as the basis of a democratic public. Justice as fairness supplies "a principle of conduct that applies to a person in virtue of his nature as a free and equal rational being."[29] The cost of ascertaining "the virtue of practices where there are competing interests and where persons feel entitled to press their rights on each other," however, is unmeasurable. It remains an absolutely abstract concept.[30] By presupposing ignorance of contradictions in the structures of accumulation (and other social forms) in the name of Kantian individualism, Rawls denied any chance of establishing a bridge between "what is" (which his theory ignores) and "what ought to be" (which his theory suggests, but only in a vacuum). His insistence on this "original position," where individuals are utterly stripped of all knowledge regarding their particular circumstances and interests and forced to decide on the basis of what they must assume universalized interests to require, is especially problematic here. Rawls assumed that stripping people of all possible particularity would allow universal reason to prevail. But if people's "desires and aspirations" must be "restricted from the outset by the principles of justice which specify the boundaries that ... systems of ends must respect," commonality can only be stipulated on an abstract plane of formal logic.[31] Any concept of the public or public knowledge must, therefore, remain so far removed from concrete reality as to be virtually meaningless. Here, possibilities for democratic educational reform and critical literacy are as truncated as they are in communitarian theory, although for different reasons.

The difficulties of deriving effective *praxis* from a neorationalist position are especially apparent in Gutmann's attempt to articulate a democratic theory of education. She believed that democratic education is "a political as well as an educational ideal," holding that "education not only sets the stage for democratic politics, it plays a central role in it. Its dual role poses one of the primary moral problems of politics: who should share the authority to influence the way democratic citizens are educated?"[32] Gutmann would appear to have hit on the central point of the curriculum debates: By whose authority should the form and substance of education be decided? Although she *hinted* at the moral implications of this very political question, she immediately backed off from this stance, claiming that there "is no morally acceptable way to achieve social agreement on a moral ideal of education, at least not in our lifetimes."[33] Thus, she posited an abstract ideal but refused to explain it or apply it as a standard for judgment at a critical juncture.

Gutmann suggested that the "separation between a moral and a political ideal of education is often hard to accept," especially "when we are convinced not only of the correctness of our moral ideal but also of the beneficial social consequences that would follow from its implementation."[34] She offered her own feminist commitment to the ideal of an egalitarian family as an example of this kind of thinking. She saw the chasm between the moral and the political as reflected in the way in which this desirable moral ideal "does not simply translate into a political ideal that sanctions state intervention into the family for the sake of making it more egalitarian."[35] Yet, rather than confronting the challenge of building a theoretical bridge between the two realms, she simply elided them, preferring "to concentrate on questions concerning how democratic governments should furnish the educational room unoccupied by parental discretion."[36] Because she drew such a sharp separation between categories, on close inspection this room turns out to be very small; a great deal of content is to be sacrificed here for the sake of theoretical form.

Gutmann tried to distance her work from Rawls's more extreme abstractions, suggesting that the method she used to explore the relationship between democratic theory and educational policymaking "is akin to what John Rawls calls 'reflective equilibrium,' but it does not require us to separate ourselves from our particular interests or our moral convictions by entering an original position."[37] This statement contradicts her prior suggestion that radically dissociating moral and political ideals of education ought to be acceptable. Still, the contradiction is not readily apparent, for Gutmann's analysis is continually driven back upon a set of ahistorical concepts and definitions. She premised her theory on the notion of a "democratic state of education," which putatively "recognizes that educational authority must be shared among parents, citizens, and professional educators even though such sharing does not guarantee that power will be wedded to knowledge, that parents can successfully pass their prejudices on to their children, or that education will be neutral among competing conceptions of the good life."[38]

The cooperative or collaborative processes by which such public authority would be constituted are never addressed here. Presumably, "parents," "citizens," and "professional educators" are representative labels for monolithic groups whose various interests can be depended upon to check and balance each other. Again, as with Rawls, questions of intragroup diversity and the possibility of fractions having conflicting or irreconcilable interests can be neither asked nor answered. And the larger question of how, in history, such a state might evolve—or how the conditions for its constitution might be specified—cannot even be approached.[39]

The failings of the neorationalist stance came into sharp focus when Gutmann addressed the relationship between public and private schooling. She raised a provocative question of whether "access to public schooling" is "a necessary or desirable limit on democratic authority over primary education."[40] In other words, should democracies ban private schools? This question strikes at the heart of how educational authority may be privileged by nondemocratic interests, as it often has been in capitalist democracy. Gutmann's response was negative; in the process of defending it, she reduced a potentially rich debate over the relationship between privileged economic

power, schooling, and public educational authority to a broad—and remarkably sterile—category of "dissent."

"Private schooling in the United States serves primarily to permit Catholic
and other religiously committed parents to send their children to schools that
teach their faith," Gutmann claimed, conflating all choices to opt out of public schooling into the category of dissent founded on religious faith.[41] The
problem here is that the logic behind this category is fundamentally flawed.
Actually, the communitarians would develop a better response on this point
than Gutmann was able to provide, because they are far more aware of the
web of fears and judgments people face when deciding the future of their
children—and how such concerns are often rooted in the historical traditions of a given community.

Although many parents certainly send their children to denominationally
affiliated private schools because they support religious education, this is not
the sole motivating factor for all parents who reject public education. Private
schooling—religious or secular—clearly allows a greater degree of parental
control over the racial, sexual, class, and cultural mix of children (and teachers) with whom their own daughters and sons will associate. There exists today a common perception, especially among the educated middle class, that
public schools, particularly in urban areas, are intransigently dangerous,
substandard institutions. As J. Anthony Lukas pointed out in his analysis of
the effects of court-ordered busing on the Boston public schools, middle-
class flight from the public schools was a factor before Judge Arthur
Garrity's desegregation order in the early 1970s and would have gone on
even if there had been no busing.[42] Yet Gutmann ignored this entire spectrum of issues, along with the larger questions of allocation of power and
privilege in society, institutionalized racism, and control of economic resources for education that they incontrovertibly reflect.

Gutmann's analysis in this area collapses too many categories and elides
the value-loaded issues of class and race. By her logic, the "Saint Grottlesex"
constellation of exclusive and expensive preparatory schools analyzed by Peter W. Cookson, Jr., and Caroline Hodges Persell is categorically no different
from the Catholic schools in Boston—highly disciplined bastions of basic education and sternly traditional values—to which the white working class fled
rather than accept forced busing, or from the all-white Protestant academies
that blossomed across the Deep South in the wake of Little Rock.[43] By her
logic, we must see parental decisions to send their children to any such
schools rather than to local public institutions as motivated by nothing more
than a preference for *religious* education.

At first glance, such assumptions appear rather silly. After all, Joseph P.
Kennedy sent his Roman Catholic sons to Episcopalian Groton because it
promised acceptance to Harvard College and a ticket to elite society, not because of any deeply felt conviction about religious education. However,

there are more serious issues at work here. Much as the communitarian celebration of an abstract ideal of community serves to mask the real social conditions of modern life, metaphorically replacing affective bonds eroded by
the intrusion of the market, the neorationalist approach evades critical political questions of power, conflict, and social antagonism. It does insist that
because modern, pluralist democracies cannot agree on a single public good,
they are therefore unable to derive politics from religious, moral, or philosophical conceptions of the good life. But neorationalists all too often mistake the *beginning* point of democratic discourse for its end.

If what is really at stake—for democracy and education alike—is the question of social unity, then what is called for here is a *transformation* of social
values and reform of structural constraints on equality, autonomy, and
choice. It is not enough merely to articulate such values or reforms in the abstract or to valorize the status quo. The neorationalist position, at best, may
be able to describe formal preconditions for such a transformation, yet it
cannot account for how newly articulated democratic demands might be
substantiated through praxis. In the end, because they have sacrificed substance for the sake of form, the neorationalists are no more able to derive
meaningful standards for public knowledge than their communitarian opponents.[44]

Both sides in this debate fail to recognize that the public is a critical conceptual foundation of democratic theory and education. Communitarians
simply assume the public as a given aspect of social organization, culture,
and tradition; neorationalists implicitly posit its theoretical necessity without articulating it among their a prioris. Each position is therefore equally
unable to conceptualize reflexively this most basic component of democratic
theory and practice; neither can confront the essential contradictions of capitalist democracy. A dynamic, reflexive notion of the public must precede any
discussion of education in and for democracy. Attention to this detail, however, has been spectacularly absent from contemporary policy debates.[45]
Voices from the left and right alike have, in one way or another, followed
communitarians and neorationalists in taking the public as either given or
necessary. All fail to recognize that this concept is a product of historical con-
junctures that may be manifest differently at various times and places.[46]

By taking the public as given or necessary and assuming cultural commonality, the communitarian and neorationalist theories of democracy and
democratic education simply deny reality. The consequences are made manifest by the ethnographic research of sociolinguist Shirley Brice Heath, who
has written extensively on the differential valuation and use of literacy in
three culturally (and class) distinct communities in the southern United
States.[47] She suggested, for example, that in the two working-class communities she studied—one African American, one white fundamentalist Protestant—people generally do not feel that schooling makes, or might make,

much difference in their lives. Most working-class jobs offer few opportunities to read or write creatively and present few occasions where the use of oral language might be critical for success.

The workers Heath studied spent "their days and nights at work making few instrumental or heuristic uses of language." Most were simply told what to do by supervisors; they were unable to make changes in procedures and seldom aware of the outcomes of projects. Thus, it made little sense to them to question the reasons behind a particular task or to form opinions about the role that the task might play in the overall process and even less sense to articulate such concerns.[48] It requires no great leap of logic to suggest that there are political consequences attendant upon such sociolinguistic differentiation. I will elaborate upon these in my discussion of "critical literacy" in Chapter 6, but analyses like Heath's serve here to bring the deficiencies of the political and educational theories shaping current debates into sharp focus. Not only do they make it evident that there is no common culture, but they also undercut a priori attempts to elide distinctions and difference. How, the question becomes, could one even articulate an a priori notion of universalized interests without implicitly privileging some linguistic forms over others? Once again we find ourselves on barren terrain indeed.

Socialist theory provides the vital link between theory and practice that overcomes the emptiness of these debates, however. It conceives of democracy as a fluid process aimed at overcoming the demarcation between politics and everyday life and constraining arbitrary exercise of socioeconomic and political power. Unlike the liberal theory that undergirds capitalist democracy, socialist theory is not premised on individualism but rather grounded in the collective. Unlike communitarian and neo-Kantian theories of democracy, it locates this collectivity within a historical dynamic that refuses to accept the limitations of the present. At the same time, socialist thought grounds the civic activity of individuals or groups within communities according to values that are both universal and particularistic.

Here, the whole concept of democratic accountability demands that issues be evaluated in terms of how they are likely to affect those who are least able to protect themselves in society—those who, for whatever reasons (social, political, economic, and so on) are least empowered to make autonomous choices. Because democratic accountability inherently provides the basis for an immanent critique of existing conditions and for envisioning the conditions of freedom, it provides a baseline for establishing standards by which to judge the character of public life. Or, as Bronner put it: "If this ethical fulcrum enables socialist theory to stand in a coherent relation to the revolutionary heritage of bourgeois philosophy, it also helps in the formation of judgments regarding past practices and facilitates the creation of a socialist tradition that will speak to the current age."[49] A socialist theory of democracy, therefore, has immediate relevance for the concept of public knowledge as the ground for democratic education; here, we find a way out of the dilemmas of liberal, communitarian, and neo-Kantian thought. The ethic of democratic accountability provides a basis for overcoming the tensions between universal and particular demands, which currently limit possibility by privileging certain forms of knowledge over others on the basis of class (and race) distinctions.

The socialist conception of democracy contests both the arbitrary exercise of state power and the inequities of the accumulation process, with which existing political institutions have—as Henry Adams (no radical himself!) so pungently pointed out a century ago—become deeply intertwined. But socialism does this in terms of a process that is ongoing, linked to historical traditions—a process whose outcomes cannot be predetermined. The socialist premise of democratic accountability relies on the formal and universalist assumptions that support the rule of law while at the same time incorporating a specific class standpoint that challenges the structural contradictions of capitalist accumulation. Thus, all existing institutional arrangements—including those surrounding capital—are held accountable in terms of both the universal and generalizable concerns of public life and the particular interests of workers[50]—and they are held accountable to democracy.

The project of democracy becomes a class issue, focused on the task of developing new means by which reasoned debate among citizens facilitates the development of a new logic of accumulation, one in which "subjects can reassert their control over the objective world which they produce as well as the institutions in which they function." This entails a continuing effort in the workplace and other social institutions to make instrumental decision making accountable to democracy. Instrumental logic would be subordinated to decision making that was aimed at expanding the available range of public goods instead of the private profits central to capitalist accumulation. Institutional arrangements here are predicated on expanded individual choice: Institutions are places where each person in society can realize his or her subjectivity formally and substantively. Thus, socialist democracy relies on a conception of the world as a place where no individual will be treated either as an object or as a means to some instrumental end.[51]

Following in the tradition of the Enlightenment, socialist theory insists on regarding individual self-determination as an integral part of democratic politics. By seeking to subject all values and decisions to constant scrutiny, debate, and accountability, socialist theory challenges the instrumentality of capital and provides an inherently public context for political and educational practices. Thus, the task of democratic education becomes not only that of making schools institutionally inclusive or representative but also of holding them democratically accountable for the development of autonomous, rational citizens. Accountability here involves the provincialism inherent in localized standards for funding and curriculum as well as adherence to *universal* ideals of freedom, equality, and mutual respect—ideals that are not fixed or given, but elastic.

Earlier in this chapter I cited the objective conditions that cry out for a realignment of priorities aimed at bringing educational practices in line with the rhetoric of democratic political culture. A socialist theory of education would call upon national, state, and local authorities to abolish all practices based upon or furthering privilege in any form. Current right-wing fears that the task of establishing equity means leveling or "dumbing down" are founded in conservative fears that "haves" must surrender the fruits of their privilege to "have-nots." Indeed, there is a long tradition of such concerns expressed in political theory—beginning with Plato and running through Tocqueville, Adam Smith, and John Stuart Mill. This rhetoric successfully cloaks the real issues of class and race while furthering inequity. There is no objective reason why, in a society of abundance, any child, any individual, should be denied the right to develop to the fullest extent possible or the opportunity to do so in schools that are clean, fully staffed, and fully equipped.

Because it is grounded in the notion that democracy is not just the formal preserve of politics, but part of everyday life, a socialist theory of education demands a developmental pedagogy that links individual experience and growth with social problems and needs. The elementary and secondary curriculum would, therefore, be devoted to expanding cosmopolitanism and the realm of individual and collective experience so that all children could come to maturity believing that they have the right—and the responsibility—to participate in society, helping to shape the very intellectual and cultural traditions they study rather than being little more than passive receptors of least-common-denominator cultural forms. Such a pedagogical outlook would, of course, go a long way toward overcoming the dichotomy between mental and manual labor and would challenge the existing division of labor—in schools, and beyond.

# 5

## Public Intellectuals
## and Public Knowledge

Over the past decade, the question of what it means to be a "public intellectual" has been debated both on its own merits and as part of the larger controversies that have raged over the form and content of higher education in the United States. At least one extended obituary mourning the collective demise of public intellectuals has appeared, generating a broad spectrum of response.[1] In another set of narratives, powerful cabals of faculty "radicals" are accused of taking over the universities and implementing pernicious educational doctrines that place not only the economy but civilization itself at risk.[2] Throughout the 1992 presidential campaign, a cultural elite comprising an odd mixture of professors, journalists, and television sitcom producers was repeatedly blamed for declining "family values" and otherwise held accountable for the decay of democracy in America. Yet much of what has been said recently with regard to public intellectuals has been articulated before.

As the ninetenth century drew to its close, Henry Adams mused that "one knew no better in 1894 than in 1854 what an American education ought to be in order to count as a success."[3] By 1892, he had become completely estranged from public life in the nation's capital; he felt that it no longer provided any semblance of a social medium where the ideas of "men of discernment and refinement" could influence public affairs.[4] Those few who persisted in the attempt were simply ignored, by the president and Congress alike. As Adams put it: "No one in society seemed to have the ear of anybody in Government. No one in Government knew any reason for consulting any one in society. The world had ceased to be wholly political, but politics had become less social."[5]

Indeed, by the time Adams sat down to write his narrative of intellectual decline in the post–Civil War United States, the model of the intellectual gentleman that prevailed during the revolutionary era had been quite effectively marginalized in politics. For a brief moment in time—one perhaps more immediate to Adams because of his family connections than to others among his generation—the nation's leaders had been, for the most part, intellectuals. Sages and scientists, conversant with classical languages and learning, they had brought their wide reading in history, politics, and law to bear upon the political problems of their day. Historian Richard Hofstadter has suggested that no other historical moment "has produced so many men of knowledge among its political leaders as the age of John Adams, John Dickinson, Benjamin Franklin, Alexander Hamilton, Thomas Jefferson, James Madison, George Mason, James Wilson, and George Wythe."[6]

Indeed, these eighteenth-century men had been bound together, if not by common agreement on all political questions, then by the fact of their active participation in the public sphere during a time of revolution. Society and politics, if not seamlessly interwoven, certainly meshed in their day to a degree almost unimaginable in Henry Adams's time—let alone a century later. But that day had passed. The presidency of Henry's grandfather, John Quincy Adams (1825–1829) had, in fact, served as "the test case for the unsuitability of the intellectual temperament for political leadership in early nineteenth-century America." While in office, John Quincy "had the temerity to suggest that some policies of the governments of France, Great Britain and Russia could well be emulated" in the new nation; having studied in many of the great European cities, as well as at Harvard, he enjoyed a wide range of literary and scientific interests, from writing epic poems to reporting on systems of weights and measures. In suggesting that Washington should become a cultural capital, however, President Adams "became the symbol of the old order and the chief victim of the reaction against the learned man."[7]

Intellectual cosmopolitanism was unpopular then as now; John Quincy Adams's suggestions that the federal government should become involved in national programs aimed at educational and scientific advancement, including the establishment of a national university, were sneered at by members of Congress and fueled popular fears of a strong central government in the rapidly expanding, but still young and insecure, nation. President Adams was thus forced to abandon his plans; he represented a kind of aristocratic intellect and leadership whose time had passed, to be eclipsed soon by the egalitarian and anti-intellectual impulses of Jacksonian Democracy.[8]

So, when the young Henry Adams returned to Washington from England after the Civil War, he found a very different sort of person in political ascendancy. President Grant and his cronies were despicable examples of the prevailing economic and political opportunism; Adams scathingly criticized them as "men whose energies were the greater, the less they wasted on thought." They might be "forces of nature ... but they made short work of scholars."[9] The bourgeois public sphere that had sheltered and fed political aspirations in the revolutionary and republican eras was in decline; not only had politics become "less social," but so had intellectual endeavor. As Adams was quick to point out at every opportunity, the qualities of intellect and leadership seldom overlapped in the real life of practical politics.

Adams, however, would never have referred to himself as an "intellectual"; the term did not come into use until the famous "Manifesto of the Intellectuals" at the height of the Dreyfus affair in France, in 1898. The term most likely originated "from the pen of Clemenceau in an article in *L'Aurore* of January 23, 1898, as a collective description of the most prominent Dreyfusards" and quickly came to connote a pejorative disloyalty to the nation itself. Thus, in its earliest usage, *les intellectuels* was politicized—as a term of contempt employed by the Right against the Left. The appellation quickly became indicative of a particular political slant and style: *Les intellectuels* were cosmopolitan, rational, elitist, and formal in their approach. As autonomous individuals, they took a critical view of the world, seeing that modernity had broken forever the old bonds of place and tradition. Partisans of the Right, on the other hand, gloried in being rooted to tradition; they chauvinistically celebrated nationalism, emotionalism, popularity, and contextuality.[10]

The tension between the autonomous—or, in Karl Mannheim's famous phrase, "free-floating, unattached"—intellectual and the "engaged" (Sartre) or "organic" (Gramsci) intellectual attached to a specific social project or movement has been a hallmark of the problematic position of intellectuals for nearly a century. The notion of a detached, classless individual willing to forgo all partisan involvements for the sake of a quasi-religious commitment to pure thought was, of course, central to Julien Benda's indictment of the *trahaison des clercs*. To Benda, an intellectual's involvement in politics constituted a betrayal of the sacred that far outstripped any forms of treason against governments or individuals.[11]

Benda's conception of the political role of the individual has often been misread. Bruce Robbins, for example, claimed that Benda's charge of treason "names not a violation but the essence of the intellectuality thus conceived." If being an intellectual involves renouncing all that is partisan for the sake of higher things, then "the 'clerc' must *always* 'betray' from the moment his ... thought assumes any social embodiment." The world is thus inevitably engaged, and any "wishful incongruity between intellectuals and politics dissolves into a historic intimacy."[12] Robbins insisted that the notion that intellectuals could or should remain "unattached" is an illusion; by omission or commission, the life of the mind—once articulated and made social through linguistic activity in communication—is inherently political. But this is not the real issue; Benda, a humanist, was committed to the values of free inquiry and undistorted truth. He took part in anti-Fascist conferences at a time when many of his colleagues chose to take the line of least resistance. His critique was aimed at those who would *betray* the truth for the sake of party

(Communist or Fascist) ideology. The question he addressed was whether truth could be reduced to such ideology—whether intellectuals should blindly toe the party line in scholarship and teaching or instead be willing to admit to truths that might call one's party—along with its programs or actions—into question.

The question then becomes not merely one of political *engagement* but one of the extent to which such engagement can be maintained in conjunction with scrupulous intellectual honesty. Without such linkages, without the kind of collective expression and contestation of positive ideas inherent in any progressive movement for social change, the intellectual will give way to the elitist. This too is a legacy of the Dreyfus affair. The right-wing nationalists who attacked the Dreyfusard *intellectuels* were elitists masquerading as populists. Yet, the defenders of Dreyfus on the left, such as Leon Blum and Jean Jaures, were, however loosely, linked to international socialist movement—or they were honest humanists, like William James.

The dangers of elitism readily become apparent on right and left alike. While it is not difficult to think of contemporary examples of conservative elitism—the names William Buckley and George Gilder, for instance, spring to mind—it is equally important to remember that merely being positioned on the left does not guarantee freedom from this taint. Here, the negative critical theory best exemplified by the work of Max Horkheimer and Theodor Adorno comes to the fore. The notion of the "culture industry" held by these two thinkers is abstract and ahistorical, permeated by a conservative nostalgia for "high" cultural forms and exalted individualism. On this terrain, left and right analyses of cultural decline arrive at a consensus; both hypostatize a degenerate present and deny history. Of course, Horkheimer and Adorno were not alone in their elitism; a similar problematic informs the work of thinkers as diverse as Henry Adams, José Ortega y Gasset, and Allan Bloom.[13]

Indeed, Adams's *Education* demonstrates, along with contemporary narratives of decline like Allan Bloom's *The Closing of the American Mind* and Russell Jacoby's *The Last Intellectuals*, that the concept of the intellectual cannot be judged in terms of some idealized historical past from which people have, sadly, fallen.[14] Perhaps there is something in the final decades of any century that fosters this preference for the obituary form, whether from the perspective of the liberal elitist (Adams), the conservative elitist (Bloom), or the left elitist (Jacoby). Despite the fact that nearly a century separates Adams from Bloom and Jacoby, the arguments forwarded by these three men are curiously—in many respects, even remarkably—symmetrical.

Allen Bloom's *The Closing of the American Mind*, which rose meteorically on the best-seller lists when it appeared in 1987, is a scathing attack on higher education in America today. The book is subtitled "How Higher Education Has Failed Democracy and Impoverished the Souls of Today's Students." In it, Bloom claimed that American intellectuals—the university professors who shape contemporary higher education—have closed their minds to two and a half millennia of hard-minded thinking about absolute truth and have replaced philosophy with an unthinking tolerance based on the "openness" of social science, relativism, and hedonistic emotional satisfaction. His central argument is simple: People tend to think and act as they have been taught, and what Americans are taught in schools is primarily influenced by what happens in elite universities—a "trickle down" theory of educational practice.

Bloom argued that the content of a university education today is simply awful. Under the pernicious influence of thinkers like Marx, Nietzsche, and the postmodernists, professors have abandoned concepts of truth, justice, and beauty as outdated historical myths and embraced arbitrary, relative ideas about morality. They have abdicated their responsibility of teaching traditional values and beliefs, thereby closing students' minds to the possibility of virtue.[15] It is thus hardly surprising that Bloom's prescription for curing America and its youth of this corruption is renewed attention to philosophical thought and reverence for heroes—a return to the reading of "great books," which are vaguely defined as Plato, Aristotle, Shakespeare, and the Bible. "Men may live more truly and fully in reading Plato and Shakespeare than at any other time," he told us, "because then they are participating in essential being and forgetting their accidental lives."[16]

Bloom never made clear just what he meant by phrases like "essential being," but that is hardly the only problematic aspect of this diatribe. He also failed to distinguish any real difference between, say, Marx and Nietzsche; he dismissed both thinkers more for being German than for anything substantive that either might have said. Marxists and postmodernists are likewise indistinguishable; Bloom wrote off both camps for blindly succumbing to the seduction of foreign intellectual fads. To understand Bloom's positive prescriptions for the academy—not to mention the whole of Western civilization—one has only to imagine a parcel of "great books" taking transhistorical flight in Greece a millennia or two ago, hopping over the Aegean, making a quick stop in the westernmost reaches of northern Europe, and finally landing, once and for all time, on North American soil as the twentieth century draws to a close.

It is only on very special plots of this soil, however, that the parcel can land and be opened to reveal its "truths." The "greats" Bloom valorized can only be appreciated by affluent white males (youthful students or their older, well-tailored professors). These are ideas doomed to wither and die on any but "the very best" college and university campuses. Bloom's concern was not really with higher education (or democracy) in general but with the relatively few elite institutions found at the very top of the educational hierarchy. These are, of course, the four-year liberal arts colleges traditionally favored by wealthy families and the research universities with which such colleges are often integrated, for example, Harvard, Radcliffe, and Columbia. Such schools emphasize graduate and professional training; whether publicly funded, like Berkeley, or privately endowed, like Stanford, all have close ties to the major government and corporate interests that provide significant funding for research. Here, Bloom demonstrated his awareness of something many political scientists seem to have forgotten: It is the products of the top twenty or thirty such schools who generally run social, political, and economic institutions in the United States (and abroad).

Bloom bewailed the decline in educational standards that accompanied the expansion of higher education over the past three decades; he wished to return to a golden age of higher education by rolling back the democratizing elements of coeducation and affirmative action. Many beneficiaries of these trends were, in his view, simply incapable of reading, let alone appreciating, "great books." It is the privileged few who are most in need of education; groups and individuals traditionally considered disadvantaged lack talent and refinement and, therefore, possess much simpler needs.[17] Bloom was uncomfortable with any hint of substantive democracy; he much prefered to keep the discourse on a formal plane, where only the best and brightest are in charge, and the rest know their place and keep to it. He ascribed the contemporary malaise to a set of intellectual failings concentrated in America's elite colleges and universities. It is not democracy that is bad but the people who rule, along with those who have taught them what they know. Only by limiting enrollments at top institutions to those chosen few capable of entering the "great conversation" on his terms and becoming, in the process, something akin to Plato's philosopher kings—or perhaps to Bloom himself—could a cure can be effected.[18]

Although Bloom's jeremiad can be justly criticized—and has been, on a wide variety of counts—for now, I will refrain from doing so, turning instead to consideration of Russell Jacoby's *The Last Intellectuals,* which was also published in 1987.[19] Jacoby shared Bloom's preoccupation with the role of left intellectuals within the university, although the two approach the problem from opposite ends of the political spectrum. "If Bloom blames the decline of the university on the left," as Jeffrey Escoffier put it, "Jacoby ... seems to blame the decline of the left on the universities."[20] A simple, broadly stated question appears to guide Jacoby's narrative. "Where," he asked, "are the younger intellectuals?"[21] He argued that there is a whole generation missing from the history of American intellectuals. Those who came of age during the 1960s and 1970s opted to enter the academy, forsaking public life to become university professors rather than risking the insecurities of trying to earn a living outside the universities. In part, such choices were structurally influenced, for suburbanization and urban gentrification had destroyed the bohemian enclaves in large cities, which in earlier decades had enabled creative writers, thinkers, and artists to live cheaply in proximity to one another.

There is a larger element of voluntarism in Jacoby's analysis: Seduced, as it were, into the job security offered by faculty lines in the universities, members of the "missing" intellectuals refused to write for the general public, finding an audience instead in the specialized professional journals of academic disciplines. Thus, "eschewing 'public prose' for specialist jargon, they became invisible to the public at large. Unlike Daniel Bell or Edmund Wilson, intellectuals of the New Left ceased to be 'public intellectuals.' In fact, in becoming academics, they ceased to be intellectuals at all."[22] This movement of left intellectuals into the universities has been, in Jacoby's view, an unmitigated tragedy, for it has engendered "academic Marxism," an intellectual environment in which political struggles are absorbed by specialization and professionalization. He sneered at how "the 'politics' of academic life supplant larger politics" and castigated "no-nonsense Marxist academics" who forsake revolutionary solidarity and ideals in a self-aggrandizing quest for "institutional clout and prestige."[23]

Of course, there was a golden age before the Fall, when intellectuals were independent, public, and, perhaps needless to say, almost all male.[24] Jacoby established the meaning of these terms by uncritically comparing the "missing" youngsters who have been consumed by academia to the "last" generation of intellectuals, essentially (although not exclusively) represented by a group of New York intellectuals—Lionel and Diana Trilling, Norman Podhoretz, Daniel Bell, C. Wright Mills, Sidney Hook, Midge Decter, Norman Mailer, Irving Kristol, and Philip Rahv—to cite only a randomly chosen few from the many named. These "last" intellectuals, who flourished during the late 1940s and early 1950s, define Jacoby's ideal type:

> As the last public intellectuals they loom large in the cultural firmament. They have viewed from outside, as their successors could not, the professionalization of cultural life; and perhaps because of their origins as free-lance authors, their writings often shine. They write to be read. Many continue to play active roles in letters and politics. They have presided over the intellectual scene for decades.[25]

This celebration of the "last" generation of intellectuals rests on shaky ground, however. As Lynn Garafola pointed out: "Jacoby rues the fact that the New York intellectuals failed to reproduce themselves. But he overlooks the abysmal record of their behaviour in the 1960s—the fulminations against the counterculture, the denunciations of the New Left, the jeremiads against feminism. If the New York intellectuals left no heirs, the fault is largely their own."[26]

The significant questions here have to do with the social role of intellectuals and their attendant political obligations. What does it mean to be an independent or public person in the 1990s—or, for that matter, at any other moment in history—let alone an *intellectual* person? Barbara Ehrenreich, for example, admitted to being "a little afraid that Jacoby's 'public intellectual' is really a *famous* intellectual," adding that "many fine thinkers strive to have a political impact through their writing and do not ever become as visible as, say, Irving Kristol."[27] Preferring to think of herself as a *political* intellectual, she described the responsibilities she considered integral to her ongoing efforts "to 'shift the discourse' through every available medium and, equally important, keeping in touch with all kinds of streams of protest and dissent so as to know what's important to say. ... Being a political intellectual means keeping abreast of all kinds of struggles, trends, ideas, people. Then you have something to be 'public' about."[28]

What is really at stake here is neither fame nor the popularity that Jacoby held out as a desirable endpoint of critical and literary endeavor. None of the "last" intellectuals Jacoby cited as paragons of public approbation could compete with Jackie Collins, James Michener, or Stephen King in reaching the masses. Jacoby's contention that there was something inherently wrong with pursuing a specialized area of interest and thus addressing a limited audience (inside or outside of the university) is really beside the point. The world is complex; no one can master it as an undifferentiated entity; specialization is even more necessary today than in the (largely imaginary) past when, it is assumed, public intellectuals were *generalists* first. Jefferson's interests and talents ranged from architecture to zoology, but he is best remembered for his contributions as primary author of the Declaration of Independence and later as president of the United States. Was he a specialist or a generalist? Einstein revolutionized physics, wrote eloquently about and worked for world peace, and played the violin. Where does he fit?

Perhaps there is something beyond popularity that marks a public intellectual today; after all, Sartre never sold as many novels as Harold Robbins. People like Paul Kennedy, Adrienne Rich, Audre Lorde, Leslie Marmon Silko, Milton Friedman, Jürgen Habermas, Barbara Ehrenreich, Frances Fox Piven, and Noam Chomsky—not to mention Margaret Mead and James Baldwin—provide only a few examples of public intellectuals who have engaged the world and the word from a critical stance, whether within the university or not. Their work may not be popular by the standards of mass culture, but neither has it been without influence. By their lifework, such public intellectuals contest the privileging of knowledge; they articulate and engage ideas; they challenge the status quo. Their work is debated and discussed. It is provocative. Its importance does not rely on being popular. Rather, since most people are denied access to any kind of a public audience, as Chomsky suggested, "it is the responsibility of intellectuals to speak the truth and to expose lies."[29]

Here the commonalities in Bloom (himself a public intellectual in the university) and Jacoby begin to come clear. Both repeatedly evoked images of decay in American intellectual life without analyzing the economic or political sources of that decay or suggesting any meaningful alternative. Both narratives proceeded from the notion of a mythic past, a golden age when things were better than they are today, so that a myth of generalized decline substitutes for an extended defense of extremely particularistic and privileged groups. On the right, Bloom mourned the democratic erosion of "high culture"; on the left, Jacoby castigated other intellectuals for selling out on the academic market. They reached consensus on a transhistorical plane of contemptuous elitism.

Bloom assumed that elite youths capable of appreciating "the higher values" are today no different than they were in Plato's time. It is, to say the least, difficult to cast Glaucon and Adeimantus in the same light as "Master of the Universe" Sherman McCoy, from Tom Wolfe's *The Bonfire of the Vanities*. Yet McCoy (schooled at "Buckley and St. Paul's and Yale") represented, and in many respects spoke for, many, if not most, of the "best and brightest" graduates of elite colleges today.[30] Not the life of the mind but making money and achieving a high-profile consumer lifestyle has been the ideal.[31]

Jacoby condemned an entire generation for failing to match its predecessors' commitment "to a public world—and a public language, the vernacular."[32] He ignored the simple fact that intellectuals have less clout today than in the past because of mass culture. There is also no movement, in the old sense, with which to interact, no movement that would provide a context for cultural struggle and production. This is a historical development whose entrenchment in society has deepened steadily for well over a century—as was noted long ago by Rousseau, Balzac, and, of course, Flaubert.[33] Here, it is important to remember the response to Frank Sinatra in the 1940s, Elvis Presley in the 1950s, and the Beatles and Rolling Stones in the 1960s: All quickly became icons of popular culture and, far more than any of Jacoby's public intellectuals, defined the public language, the vernacular of these decades.

Honesty must never be sacrificed for the sake of gaining publicity or some political end—not matter how desirable either (or both) goals may appear. Both Bloom and Jacoby elided the clear connections to be drawn between the elitist forms of intellectual endeavor that they emphasized and the sociopolitical distribution of power—just as Henry Adams did a century ago. Both relied on a static, transhistorical concept of the public, which only served to obfuscate matters further. Throughout this work I have discussed how Jürgen Habermas, himself a public intellectual of the first rank, analyzed the emergence of the bourgeois public sphere at just the moment when a newly organized class, the bourgeoisie, was coming into its own and claiming first economic, then political, power.[34] Those in the public sphere—mainly educated, propertied "men of affairs," but also poets, journalists, philosophers, artists, and perhaps even a token woman or two—who met at coffeehouses and salons to discuss the affairs of the day were, in the Gramscian sense, "organic" to this rising class.[35] Thus, there is something fundamentally dishonest about calling upon intellectuals *today* to replicate these forms of "publicity" without at the same time asking questions like On whose terms? or In whose interests? The blunt fact of the matter is that one can neither be nor become a public intellectual without the credibility that attaches to participation in open discourse on issues of interest to others in society. It is the constellation of institutions of higher education subsumed by "the university" that today provides both an arena where such discourse can take place and the recognition that lends credibility to both process and participants.

In the eighteenth century, public intellectuals could find their credibility in an emerging print media and the discursive communities available in coffeehouse, salon, or table-talk environments. But today, the appropriation of these opportunities for free expression by the culture industries of late capitalism has necessitated a shift in the locus of intellectual credibility and intellectual identity. At stake here is the changing role of universities as sites for public discourse in advanced industrial societies. There is a fundamental dishonesty attached to the elitist vision of the university espoused by Bloom and Jacoby. They (and others) saw such institutions as havens for the elite, ivory towers more or less removed from the exigencies of everyday life and unsullied by public debate. Many years ago, Karl Jaspers articulated this concpet in *The Idea of the University;* ironically, Bloom castigated the German philosophical tradition, of which Jaspers was very much a product, at the same time that he all but recapitulated Jaspers's ideas.[36]

In light of contemporary realities, this elitist view is not merely anachronistic but also fantastic. On one level, it overlooks how, in the structural sense, all institutions of higher education serve a crucial socioeconomic function by keeping large numbers of young people off the labor market while at the same time socializing them to the roles and values they will need to rely upon when they do take up their places in the economy.[37] More significantly, this view ignores the substantial role played by these institutions as the only places where people can talk about ideas and principles and the institutional role in facilitating mass access to public knowledge. And it also ignores the long-standing and overarching tradition of the university as a place where not only new forms of public knowledge but truth itself can be constantly created, debated, engaged, encouraged, and recreated by individuals who are themselves dedicated to this intellectual endeavor.

Indeed, it is a testament to the power of public knowledge that so much of the struggle for democracy has taken place within the university. That is where much of the collective historical memory of a particular culture is generated, collected, analyzed, and preserved. As institutions, universities are distinguished from other public and private arenas because of venerable traditions of intellectual autonomy and academic freedom, which have formally, if not always substantively, shaped the quest for knowledge and truth.[38] Although this history has hardly been unproblematic, the institutional constellation of higher education offers an existing framework within which individuals can work toward thinking, debating, and implementing a *praxis* of democratic public knowledge to inform a much larger, and ongoing, process of recognizing and extending the range of social, economic, and political possibilities and choices.

As Clark Kerr put it thirty years ago in his now-classic discussion of the "multiversity": "Knowledge is now central to society. It is wanted, even demanded, by more people and more institutions than ever before. The university as producer, wholesaler, and retailer of knowledge cannot escape service."[39] Daniel Bell said much the same thing when, in 1976, he described the university as "the primary institution of post-industrial society. In the past twenty years, the university ... has taken on a vast number of functions: in basic research, as a service institution, and in the expansion of general education."[40] In other words, given their role in the generation and preservation of knowledge, in providing spaces where mass constituencies can forge linkages with civic and corporate concerns, and—especially since the 1960s—in mediating between the state and civil society, universities have become important public spheres in their own right. To suggest this is not, however, to adopt or endorse Bell's sanguine stance toward these institutions. The idea of the university as a potentially viable public sphere today represents not an end but a beginning.

From the conservative standpoint, the university resembles a museum, a place to which only the chosen few can be granted access and where knowledge and truth are artifacts to be preserved under glass in a strictly climate-controlled atmosphere. Instrumentalists—liberals and leftists alike—define the university as nothing more than a locus for ideological and practical legitimation of the status quo, viewing it as a production site for scientific and technical skills, innovations, and information, which, fueled by state funding and private grants from corporations (or corporate philanthropy), serve the military, the state, and capital interests alike.[41] But this is only one side of the story. Although universities do serve as "knowledge factories" that benefit corporate interests and the capitalist state, they are also potential locations for developing critical self-knowledge of "the system" itself. The liberal arts buttress bourgeois claims to the inheritance of Western culture, but they also provide a tradition of critical thought and an effective set of tools by which such habits may be acquired. Thus, in the absence of a proletarian public sphere, and with the old bourgeois public sphere eclipsed by the culture industry and its commodity forms of news and entertainment, a new terrain of cultural struggle has taken shape within the universities, especially with re-gard to the struggle over the curriculum.[42] From a socialist perspective, the university is not part of the problem for public intellectuals but part of the solution.

Battles over the curriculum are, of course, nothing new in higher educa-tion. President Charles W. Eliot's introduction of the elective system at Har-vard in the 1870s is only the best-remembered moment of a protracted de-bate that raged between reformers and advocates of the traditional college curriculum (consisting of Greek, Latin, mathematics, and moral philoso-phy). According to historian Laurence R. Veysey, this debate "extended from before the Civil War to a culmination in 1884–85, when the forces of ortho-doxy made their last notable effort to stem the tide of change."[43] Although critics castigated the elective system as the academic corollary to laissez-faire capitalism and a capitulation to the fickle whims of the student body, the idea caught on in one university after another, for the elective system fit neatly with the increasing professionalism and specialization of faculties and departments.[44]

But the idea of specialization as innovative and desirable became in its turn controversial when, a few decades later, universities struggled, first, to as-similate the rush of new knowledge in the recently developed social sciences and, second, to cope with the nation's entry into the First World War. In 1910 Alexander Meiklejohn, then president of Amherst, initiated a general course for first-year students. Entitled "Social and Economic Institutions," the course aimed at unifying and integrating social studies. At Columbia, a course in "War Issues" generated a call for a corresponding offering in "Peace Issues"; the result was a course in "Contemporary Civilization," which was for many years required of all freshmen.[45] It was not until the end of the Second World War, however, that general education fever would re-surface with the publication of the famous Harvard "Redbook" (actually en-titled *General Education in a Free Society* but commonly known by the color of its cover).[46] Twenty years later, sociologist Daniel Bell would also explore the challenges of general education in a report entitled *The Reforming of General Education: The Columbia College Experience in Its National Set-ting.*[47]

Cycles of tension between advocates of specialized and general education in colleges and universities were broken, perhaps once and for all, by pres-sures for expansion and reform in the 1960s and early 1970s and by the po-litical effects of decay reflected in the many varieties of postmodernist thought; the generation of the 1960s made higher education a base for forms of political and cultural opposition that have markedly altered the face and shape of institutions and curricula. The student population of American uni-versities has changed rapidly and dramatically in recent decades, largely as a corollary of the civil rights and women's movements. Throughout all this, the position—and the identity—of intellectuals within these institutions has become a matter of no small controversy.

Since 1950, undergraduate enrollments in higher education in the United States have increased by nearly 400 percent; at the same time, the number of institutions has grown by 60 percent. (By comparison, between 1870 and 1940 student enrollments grew by 3,000 percent.) Forty percent of the nation's college and university undergraduates are twenty-five years of age or older; fewer than 60 percent study full-time. About 55 percent of college students are women; almost 20 percent are nonwhite or Hispanic.[48] These changes, about which both Bloom and Jacoby were remarkably silent, reflect consensus on many levels that higher education is a fundamental human need, one that should be broadly available to all. Furthermore, many talented students are unable to attend the kind of elite institutions on which Bloom focused; many find it necessary to hold down full- or part-time jobs and attend school part-time, a practice discouraged by many selective liberal arts colleges. Other students must live with or near parents to share family responsibilities and find that no such school as Bloom described is available within commuting distance. Although it is true that the structural need to keep young people off the labor market for longer periods of time and the growth of "credentialism" have in part motivated the expansion of higher education, it is equally true that simply gaining access to higher education has represented a major victory for groups and individuals whose educational options were formerly circumscribed by race, gender, ethnicity, poverty, or any combination of these factors.[49] The project of opening the universities to workers, women, and previously excluded minorities—far from completed today—further supports the argument favoring the university as a potential public sphere. Far from being elitist ivory towers where leftists go when they want to sell out, the university today provides one of the few arenas where the struggle for democracy is active and continuous. The task for public intellectuals is therefore not to close the university gates, limiting culture to the study of dead yesterdays, but to make them ever more open, more accessible, and more fully public institutions. The magnitude of this task cannot, however, be underestimated, especially with regard to the issue of making university faculties more democratic than they presently are.

Whereas, as we have seen, the student population of higher education has changed fairly dramatically in a rather short span of years, faculty diversification has proceeded much more slowly: "In the early '60s ten of the top history departments in the country had 160 professors, all of them men, and 128 assistant professors, four of them women. Ten years later there were 274 professors, two of them women, and 317 assistants, 314 men. By the mid-1980s, 11.7 percent of all full professors in the country were women. Only 2.2 percent were black."[50] "Glacial" seems to be an appropriate adjective for this pace of change, yet the real or perceived influx of women and other "others" (including people of color, lesbians, gay men) into faculties, combined with the democratization of student bodies, has been the motive force behind a conservative counterrevolution against the changes in American higher education and cultural life that have taken place over the past thirty years. Beginning with Bloom, and more recently evidenced by John Searle's essay "The Storm over the University," in the *New York Review of Books,* Roger Kimball's *Tenured Radicals,* and Dinesh D'Souza's *Illiberal Education,* the neoconservative response has consistently excoriated the democratic impulse toward reform witnessed in recent decades.[51] This is no coincidence or caprice but rather an attempt to rally state and popular support for reasserting conservative claims over a realm that increasingly appears to be slipping from the conservatives' formerly all but exclusive control.

The rather crude right-wing critique of education that initially linked reform to the needs of big business has been superseded over the past decade by an emphasis on colleges and universities as locations of cultural production.[52] Conservatives have demonstrated this over and over—by attempts to define issues of cultural literacy; by the canon debates in higher education and calls for national curriculum review boards; and by initiatives designed to preserve the essential traditions of Western civilization.[53] As the story goes, faculty radicals have, since the 1960s, taken over the universities, implementing pernicious educational doctrines that place not only the economy but civilization itself at risk. These doctrines include cultural relativism, which systematically degraded the curriculum; the idea that student experience might qualify as a viable form of knowledge; and the notion that ethnic, race, gender, and other identifications have played an important role, whether by commission or omission, in the development of literary and intellectual culture.[54]

It is certainly true that there are some tenured professors who are readily identifiable today as veterans of activism of the 1960s. It is equally true that because of the very traditions of academic freedom and free speech the Right would seemingly prefer to monopolize, Marxist and other radical ideas have found currency—in *some* departments, among *some* (but by no means all) professors. Yet the difficulties of earning tenure in the tight market of recent years are becoming legendary—and tenure has been no less difficult for leftists to achieve than for any others. The classification and description of tenured radicals favored by Kimball and D'Souza reflect the sloppy research and thinking characteristic of the conservative stance. Of course accuracy is really beside the point if the main goal is to discredit the university—along with its public intellectuals. Thus, it matters little *whose* names are named in the process of creating the illusion that a new form of "clear and present danger" exists; what counts is *the perception that an enemy exists.*

The notion that "once upon a time" things were better than they are at present is common to both Bloom and Jacoby. The real source of conservative distress is an unrequited desire, a longing, to return to the good old days when women, working people, and people of color simply were not present at universities in large numbers.[55] But the conservatives' charges against all the "radical" intellectuals who have invaded the ivied halls, disrupting the curriculum and corrupting the students, are more than just wishful thinking tinged with nostalgia. They are a pack of outright lies. And here we come round once more to the issue of honesty and the responsibility of public intellectuals to tell the truth, with unflinching rigor, regardless of the context or consequences. We are back to Benda's cautionary tale.

The conservative educational agenda serves as a thinly veiled apology for a highly dogmatic, elitist, and reactionary politics that is antithetical to democracy and unabashedly premised on privileged forms of public knowledge. However, it ought to be taken seriously by the Left, for there is something to the substance (if not necessarily the forms) of the Right's critique of postmodernist relativism. Critics like Kimball and D'Souza correctly charged that many left intellectuals, in the rush to embrace postmodernist conceptions of a "politics of difference," have contributed, often enthusiastically, to the intellectual relativism currently pervasive within the academy. Here, D'Souza in particular had a point when he addressed the destructive tendencies that attend the emphasis on difference.[56] What the concept of "difference" teaches to women, people of color, ethnic minorities, lesbians, and gay males—any groups or parties traditionally excluded from the dominant society as well as from academia—is a form of counterhegemony that exemplifies many of the most destructive aspects of the dominant tendencies that are being called into question. Having decided, for the best of reasons, that it is a mistake to discount the importance of such ascriptive characteristics as gender or race, many left intellectuals have now swung entirely to the opposite pole. Here, the very ascriptive characteristics previously elided by false "universals" now become paramount. The tables may be turned—but little else has changed. Put bluntly, this represents adoption of the oppressor's tactics—a tendency to which, as Rosa Luxemburg always knew, even the most committed revolutionaries are never automatically immune.

There is more at stake here, however. Many left intellectuals have abandoned the socialist tradition of contesting capitalism. At the same time, reformers in Eastern Europe and the former Soviet states are looking westward for models of economic or political transformation and achievement. Post-Marxist attempts to conceptualize away the ruthlessly totalizing tyranny of the capitalist marketplace, with its global commodification of all aspects of life, make a travesty of efforts to promote values of freedom, autonomy, and democratic self-government anywhere on the planet. Especially from a socialist perspective, it is morally reprehensible to put forward theoretical frameworks that render such exploitation invisible or reduce it to just one among many fragmented experiences, at the very moment when this system is expanding to become more widely entrenched than ever.[57]

Many left intellectuals have been busy defending what they ought to oppose instead of developing and presenting ethical alternatives to the cynicism and opportunism that have accompanied the increasingly global depredations of capital, especially throughout the decade of the 1980s. With regard to public knowledge, the articulation of alternatives would enable the development of standards and categories by which the concrete contribution of different works from the vast cultural inheritance of the past in all its various traditions could be analyzed, debated, and utilized to further democratic values.[58] Yet, the Left has not articulated a positive response that promulgates values of democratic accountability through the critical history of left social and political struggles, such as rationalism or humanism, with the goal of extending public knowledge and locating public intellectuals within the university. Instead, the Left has largely ceded the terrain of discourse to the Right in debates over the university curriculum and the role of intellectuals. This failure to provide a unifying alternative vision is especially disturbing in the face of attacks on democracy being made, concurrently, by the Right—exemplified during the 1992 presidential campaign by the demonization of a cultural elite and the rhetorical promotion of a thinly veiled racist and sexist social agenda under the rubric of "family values."

Nevertheless, many left intellectuals have remained locked into a defense of postmodernist fragmentation and a valorization of potsherds of "difference" shaped by the multiple social realities of cultural and intellectual pluralism, defying attempts at unifying discourse.[59] What seems to be lost amidst the rubble is the notion that recognizing and respecting differences need not preclude the articulation of solidarity and unity; the attempt to get beyond the damage done by false universals that cloak the replication of privilege or power need not become a zero-sum game. Although unifying discourse may harbor unarticulated relations of dominance, it also harbors the critical ability to call such relationships into question—and thus to account.

The concept of "a University community given to the competition of ideas and of merit, devoted to excellence, and dedicated to the belief that freedom of choice, speech, and creed is essential to the quest for truth that constitutes its mission," as A. Bartlett Giamatti once described it, is central to the tradition of humanistic study.[60] Realization of this concept would open up opportunities for articulating and furthering values that question or contest the oppressive nature of the capitalist accumulation process and the social relationships attendant on it. Furthermore, because the cooperative search for truth is premised upon structures of public argumentation, universities today are spaces where critical discourse and debate routinely take place. This latter function is especially important in a society where the old working-class neighborhood cultures, and the socialist and radical public institutions that at one time provided alternative forums for learning and exercising these skills have all but vanished.[61]

Public intellectuals who are willing to engage in this process of seeking, articulating, debating, and re-envisioning truth simply cannot claim elitism as the cornerstone of their identity, whether as individuals or as members of discursive communities. Elitist standards for truth, as we have seen, privilege public knowledge and relegate intellectuals to the role of uncritical conservationists, guarding past legacies in glass cases of the mind. It is, after all, the *quest* for truth that, traditionally, has been fundamental to the very idea of the university. And this quest is dynamic. It inevitably looks forward, imagining the unknown, at the same time that it honors, respects, and preserves the inheritance of the past. In a very real sense, the university as a public space populated by intellectuals who are constantly undertaking a search for the truth of their lives in and about the world embodies the utopian impulses Ernst Bloch characterized as the "Not-Yet Become, Not-Yet Achieved … the horizon of the future to be attained."[62] This notion is grounded in the language of hope and predicated on concepts of history and culture that are open to inquiry, criticism, and change. It is intimately linked to the fundamental values of the university. Insofar as intellectuals are always looking to discover new truths, the notion is central to the tasks of research; insofar as intellectuals are also held responsible for passing on to new generations the legacy of the past and discoveries of the present, this notion is fundamental to teaching.

Politically, of course, the "not-yet" is directly linked to the "far-from-realized," but ongoing, project of making the promises of Enlightenment ideas of human freedom and dignity, of autonomy and democracy, more widely available to people around the world, without prejudice or exception. In the university, public intellectuals summarize and symbolize the interaction of "private self" and "public sphere" by the very nature of their lifework. The question of the changing role of universities as public spheres for discourse and the responsibilities of intellectuals as participants in this process becomes most salient at this juncture because what is really at stake in all the debates is democratic equality and how to achieve it both formally and substantively.

If public knowledge is a right available to all citizens rather than a privilege, and if the university is a place where such knowledge is produced and promulgated, then the struggle over the curriculum truly becomes a battle for democracy. What this entails, first of all, is the recognition that elitist conceptions of what it means to be an intellectual, whether articulated by the Left or by the Right, are antithetical to democracy itself. Beyond that, where questions of intellectual identity and responsibility are concerned, this struggle for democracy involves linking the utopian impulses of the "not yet" to what Václav Havel has eloquently described as "living in truth." This entails consistently and courageously taking "the side of truth against lies, the side of sense against nonsense, the side of justice against injustice," wherever and whenever possible.[63]

Intellectuals committed to reclaiming the public sphere for progressive ends cannot afford to promulgate or participate in distortions of the truth. In order to count as a success, an American education today must begin with the premise of freely available public knowledge; it is the responsibility of intellectuals to articulate and implement the standards for cultural unity integral to this task. This does not require starting from ground zero but rather building upon what has already begun within the public sphere of the university. The task would, in effect, become a *political movement for democracy,* integrating the original meaning of the term "intellectual" with contemporary social realities. Jacoby's elegy for the public intellectual emerges, in this light, as a misdirected lamentation. What he mourns has not been lost. The issue is not the decline of some romantic ideal type, nor is it the co-optation of left intellectuals within the academy. What is at stake here is the courage, commitment, and values that guide the work of all public intellectuals. If these further the emancipatory project, inside or outside of the university, what is there to eulogize?

# 6

## *Literacy for What?*
## *Critical Literacy and*
## *the Power of Public Knowledge*

Picture, if you will, a scene from an ordinary American household in the early 1950s. Dad—a sergeant in the Air Force—is overseas at the height of the Korean War. Mother's enjoying a rare evening out at her high school reunion and Grandma's minding the kids—two of them, a four-year-old girl and a baby boy. I'm the girl in this picture. Precocious, I'm already reading, hungry for books, billboards, and the backs of cereal boxes. I come by this craving honestly; my mother reads voraciously and shares her passion with us. Decades later, she still tells of sitting with me as an infant, reading stories out loud from the *Ladies' Home Journal*—just to ease the loneliness of my father's many absences by hearing the sound of her own voice. It hadn't surprised anyone when one day I took a book off the coffee table and started reading, out loud, quite naturally with no prior (or formal) instruction.

In the scene I want you to imagine, it's bedtime—always the moment for a story. I'm in my pajamas, snuggling against my grandmother's bulky, comfortable body and luxuriating, as always, in her smell—a mix of Jergens soap, Cashmere Bouquet talcum, and line-dried nylon housedress. This is the best part of the day; sleep beckons, but there's still the magic of the story to come before the light goes out. *Finally* my grandmother opens the book and starts speaking, her voice a little fluty, with the oddly accented speech of Newcastle in the North of England that always fools strangers into guessing that she's from Scotland or even Sweden.

And that's the problem: She's *talking*, not reading. I know the difference because I recognize all the words on the page. She's holding the book so that my brother and I can see the brightly colored pictures, but the story she's telling doesn't match the printed text. I feel a surge of rage and squirm against her, angrily grabbing the book out of her hands. I begin reading the words—the *real* story—in a loud, clear voice, demanding, impatient to prove that *I* can get it *right*. There is a sudden stillness in the room. I feel my grandmother stiffen against me, and she stays very quiet until I have finished. From that moment on, there is always a strangeness between us, a distance that cannot be bridged.

Twenty-some years later, my grandmother is dead, and I am studying reading and sociolinguistics at the Harvard Graduate School of Education. We students are asked to recall how and when we learned to read. I call up the memory of this scene for the first time and go cold when I realize that my grandmother *could not* read the words of that bedtime story.[1] It stuns me to think that she must have been illiterate—and yet I never knew, or noticed. When I telephoned my mother to ask about all this, she at first denied, but then corroborated, my memories—admitting with shame that she and other relatives preferred to keep this aspect of family history a secret.

What innocent cruelty there had been in my drive—as a reproachful four-year-old—to set the story right. What my grandmother must have felt that night! How this incident would come to symbolize the gulf between her life, her work—as miner's daughter, chambermaid, charwoman, pastry cook, wife, mother—and mine, as college professor. How those differences hung between us, frozen in the air, for decades. How they hang there still, even now that she is long dead.

Thus, the politics of literacy stand out in hard relief against two lives, my grandmother's and my own. Yet I get stuck here, puzzling over the meaning of the phrase "the politics of literacy" that I've glibly typed. My fingers stumble a bit on the keyboard; I want to say something profound and find that I cannot. I try out sentences, deleting them wholly or in part, dissatisfied, uncomfortable, confused. I'm nervous because I've been speaking in a very personal mode, approaching intimacy—something best edited out of scholarship. I feel vulnerable, having just made a confession of sorts: At the very least, I've written a skeleton out of the family closet. And in the effort to think through these problems, I realize that my discomfort, in itself, reflects the many, separate strands of complex meaning that twine together and around this catchphrase—"the politics of literacy." Either noun alone speaks volumes; put them together and you have a wealth of concepts to untangle.

*       *       *

To many people, the term "literacy" means little more than the ability to read and write, an unproblematic process of decoding and encoding oral language symbolically. But things, as we shall see, are not nearly so simple. When corollary questions are asked, such as Read and write what? How? Under what conditions? For what purpose(s)? a set of complex linkages emerges. James Gee catalogued the breadth and depth of the connections by which literacy is construed as both the agent and the by-product of individual and social transformation:

Literacy leads to logical and analytic modes of thought; general and abstract uses of language, critical and rational thought; a skeptical and questioning attitude; a distinction between myth and history; the recognition of the importance of time and space; complex and modern governments (with separation of church and state); political democracy and greater social equity; economic development; wealth and productivity; political stability; urbanization; and contraception (lower birth rate). It leads to people who are innovative, achievement oriented, productive, cosmopolitan, politically aware, more globally (nationally and internationally) and less locally oriented, with more liberal and humane social attitudes, less likely to commit a crime and more likely to take education and the rights and duties of citizenship seriously.[2]

Not at all surprisingly, investing such an apparently simple concept as literacy with wide-ranging powers leads to a great deal of confusion when one attempts to get beyond the surface of its usage. In just one example from among the wealth of possibilities, historian Lawrence Cremin defined literacy as "a fundamental index of cultural vitality."[3] He distinguished between two forms of eighteenth-century literacy practice. On the one hand, there is "inert literacy, in which a minimum technical ability is combined with limited motivation, need, and opportunity (the literacy of the sixteenth-century yeoman who learned to read the Christian liturgy and nothing else would be an excellent example)." On the other, there is "a more liberating literacy, in which a growing technical ability is combined with expanding motivation, need, and opportunity (the literacy of the American colonists following the Stamp Act crisis of the 1760s is a useful case in point)."[4]

Cremin's second definition of literacy as possessed of "liberating" attributes and powers is profoundly ideological. Attached to it is a constellation of concepts promoting political democracy, social equity, and many other elements from Gee's catalog. There is an element of faith involved in all this: The ability to read and write becomes a powerful agent of social transformation in and of itself. The reading and writing individual is both agent and locus of change; all structural constraints and considerations drop out of the equation.

Extending Cremin's logic, it becomes easy to assume that democracy, freedom, equality, and heightened social consciousness will all magically (and automatically) accrue with the spread of literacy. The march of literacy throughout American society over the past two centuries is inescapable, inevitable, and progressive. This depiction is consonant, of course, with Cremin's belief that "on balance the American education system has contributed significantly to the advancement of liberty, equality, and fraternity."[5]

Harvey Graff, in contrast, suggested that this kind of exalted faith in literacy constitutes a "literacy myth." In an encyclopedic survey that treats literacy from the time of Plato to the present, Graff argued that there is little historical evidence for these beliefs; literacy alone cannot be, and has not been, a powerful engine of social change. Nor can it be construed as a redemptive panacea for social ills. "Literacy crises," he suggested, have, however, been a recurrent motif in the history of reading and writing. They tend to turn up concomitantly with moments of social and economic crisis.[6]

If solutions to complicated economic issues or social problems are not readily or cheaply available, it is easy to turn to literacy. On the one hand, looking to literacy as the panacea can serve as a fall-back position: if people were smarter (that is, could use literacy more effectively—the tendency here is to conflate "literacy" and "intelligence"), we would have solutions—to the deficit, to jobs lost to restructuring, or whatever. On the other hand, literacy can serve as a diversionary tactic: *Why Johnny Can't Read* was a best-seller at the height of the cold war. In either case, the logic is simple. Reading and writing are skills that can be taught; teach them and you have resolved the crisis—without questioning national goals or priorities or allocating large amounts of resources. Graff argued against investing literacy with highly charged political symbolism, whereas optimistic accounts such as Cremin's took such investment for granted. Yet, the conclusion to be drawn in either case is the same: For well or ill, on the basis of sound historical evidence or spurious conflations of fact and illusion, literacy and politics are, in the modern world, inseparably linked. Neither can be reduced to the other, but the connections between them are inescapable; public knowledge must be located squarely at this juncture.

Indeed, the politicization of literacy—along with awareness of its actual or potential public impacts—is nothing new. For example, a bill for universal elementary education was introduced in the British Parliament in 1807, reflecting the view of many members of the ruling classes that the industrial revolution would demand more widespread literacy of workers. The bill was, however, defeated in the House of Lords; among its vigorous opponents was the president of the Royal Society, who argued that

> the project … of giving education to the labouring classes of the poor … would in effect be found to be prejudicial to their morals and happiness; it would teach them to despise their lot in life, instead of making them good servants in agriculture, and other laborious employment to which their rank in society had destined them; instead of teaching them subordination, it would render them factious and refractory, as was evident in the manufacturing counties; it would enable them to read seditious pamphlets, vicious books, and publications against Christianity; it would render them insolent to their superiors; and in a few years the result would be that the legislature would find it necessary to direct the strong arm of power toward them.[7]

Here we find two central arguments that remain current today. There is the worry that educated workers might not remain "good servants," content with their lot, and there is the concern that "seditious books" might lead people to begin questioning the structural conditions that keep them in servitude. Two sets of dualities are at work here. In the first case, there is the Janus face of literacy: If one learns to read the Bible, one can also read pornography or the "seditious pamphlets" that so disturbed the President of the Royal Society in 1807. Or, "Put another way, if a man teaches a woman to read so that she may know her place, she may learn that she deserves his."[8] In the second set of dualities, all the tensions of the private/public dichotomy are recapitulated: Although reading and writing are essentially private activities, taught to and practiced by individuals, any failure or inability to read entails isolation. Those who do not, or cannot, partake of literacy in today's world are simply shut out of fundamental forms of social interchange. So a clear understanding of literacy becomes central to the discussion of public knowledge and democracy because the ability to read represents the ability to make sense of all kinds of events and circumstances. At the same time, it is quite possible that contemporary anxieties about the difficulties raised by widespread illiteracy stand in for much more complex and problematic worries about the growing proportion of persons of color in the United States, who will presumably demand more significant social and economic roles in the future as their numbers continue to increase.[9]

Of course, categories like race and class seldom emerge from behind the cloak of the "literacy myth." At the same time, they are crucial to the articulation of deep and complex questions attached to literacy. If illiteracy is generally agreed to be problematic, then what would it take to bring about full literacy? Do the people in charge of economic and educational institutions really want a totally literate work force? Or is rhetoric that connects literacy with liberation and social transformation merely an empty shell that serves to conceal the fact that in the United States the number of available jobs has been shrinking rather than expanding? Does anyone take very seriously the notion that convenience store cashiers should be able to think, read, and write in ways considered essential for students at elite colleges and universities?

The issue is really quite simple: Literacy can never be conceptualized in the abstract but only in terms of the social ends toward which literacy (and literacy education) will be directed. Paulo Freire's work with Brazilian peasants raised the central question of literacy's value to people who are oppressed, particularly when the content and conduct of learning to read and write are not under their control.[10] And, indeed, much current work on literacy focuses on the often overlooked language skills of "non-mainstream people" and how "mainstream, school-based literacy often serves, via the literacy myth, to mitigate it."[11] Reading and writing per se are not just essential forms of communicative action; the issues surrounding literacy are often fused with questions of power and control in the structuring of knowledge itself. If, following Habermas, we conceptualize knowledge not as a neutral collection of facts but as being historically generated and addressing specific interests, then literacy provides a framework for critically questioning those knowledge claims that are presented as neutral or universal, along with the ideologies that inform them, *from within language itself.*[12]

What is central here is not some immanent reduction of literacy as a political act but the ability of language to transcend the particular social context in which literacy skills are developed, shaped, and practiced. According to Karl Mannheim and Michel Foucault, language may be conceptualized as a set of practices that can be reduced to the social context in which it is framed. In other words, language reflects and/or constitutes social practice, so problems of language are problems of "immanence."[13] The alternative view, forwarded by Habermas but based on Chomsky's generative theory of linguistics, sees all language as a set of universally available symbolic structures divorced from any particular social practice and, therefore, as it were, "transcendent."[14] But there is a third way of conceptualizing language as both immanent (in the sense that it does constitute a social practice) and transcendent (in the sense that it can also be used to call such social practices into question). In other words, as we saw in Chapter 5, the discourse of politics may entail power relations, but it also carries within itself the capability to call such relations into question. And this perspective is most relevant to the issues at hand.

In order to understand this framework, however, it is necessary to explore the relationship between literacy and class. Many in the United States deny the realities of class, and traditionally, most of our educators have found the idea downright distasteful. Mortimer Adler best exemplified this tendency in *The Paideia Proposal,* where he stated flatly that the United States is "politically a classless society. Our citizenry as a whole is our ruling class." Adler concluded from this that America "should, therefore, be an educationally classless society."[15] As an ideal worth striving for, this notion has merit; Adler, however, presented it as a logical conclusion drawn from a particular perception of reality. The blunt fact of the matter is that we are far from being an educationally classless society.

Adler's blindness is representative of an egalitarian myth pervasive in American educational and political thought. His words call to mind John Dewey's confident assertions with regard to education as a ticket to upward mobility; Dewey, ever the optimist, believed that "American life offers ... unparalleled opportunities for each individual to prosper according to his virtues."[16] Both men's claims are indicative of the extent to which the rhetoric of equality is readily mistaken for reality. They placed inordinate, yet implicit, faith in the notion that declaring all Americans to be equal will simply make this so. The weight of history, however, shows pretty clearly how difficult it is to achieve anything resembling an egalitarian social order. Even limited egalitarianism has seldom been arrived at without some form of struggle. There is another dimension to this view, however, that suggests that everyone is equally capable of self-betterment, that Americans will constantly (following Dewey) be "moving on up." This emphasis on constant mobility, whether real or illusory, obviates any structural concepts of class; it becomes all but impossible to think of anyone as belonging to, or remaining attached to, a given social class when people and relationships are in a permanent state of flux. It becomes equally difficult to describe or articulate relationships between classes from the standpoint of critical reason.

Under the egalitarian myth, class is effectively trivialized. At best the concept assumes the trappings of a game where winners gain status and losers slide down into the dungheap. If you're a loser, you had bad luck, or couldn't comprehend the rules. You're probably too stupid, too lazy, or otherwise handicapped in some way that prevents you from getting ahead. In any event, you've played poorly; it may even be logical to conclude that you are somehow biologically inferior to the folks who played well and won. Thus, classlessness does the bidding of class. Moreover, mobility alone does not deny the possibility of classes. An individual may start out poor and end up an entrepreneurial capitalist, but someone else will have to take her place as a household domestic. Such upward mobility indicates only the absence of a rigid caste system; it does not signify the absence of class structures, and positivists like Adler are mistaken when they conflate the two concepts in their rush to defend the United States as a classless society. The promise of Horatio Alger's American dream, entrenched though it may be in educational thought and political culture, is illusory. What is forgotten here is that Alger's heroes—to a man stereotypical exemplars of the American dream—seldom, if ever, become millionaires; what they do become is "respectable" members of society.

The statistics cited in Chapter 1 show how sharply the idea that the United States is a classless society is contradicted in fact. In addition, we may consider that in 1988, 3.74 million families were dependent upon public welfare, double the number in 1970. Twenty percent of American children live in poverty.[17] In 1986, "the top twenty percent of all American households received 46.1 percent of all pretax and pretransfer income." In contrast, "the bottom twenty percent received 3.8 percent."[18] The rifts in economic opportunity that shape social reality in the contemporary United States have been well documented, and they give the lie—empirically—to claims of a classless society.

As I suggested in Chapter 1, significant, well-documented rifts in economic opportunity exist in America today.[19] The efforts involved in simply sustaining everyday life demand that people interact, forming families and larger social networks through which human economic and affective needs may be met. This interaction involves sophisticated forms of sharing and cooperation, whether the task at hand is finding safe and reliable day care for small children, picking up the week's groceries at the supermarket, or making arrangements for a Friday night get-together. Today, everyday life depends on multiple—and often intermeshed—networks of social interaction, not on the rugged individualism that undergirds the rhetoric of meritocracy and upward mobility.

Success and failure alike are social, not individual, phenomena. Ethnic enclaves in the economy—Korean greengrocers, Ethiopian cabdrivers, Filipino health-care workers, and so on—are further evidence of this. Moreover, people who lack food and shelter in a society of plenty are not just hungry and homeless; nor are they, in all but the most extreme cases, individually responsible for their fate. Rather, they have been socially classified as the losers in a competition over which they have no individual control. In a profit-driven economy, this process of classification operates according to its own dynamic, founded on control over the means of production. Marx, of course, worked out this concept in detail, but it need not be viewed as either complex or mystified. All too often, however, "class" is misconstrued as a *variable* rather than the conceptualization of specific social relations.

What does this have to do with literacy? In the early, industrializing capitalism Marx and Engels analyzed—not much; in fact, there appears to be some evidence that "in the short turn, at the local level, the onset of factory production often inhibited literacy training ... because of child labor and immigration patterns."[20] But today, the high profile of literacy is emblematic of a swift and ruthless transition from industrial capital to an information-based economy; this shift accentuates the role of literacy in economic growth, class structure, and social estrangement. Although literacy cannot be conflated entirely with economics or politics, its salience as a potential or actual tool furthering either exploitative or liberatory ends is unmistakable.

Daniel Bell is representative of those who welcome—or at least see little to be concerned about—the economy's shift from industry to "information." He saw that the information society was entirely consonant with an already established meritocracy. According to Bell, people gained knowledge through education; those who had the best educations would know the most and, moreover, be ready to handle what they knew effectively and efficiently. They were the winners; they sat atop the social heap, but the heap itself would continually get smarter—if, that is, education did its job. Bell believed that American society would need an intelligentsia who could handle concepts through the possession and utilization of sophisticated literacy. An entirely separate, and much larger, social formation would be made up of those who were unable to deal with concepts but merely process data—keypunchers, video display terminal operators, and the like.[21]

Although fundamentally meritocratic, this distinction is not necessarily problematic; as Bell put it, "Questions of inequality have little to do with the issue of meritocracy—if we define a meritocracy as those who have earned status or have achieved authority by competence."[22] In such a system, unsuccessful, incompetent, or unimaginative people get what they deserve; the presumption of equal opportunity to gain status or authority through competence allows for a fair separation between go-getters and those who are willing to settle for mediocrity. Here, knowledge (and by association, sophisticated literacy skills) creates and defines both structures of power and domination and an underclass standing forever outside of these structures. Those who fail to take advantage of the new knowledge drop out, or down, to the levels of the perpetually un- and underemployed.

Bell saw information as interchangeable with knowledge or with science and technology; knowledge is simply "a set of organized statements of acts or ideas, presenting a reasoned judgment or an experimental result, which is transmitted to others through some communication medium in some systematic form."[23] Information, knowledge, and literacy here collapse into the concept of a body of information that one either possesses or does not and that may be obtained by command and demand. In other words, a person who wants knowledge—who wants to participate in the economy, to hold a job, to work—is a person who gets it. Class relationships stay the same; the only issue becomes how to distribute the new commodity. And, in the process, public knowledge conflates with the political economy of the capitalist status quo.

Bell's analysis is hard to beat. In a putatively free market economy, public knowledge is useful insofar as it accords with the needs and aims of private profit; the way to control knowledge is to regulate access by co-opting the context. American society is literate; it relies on written records, whether set down in ink on paper or filed in computer memory banks or on floppy disks. Indeed, the spoken word today lacks the validity stamp of literacy. Legality demands written records; written records demand to be read; the link between economic and social decision making is literacy–the language of profit. Yet here, as elsewhere, the preconditions for a truly free market, such as relatively free entry and exit, uniformity of goods, and unrestrained competition, remain unmet.

Literacy is the condition of postindustrialism; a worker's possibilities are contained within her ability to negotiate the various, and labyrinthine, hallways of the capitalist system. Thus, literacy and class are, to some extent, fused—with both currently undergoing a process of restructuring. In Chapter 2 I discussed the relationship between the contradictions of capitalist democracy and the privileging of knowledge throughout a stratified educational system. Now it also seems clear that the literacy skills that facilitate the acquisition and utilization of such knowledge are themselves privileged by contemporary educational practices.

The politics of literacy must, therefore, be analyzed in tandem with the politics of class and will be subject to similar forms of obfuscation. Yet at the same time that literacy serves a socially and economically regulative function it is also pedagogical. Literacy education begins in the ideas of the socially and economically dominant class and emphasizes the development of stylistically acceptable forms of reading, writing, and speaking. Becoming literate at a highly sophisticated level signifies in large measure the ability either to conform in fact or to maintain an illusion of conformity to the values, norms, and practices of capital. In turn, as we have seen, literacy serves as a means of regulating access to social, economic, and political goods. Literacy is as powerful a sorting mechanism as it is a technology; indeed, it is the very means by which public knowledge may be instantiated in the modern world. Yet the major strands of theorizing about literacy—and literacy education—generally fail to acknowledge this or, if they do, fail to address its implications in a manner amenable to overcoming the difficulties presented by the privileging of literacy skills and public knowledge alike.

Contemporary theorists of literacy provide very different visions of literacy pedagogy. One influential North American approach draws on the positivist tradition of twentieth-century social science. Within this paradigm, educators regard literacy as a collection of discrete skills that are context neutral and value free. These skills, it is assumed, are readily broken down into discrete sets of measurable subskills that can be taught to children with near-scientific precision, in much the same manner as Taylorism promoted organization of assembly lines in factories by breaking tasks down into their smallest or least-demanding parts. This approach regards literacy as something akin to the stimulus-response model of behaviorism. The stimuli (linguistic and ideational features of a text) can be configured and manipulated to evoke specific responses on a continuum from crude decoding to sophisticated levels of comprehension. Measurement of student responses, then, determines the level of language development.[24]

Putatively value free, this research is closely allied to the technocratic value system of late capitalism, which permeates centralized public school systems organized along lines of managerial efficiency. It is also extremely reductive; the rich magic of language is removed to a sterile plane of "skills transmission," where instructional materials are blandly superficial and conservative. Geared to a multinational market, educational publishing in this mode strives for the least common denominator, fearful of offending the diverse sensibilities of parents, teachers, administrators, politicians, and interest groups.[25]

All of this evokes Adorno and Horkheimer's analysis of how the culture industry, driven by a similar demand for profit, seeks the least common denominator of popular taste in the arts.[26] Clearly, the "skills" approach parallels the demands of contemporary capital, not insignificantly in that it encourages the denial of difference—particularly where class differences are concerned. The technocratic paradigm emphasizes a limited set of surface features linked to a predominantly middle-class worldview, thus truncating any possibilities for the development of a critical literacy wherever it dominates—even, or perhaps especially, among the very class whose values it supposedly furthers.

Although there is some evidence that there may be limits to homogeneity, attested to by recent efforts in New York State to change the elementary and secondary social studies curriculum so as to assure greater sensitivity to and study of previously underrepresented groups (Native Americans, women, ethnic and racial minorities), there is no reason to suppose that the market is too inflexible to incorporate such change. Publishers of school texts will quickly realize that if they remove the critical or radical elements, even the most progressive curricula can be reduced to a mushy pluralism where everyone "feels good" and no one contests received reality. In addition, given the newly available production and marketing techniques aimed at segmentation and customizing rather than at mass markets, publishers will most likely attempt to tailor content to a wide spectrum of possibilities simply as a routine method of doing business. To say the very least, under such conditions it is impossible to articulate forms of public knowledge founded on the critical use of reason.

Whereas the behaviorist approach aims to remove the skills of reading and writing from any social context, Paulo Freire's literacy theory is deeply rooted in the social aspects of language and human individuality. Drawing on experiences with peasant literacy projects in Brazil, Chile, and elsewhere, Freire articulated a revolutionary stance founded on culture and consciousness. His work has become very popular in the United States over the past twenty years, but it is far from unproblematic. If the behaviorist models of literacy can be accused of forsaking the forest for the sake of the trees (or leaves), Freire's theory leads to the opposite position, where the outlines of individual trees (specific students, contexts, practices) are utterly blurred by the totalizing emphasis on the forest (the ideological context of literacy).

From the time of his first and probably best known book, *Pedagogy of the Oppressed,* translated and published in English in 1968, to the present, Freire has consistently emphasized the relationship between language and ideology.[27] Language is never simple, never just a passive tool of communication; rather, it is ripe with the concepts of social reality. Literacy is a form of constructing that reality; it is, in a sense, knowledge *making*. As people become literate, they construct new forms of knowledge and, in the process, "begin to know what before they did not know." Class consciousness is both the process and the product here; it is neither a "psychological state" nor a mere sensitivity to opposing interests but rather a new, "nontransferable" form of knowledge "born in and through action on reality."[28]

Literacy serves as an invitation to the comprehension of revolutionary truth, but when literacy is manipulated by dominant classes who enhance their power by mystifying unread words, it may also cloak the realities of human existence. Freire suggested that it "would be extremely naive to expect the dominant classes to develop a type of education that would enable subordinate classes to perceive social injustice critically."[29] Of course it would. But what is necessary and absent here is an indication of practical guidelines for overcoming class dominance and manipulation of literacy education; grand, abstract claims are far more typical of Freire's analysis than concrete recommendations for effecting substantive change.

Freire promoted a pedagogy that respects students' culture and includes them as subjects in directing the process of their own education. Therefore, literacy instruction should be based on words "laden with the meaning of the people's existential experience" instead of that of the teacher.[30] He insisted that literacy empowers only when it actively engages individuals in a process of relentlessly questioning social reality:

> Reading the world always precedes reading the word, and reading the word implies continually reading the world. ... In a way, however, we can go further and say that reading the word is not preceded merely by reading the world, but by a certain form of writing it or rewriting it, that is, of transforming it by means of conscious, practical work. For me, this dynamic movement is central to the literacy process.[31]

The notion of how, precisely, this is all supposed to work is never really entertained, however.

Many who have enthusiastically embraced Freire's pedagogy in this country have failed to ask whether a model of putatively liberating "critical" literacy designed for rural peasant cultures can have much resonance in the infinitely more complex environments that shape even the most degraded educational experiences available to public school students in the United States today. The question of whether guidelines can be drawn to ensure that the empowering components of literacy will not be reduced to a crude formalism (for example, the claim that reading and writing are empowering substitutes for substantively instantiated, egalitarian social and political change) is seldom even addressed. Indeed, the question of whether Freire's practices are fully in accord with his principles is not raised. As Peter Elbow asked of *Pedagogy of the Oppressed*, "Isn't there something suspicious about a book which emphasizes so much the importance of concrete reality, and yet in its language, style, and structure is so wholly abstract, deductive, and without *any* concrete people, places, or incidents?"[32]

From the perspective of public knowledge, Freire's work recognizes the problems of class domination in literacy education and thus represents an improvement over the behaviorist approach, but it is by no means an adequate answer to the difficulties of literacy education. Freire offered no standards for judgment, nor did he suggest any means by which such standards might be democratically arrived at or critically evaluated in practice. Regardless of how open and liberating Freire's theory sounds, we still come up against the problem Plato faced in the *Phaedrus* and the *Republic:* how to ensure that when people read (a text, the world) they will come to a "correct" interpretation.[33] For all Freire's rhetorical insistence on dynamism, the suggestions presented in his exercise workbooks for adult literacy programs indicate at least one major ideological constraint. Over and over, students are enjoined to "think correctly" by reflecting upon their everyday lives and their work and to complete exercises by "attempting to think correctly."[34]

Such injunctions tend to contravene Freire's emphasis on pedagogical forms that are "less certain of certainties" than the more traditional "social science," models.[35] What does it mean, for example, to think correctly? Perhaps his fundamental notion of experience is itself an ideological construct; if this is the case, what about the question of standards? Perhaps Freire, too, is really presenting us with a "Republic." Perhaps there "is no way out of having an opinion, an ideology, and a strong one—as did Plato, as does Freire." If this is the case, we can only conclude, with Gee, that "literacy education is not for the timid."[36] LoL

Nor is it for the overconfident. But that has not deterred proponents of right-wing political and educational theories, whose basic claim is that literacy serves a specific cultural function of civilizing the barbarians. At the same time, however, literacy reserves for an elite few its "highest" rewards. Allan Bloom was quite specific about this; he acknowledged that the whole of education cannot be reduced to literacy but insisted nonetheless on the necessity of book learning, especially "when there is a poverty of living examples of the possible high human types." It is for these few, the best and the brightest, who can read and comprehend sacred texts, that liberal education exists; indeed, lacking the presence of this elite, "no society ... can be called civilized."[37]

E. D. Hirsch, whose *Cultural Literacy* joined Bloom's book on the bestseller lists in 1987, pulled even fewer punches. Hirsch told all who would be literate to simply consult the vocabulary list of civilization, "What Literate Americans Know," appended to his book. They had to do so quickly, for civilization was already imperiled. The tendency of U.S. educators to focus on skills rather than "the traditional materials of literate culture" was a tragic mistake, for it brought about "a gradual disintegration of cultural memory, causing a gradual decline in our ability to communicate" with each other, thus becoming "a chief cause of illiteracy, which is a subcategory of the inability to communicate."[38] Whereas Bloom attacked cultural institutions, social practices, and ideas that challenged his assumptions regarding the decay of contemporary civilization, Hirsch aimed "to enlist the language of culture and the culture of literacy as a basis for rethinking the American past and reconstructing the discourse of public life."[39] He argued against teaching skills in schools, but he totalized "culture" as having a monolithic, durable history—obviating any notion of how different and competing interests might attempt to make sense of varying circumstances and conditions of life—in much the same manner as Bloom.[40]

Hirsch argued that human knowledge cannot be reduced to discrete facts; it is always deployed according to schematic patterns. These patterns allow people to store and retrieve knowledge and to organize what they know efficiently; lacking appropriate background knowledge, they will be unable to understand either written or spoken language. Furthermore, to the extent that they cannot deploy background knowledge rapidly and efficiently, they will be unable to perform complex reading tasks.[41] Given what is known about how class impacts upon children's use of language, from the work of sociolinguists like Basil Bernstein, Shirley Brice Heath, and others, this argument seems fairly convincing.[42] Of course, the background knowledge that shapes people's ability to understand written and spoken language will vary in class-stratified social and educational systems such as those that exist in the United States today. As we saw in Chapter 2, the children of privilege develop different "conceptual maps" than working-class children do—in large measure because elite families and schools are able to provide richer, more varied opportunities for cultural and linguistic practice. Such enriched opportunities for language development are, of course, closely linked to social (and political) success later in life.

Instead of critically questioning these variations in background knowledge and premising an extensive and interconnected program of linguistic awareness and activity on bridging the gap between elite and working class experiences with language, Hirsch relied on the assumption that the discrete bits of information set out in his vocabulary list (of over 5,000 items) could themselves provide the equivalent of schematic patterns and overcome any gaps. This is a curious move, to say the least. None of the items on the list of "What Literate Americans Know" is defined nor is any explained in terms of patterns or relationships. Most entries represent single words or people's names; some are two- or three-word phrases; a few are clichés like "all's well that ends well." The *longest* entry is the famous tag from John F. Kennedy's presidential inaugural address: "Ask not what your country can do for you. Ask what you can do for your country."[43] All of this points to a fundamental contradiction: Why did Hirsch, who claimed knowledge is more than discrete facts, propose nothing more than a laundry list of discrete items by way of a cure?[44]

If, indeed, reading is not a skill separable from content and substance, why did Hirsch not demonstrate how or why these arbitrarily selected and seemingly disconnected words and phrases could help individuals fill in the blanks of background knowledge and effectively forge missing links to literacy? And why did he not come clean about how students at Vassar or Harvard generally develop very different "maps" from those developed by students at Rutgers or Stockton State College? My experiences with students at these four institutions have clearly shown that such differences not only exist but may have lifelong ramifications. This is not to say, however, that state college or university students are inherently deficient or to suggest that it is impossible for any of them to function on the same sophisticated level as their peers at elite institutions. The distinctions to be made here are not individual but rather are linked to generalized patterns of how cultural capital is available and utilized. Although this concept seemed to be lurking just below the surface of Hirsch's language, he never in the least acknowledged this possibility. To do so would mean acknowledging the class relationships that today shape the privileged processes by which cultural capital is acquired and maintained.

Instead of forwarding the critical rationality that is essential to public knowledge, this kind of vacuous list making and the sterile memory work that it implies actually militate against rationality. Robert Scholes called this "voodoo education" because it offers "a quick, cheap fix for massive educational problems, while ignoring the intractable realities that underlie those problems."[45] Although Scholes did not define these "intractable realities," it is clear from the context of his critique that they incorporate the poverty, racism, un- and underemployment, teenage pregnancy, homelessness, drug and alcohol abuse, sexual battery, and violence currently endemic in American society and in the schools. It is not just conservatives who would rather ignore these things. Most literacy scholars, with views ranging across the political spectrum, seem to prefer avoiding these issues, even when their own research agendas would seem to cry out for clarity and honest confrontation.

This difficulty is clearly exemplified by the work of Shirley Brice Heath, whose already classic ethnography, *Ways with Words,* appeared in 1983 and who has published extensively on language and literacy.[46] Over a ten-year period, Heath studied the ways in which three communities in the Piedmont Carolinas used language, locating literacy within distinctly cultural contexts: "Roadville," a white working-class mill town, where many families have labored for four generations; "Trackton," a working-class African American community whose older generation was raised "on the land" but that is now characterized by light industry; and "Gateway," a mainstream, middle-class, urban-oriented, and racially integrated community.

Gateway's middle-class parents interacted with children—through examples and specific instruction—in such a way that, from the time they were toddlers, language and book-oriented knowledge natural to school and other institutional settings (banks, businesses, government offices) would be inculcated.[47] For children from Roadville and Trackton it was a different story. Despite the fact that all three of Heath's communities held success in school in high regard, the linguistic experiences of children in the working-class environments, although differentiated to some extent by racially linked cultural idiosyncrasies, served to socialize children away from academic success. Both working-class communities shared an experiential, nonanalytic view of learning, in which children learned from their parents or other adults by doing and watching; each community, through its own ways with words, fostered forms of social interaction that contravened school-based literacy.[48]

Heath was aware that the transitions these working-class children made throughout their lives were shaped by language. She believed that change for the better would be a long time coming; if it were to come at all, structural reforms of schooling, family values, and work would be necessary. However, her solutions were based not upon changing the conditions of alienating work or of impoverished communities but on changing the *conditions* for language use.[49] The question she left untouched is whether working-class children from Roadville and Trackton (and, by extrapolation, all "poor" or "minority" children—as well as others who are "nonmainstream") should adopt acquired habits of language to transform the linguistic styles learned at home and in their neighborhoods. Cultural habits do not die easily, and "parents in Roadville and Trackton will initiate changes in their cultures only when they see it as their responsibility to provide opportunities for their children to practice or to extend the ways the school teaches."[50] Parents were thus held responsible for recognizing that their cultural habits were counterproductive; they had to encourage their children to develop new, school-based linguistic and cultural behaviors that would, at some point in the future, equip the next generation to partake of privileged social, economic, and cultural practices. But this all smacks of blaming the victims; given the extent to which such "counterproductive" linguistic practices are embedded in family and neighborhood life in these two communities, it also seems a rather unlikely outcome.

Heath's work was in many respects truly groundbreaking. Her attempt to capture the class-based sets of meanings attached to and surrounding literacy practices overcame many of the deficiencies of behaviorist theories (which tend to de-emphasize language's social aspects in favor of mechanical models of cognition) and of grand general theories like Freire's (which tend to overemphasize language as a social construct). Yet she avoided the real issue at stake: She could confront the question of whether poor, working-class, and/or minority students should be provided with opportunities to be able to read and appreciate, say, Balzac or Sand, Dostoyevsky or Ahkmatova, Mahfouz or Emecheta. If the answer to this question is, "Of course they should!"—as it must be if we accept the imperative of freely available public knowledge—then Heath provided no insight into how to bring this about, given the limitations of the status quo. She could describe, but she could not confront, the constraints of cultural capital. Once again, "intractable realities" like class and race have been substantively eliminated from the discussion.

In the context of public knowledge, however, it is precisely these realities that must be recognized as central to the processes and products of literacy—and literacy education. Throughout this chapter, as indeed throughout this book, I have touched on the links between the social relations of capitalism, the culture that is produced by these relations, the language that is their primary instrument, and the literature that is one of the many, varied forms through which culture gains consciousness or self-awareness and knowledge. Literacy by itself has no intrinsic value; it is a tool by which cultural forms may be encoded and/or decoded. But literacy, as a technology embedded in the complex process of cultural production, becomes heavily value laden, just as the process itself does. An exploration of the full range of the cultural relations of capitalism is far beyond the scope of this work. However, if public knowledge and democratic education are taken as the starting point, then literacy becomes a route of access, not just to culture, but also to freedom.

Because education (along with cultural and linguistic practices) in the United States has been intrinsically class structured, the reasons why workers might want to bother with, say, Stendhal—let alone Balzac, Emecheta, or Plato—are often obfuscated. Indeed, the folks in Roadville and Trackton got along quite well, in their everyday lives, without this sort of book learning and logically saw little need to instill a desire for it in their children. Neither Heath nor Freire, both of whom recognized the impact of class upon literacy, acknowledged that issues of national culture might be at work along with class; the experiences of various immigrant groups in this country highlight the ways in which working-class cultures elsewhere may be far more literate than they are here. In any case, restricting access to any texts—of "high" or "low" culture—to any group contravenes democracy. If, as Bloom would have it, only the best and brightest products of towns like Gateway were permitted access to "high culture"—or in Bell's terms, encouraged to manipulate *concepts* instead of *data*—the possibilities for public knowledge would forever remain truncated, distorted, and deformed.

If culture is seen as something for which the working class—along with exploited or oppressed masses in general—creates the preconditions, and over which class-based struggle is ongoing, then freedom is something to be gained, not lost, from democratic access to public knowledge. Although not everyone will want to read Plato—or Allan Bloom, for that matter—in a free society, everyone should be able to have that choice. Literacy—as the technology of access—must not be mistaken for freedom, but neither can it be denied to anyone, for whatever reason. The social relations of culture, not literacy, shape a contested terrain where literacy remains at the heart of the struggle.

*       *       *

In this chapter I began this exploration of the politics of literacy by taking a risk: by speaking personally, by making public a once-private family secret. The issues I have raised are neither abstract nor objictified in the context of the real lives I write about; they are very much a part of two working-class women's experience, my grandmother's and my own. She left a life of poverty in the north of England, where her Irish immigrant father had "gone down the mine" after coal, and, in the years before the First World War, found relative freedom—through *work*—as a chambermaid in the household of wealthy industrialists in Philadelphia. I have found forms of freedom—through literacy and education—that she could never imagine and, therefore, always begrudged. But like all freedom, mine has not come without cost. The distances between my grandmother and myself, the strange dissonances I would never comprehend until some years after her death, and the many repercussions of my own education out of and away from the working class resonate on every page of this chapter. Any risk I have taken here is minuscule compared to the magnitude of risk demanded by a politics of literacy linked to critical public knowledge. Yet continued ignorance of, or inattention to, these matters can only place such freedoms as do exist in the world today in serious jeopardy.

# 7

## Framing the Question of Freedom: Public Knowledge in Practice

*This is my credo, I believe in education that never ends, that goes on thru life, an education that never hurries, crowds, or forces, that helps people learn what they like and want to know when they want to know but never forces them to learn what they don't want to know, that educates the hands and heart as well as the head. I believe the fields and gardens are as much the schools as any buildings, that play is as useful for children as work, that teachers should be the parents or the friends, should be the comrades and companions who take joy in their work. I believe in the gospel of friendship in helping each other meanwhile.*
    —-Elizabeth Gurley Flynn, "Education and the School System"

In 1906, Elizabeth Gurley Flynn submitted an essay, "Education and the School System,"[1] to a contest at William Morris High School, in the Bronx. It quickly became a cause célèbre among her teachers; shocked by her strong socialist critique of public schooling, they rejected it. Flynn, showing characteristic spunk, nevertheless presented her essay to the public, delivering it as a speech outside the school while the contest winner claimed the trophy indoors. She later repeated her speech at the Unity Congregation, a socialist church that met on Sunday mornings at the Apollo Hall, not far from the New York City Public Library. Once again the work sparked controversy, including a series of letters to the editor of the *New York Times*.[2]

Flynn's youthful denunciation of the New York City public schools remains pertinent today:

Education is exemplified by the school system. ... [Its aim] is to produce a well-trained, well-knowledged human being. Why does it fail? ...

Firstly, because you cannot crowd the *education of a life time* into a few years, or the subjects suitable for a man's understanding into a child's brain. Secondly, all human beings are not alike and just as long as the parents and teachers continue feeding us, very different tho we be, on exactly the same intellectual diet, there will be many cases of mental indigestion.

Thirdly, the whole course is a memory course and not a thinking course, it is not an incentive to knowledge-seeking but kills it and as such is bound to fall in defeat.

Fourthly, we are taught no useful work that will make us a benefit to society, help us produce more than we can consume, and cultivate the spirit of independence.

Fifthly, we go into the world from the groping hands of the educators, utterly ignorant of the world and ourselves, the relation of the two, what we must do for the world, and it for us.

Lastly, and most important they force, force, force education at us and until we know the reason or right of it the system must be a failure, because we cannot cooperate with them on any mutual basis[3]

She went on to describe in detail the stultifying nature of the academic curriculum students were forced to endure and to sketch succinctly the outlines of a socialist theory of education in terms that reflected her "gleanings from Marx, George, and Proudhon, Thomas Paine and Ingersoll, Walt Whitman and Emerson and Thoreau, Shelly, Byron, even Ibsen and Bernard Shaw." Indeed, throughout the essay it is apparent how these "canonical" authors had influenced her thinking.[4] For the moment, however, her critique of the Bronx public schools provides an excellent foil for a scene from Tom Wolfe's *The Bonfire of the Vanities*.[5] Wolfe's novel rose on the best-seller lists eighty-odd years after Flynn wrote her essay; it depicts class, ethnic, and racial relations in a cross section of New York City's social structure. Peter Fallow, an alcoholic, expatriate British journalist working for a tabloid newspaper, is fed information about a hit-and-run accident by cronies of the Reverend Reginald Bacon, an African American minister, civil rights leader, and demagogue. Bacon, of course, is manipulating the story for his own purposes. The accident victim, a young black man named Henry Lamb, lies in a coma. Fallow, hot on the trail of the story, interviews Lamb's high school English teacher, a Mr. Rifkind, on the telephone, in an attempt to discover what sort of student the youth had been. Fallow puts the question to Rifkind repeatedly, and after a series of desultory replies, Rifkind informs the reporter that at Ruppert High school "we use comparative terms, but outstanding isn't one of them. The range runs more from cooperative to life-threatening."

Fallow, undaunted, asks for a description of the young man. Rifkind can only say that Henry Lamb was a nice fellow, cooperative, not likely to get into trouble: "As the saying goes, 'Ex nihilo nihil fit.' There's not a great range of activities in these classes, so it's hard to compare performances." Nonetheless, Fallow presses on, suggesting, in the (vain) hope that this will elicit a juicy tidbit to spice up the story, to the teacher that Henry's mother had said her son was considering attending college. But Fallow's hopes are quickly dashed as Rifkind cynically fills him in on the open-admissions policy at City College, where high school graduation and New York City residence are the only requirements for admission. Lamb's academic qualifications for graduating from Ruppert High revolve around his good attendance record and not being disruptive in class.

When Fallow, still seeking positive information about Lamb, asks about the quality of his written work, Rifkind hits the ceiling: "Written work? There hasn't been any written work at Ruppert High for fifteen years! Maybe twenty! They take multiple choice tests. ... That's all the Board of Education cares about." In the end, Rifkind explains that notions of levels of excellence have no meaning at Ruppert High, where "an honor student is somebody who attends class, isn't disruptive, tries to learn, and does all right at reading and arithmetic."⁶ Even allowing for Wolfe's presentation of his characters as exaggerated stereotypes, this exchange paints a chilling picture of what passes for education in an inner-city setting. Furthermore, many of the themes evident here—the warehousing of students, the lowering of standards and expectations, teacher burnout and student apathy, the reduction of literacy to multiple-choice vacuity, and the implicit racism—are by no means exclusive to inner-city schools today, nor are they limited to the underclass.

What is most striking, however, is the congruence between Flynn's schoolgirl critique of public education in the Bronx and—eight decades later—Wolfe's depiction of a Bronx high school English teacher's attitudes toward his students and their work. Flynn argued for schools that respect students as individuals and provide opportunities for them to develop to their fullest potential through "real-world" projects and tasks. Her overarching goal was an educational system that treats students as ends, not means. But it is clear from Rifkind's comments that neither he nor anyone else at Ruppert High ever considered Henry Lamb and his student colleagues as anything other than means—to no good end. This approach represents neither progress nor democracy in education. Instead of the liberal and liberating attitudes toward education expressed by Noah Webster, Ralph Waldo Emerson, and others cited throughout these pages, Rifkind's responses to Fallon's questions reflect a fundamental—and overwhelming—cynicism. Even if the situation is in some ways a caricature, the point is clear: For the Henry Lambs of this world, such cynicism simply breeds not only educational failure but also despair.

However, Flynn's insights about the impossibility of equating a lifetime of education with a few years of schooling, the irrationality of treating students as objects, the foolishness of emphasizing memory over thought while refusing to teach people useful work for the real world, and the stupidity inherent in the notion that forced attention breeds cooperation, were all colored by hope. They stand out in sharp relief against the bleakness of Henry Lamb's life and education; although far from complete in themselves, Flynn's insights provide a point of entry for developing a socialist theory of education.

Because socialist theory subjects all decision making to ongoing scrutiny and debate, it challenges the instrumental rationality of capital, recognizing "the public" as the pivot point of democracy and theorizing it historically.[7] Here, social needs and their interpretations become both the subject matter and the motive force of discourse whose aim is the transformation of society according to rational, humane goals. And *public knowledge* provides the very foundation of democratic empowerment and citizenship.

In late capitalism it is apparent that the civic culture of democracy is in decline. Capitalist democracy's role in preserving and promoting the private accumulation of wealth retreats behind the edifice of administrative neutrality; class-based forms of power and domination, inherent in capitalism, are obscured from view. Thus, the systemic structural conflicts that are the byproducts of capitalist accumulation and the greatest source of inequities of power and privilege are also those which are most likely to be obscured by the "neutral" decision-making processes of highly technocratic and bureaucratic hierarchies.[8] If the goal of democracy entails opening up these processes to a discourse in which ordinary people are able to address the practical questions of how they want to live and reclaim the control that has been surrendered to corporate and governmental institutions, the problem must really be cast in terms of the relationship between technology and democracy. Or, as Habermas put it in *Toward a Rational Society,* "How can the power of technical control be brought within the range of the consensus of acting and transacting citizens?"[9]

Finding a solution to this problem involves "setting into motion a politically effective discussion that rationally brings the social potential constituted by technical knowledge and ability into a defined and controlled relation to our practical knowledge and will."[10] This necessitates public dialogue on the democratic uses of science and technology; ideally, such dialogue should consist of open and reciprocal communication between scientists and politicians, mediated by democratically constituted and expressed public opinion (as opposed to sterilized survey research or polls). Technical progress and questions of science and technology would thus become public, political issues instead of being relegated to the instrumental realm of "expertise." These issues would be deliberated in open forums in a process of democratic consideration of practical social needs. As I suggested in Chapters 2 and 5 universities today provide an institutional framework of public spheres within which such debates could be organized.

The radical aspect of this kind of democratic communication is its insistence on the definition and interpretation of social needs and challenges to imbalances of actual power in society as being central to the discourse. In late capitalism's technocratic societies, social needs are routinely and generally marginalized. Thus, for over a decade the discourse of education has consistently been framed in terms of the market. One recent editorial, for example, suggested:

> While the Sputnik Shock of the 1950s stirred challenge and change, the Honda Shock of the 1970s and the far more serious Microchip Shock of the 1980s only elicited ever greater consumption of the products of our better educated competitor. ... Our capacity to compete head on with the best minds in Japan, not the lowest wages in Mexico, is what will produce the value-added jobs that pay the high wages required for a middle-class standard of living. In Chalmers Johnson's phrase, we need to produce microchips, not potato chips.[11]

Setting up the discourse in this manner effectively eliminates any consideration of how the social issues like poverty, homelessness, violence, drug abuse, and teenage pregnancy—all reflected in Edelman's statistics (cited in Chapter 4)—might affect our ability to produce rational and humane citizens. When priority of the market serves as the foundation for social and cultural relations, discussion remains restricted to the instrumentality of competition and profit; education's potential as an agent of human emancipation is utterly ignored by rhetoric that links education and the job market. But within democratically accountable discourse, as Seyla Benhabib observed, social needs and their interpretations become both the subject matter and the motive force for discursive activities aimed at transforming society according to more humane values and goals.[12] Indeed, this is the point where the *socialist* aspects of theory become central, for it is impossible to deliver on these goals within a capitalist framework. Although it remains to be seen whether socialism would manage to achieve them, the speculative moment of possibility must be, at the very least, acknowledged along with guidelines and criteria for action.

A socialist theory of education calls existing educational systems into question and serves as the motive force for positive change. It incorporates Elizabeth Gurley Flynn's educational credo, although it is hardly exhausted by her sentiments. By opening up issues of social and cultural reproduction to critical, emancipatory discourse, a socialist theory of education militates against the despair and deadening of the spirit symbolized by Colonel Jacob Ruppert High School and its antidemocratic practices. Grounded in human reason and undistorted communication, it encourages educational practices that stand stalwart against both cynicism and privilege.

Indeed, the early socialists believed that human reason alone could provide the motive force for shaping a free society of equals; here, the ultimate aim of reason was the advancement of individual freedom through critical self-reflection. This utopian prospect for modernity was essential to Marx's teleology in the mid-nineteenth century. The intellectual heritage of the Enlightenment is, of course, extremely ambivalent. It is this ambivalence that forms the basis of Sheldon Wolin's metaphor of dissonance between the body politic and the political economy of modernity, or between the democratic urges of the Enlightenment and its tendency, through the appeal to human experience as the basis for all judgment, to open a path to positivism and instrumental reason. In the academy, this ambivalence has been manifest in the split between Marxian critical theory and positivist orthodoxy in the social sciences.[13] Today, however, the socialist project has taken on new dimensions. Habermas suggested that Marx's analysis of social change is useful for explaining systemic crises but not where questions of cultural change or social integration are concerned. In *The Theory of Communicative Action,* he developed a social theory that integrates his philosophical interest in human reason with his social theoretical interest in developing a conceptual scheme from which to analyze potential system crises in modern Western societies.[14]

Habermas argued that in communicative action, individuals work toward reaching agreement on beliefs subject to validity claims that entail specific relations between the self and the world. For instance, truth claims presuppose a relation between the self and the objective world, about which true statements are possible. When such claims are disputed or challenged, individuals must give reasons for their claims in order to justify them and restore agreement—which must be based on consensus, not coercion or manipulation. Thus, a democratic society is one where reasons are continuously put forward to justify behavior and where public spaces exist to permit free and uncoerced debate over questions of cognitive, normative, or aesthetic truth.[15] Moreover, the notion of "development," although absolutely fundamental to the theory of education, can be articulated only in terms of the class ideal of democracy. Thus, it is simultaneous moral and intellectual growth that is intrinsically at stake.[16] From this notion it follows that education must be conceptualized as a process of acquiring knowledge about historical traditions and developing the capacity to justify these traditions rationally. And this knowledge cannot be the privileged domain of elites: it must be *public,* in terms of access and scrutiny alike.

Nowhere is this question of public knowledge more salient than in contemporary debates over the curriculum. Within the public sphere of the university, intellectuals committed to the project of democracy today have the opportunity to engage questions of knowledge, content, and standards from the standpoint of cultural unity. A first step toward such engagement is the recognition that "the canon" has *never* been a fixed body of sacred texts (as its defenders and detractors alike tend to claim) but has been subject to constant revision and modification. It does reflect the contradictions of capitalist democracy and the privileging of public knowledge within stratified cultural and educational institutions. Yet even at its worst moments, this body of knowledge has still proved attractive to those—African Americans, women, other "subaltern" groups—whom it has most intransigently excluded. There is no real paradox here, however, for relevance is never given, but created: "The great works of the oppressor belong to the oppressed as well. ... The past always harbors a treasure for the future."[17]

This important point is missed by many on both sides of the contemporary debates. Ironically, it is often appreciated more by conservatives like Allan Bloom who work to preserve a static and hegemonic body of cultural knowledge while restricting the numbers of those granted access to its treasures. On the left, however, the tendency to equate "the canon" with *inevitably* oppressive power remains strong. Celebrations of difference that are cloaked in the rhetoric of multiculturalism or diversity militate against inclusion and often elide the historical realities of systematic denial of access to privileged knowledge to workers, women, and minorities. This blind spot is not only foolhardy but dangerous. "Divide and conquer" has, after all, been the favored technique of businesses and governments intent on breaking the power of labor unions.[18] As Hazel V. Carby, a professor of English and African American studies at Yale, recently pointed out, the current emphasis on multiculturalism has real—and often overlooked—consequences:

> Theories of difference and diversity in practice leave us fragmented and divided but equal in an ability to conceive of radical social change. ... Today we hear a lot about oppression but nothing at all about systems of exploitation. ... The concept of resistance is frequently used but the concept of revolution has disappeared. Oppression and resistance are terms more easily applied to individualist and pluralist ideals of political change.[19]

Thus, any refusal to comprehend how settling for education focused on personal autobiography or on individual identity entails acceptance—tacitly or otherwise—of the most pernicious forms of political domination.

The challenge for socialists is thus one of redefining "quality" rather than condemning qualitative forms of evaluation as undemocratic. Furthermore, it is necessary to reclaim the notion of standards and judgment as central to the project of reconstituting democracy in renewed social and political practices. Meeting these challenges will entail articulating differences without losing sight of the need for a common culture (nationally or internationally) premised on collective experience and historical memory. Thus, the appropriate demand of the "dispossessed" within the university is not a multiplicity of separate spheres within which "difference" is legitimated but a curriculum that is open to democratically accountable debate and change. The appropriate demand is for standards that acknowledge the classics as part of a cultural tradition but that also reveal the structures of power at work in an inegalitarian social order stratified by class as well as race, ethnicity, and gender, where forms of domination often cut across or within "pluralities."

The appropriate demand is for a solidarity that, while recognizing and respecting differences, nonetheless aims toward collective history and political unity.

Concretely, this would mean that Saul Bellow's snide contention, "When the Zulus have a Tolstoy, we will read him," would be unacceptable unless Bellow also supplied reasonable *proof* that there is no artist from the Zulu cultural heritage analogous to the Western world's Tolstoy. At the present, given the conservative chauvinism inherent in the Western tradition and its outlook, most "educated" people could not supply this kind of evidence. They do not know what they claim to know, and the cultural weight of this ignorance is staggering. Opening up the canon to these standards of proof and possibility need not require throwing Tolstoy's work on some ash heap reserved for "dead white men." By the same token, it need not mandate capitulation to right-wing agendas, which cloak exclusionary privilege in a veil of tradition that denies the validity of, say, workers' and women's cultural experience.

The magnitude of this seemingly simple requirement was also exemplified by the surprise and shock surrounding the announcement of Naguib Mahfouz's Nobel Prize for Literature, in 1988. Mahfouz, the author of over forty books (only ten of which were available in English translation at the time of the Nobel decision) and the creator of the novel form in Arabic, was by Western standards a nobody.[20] It is difficult for intellectuals—or anyone else, for that matter—acculturated to privileged forms of knowledge, art, literature, and so on, to see beyond the limitations of that privilege. To believe, à la Bloom, that the only "classic" cultural forms having any merit were produced, once and for all time, by the long-defunct authors of the "great books" is to believe in an illusion. To persist in or insist upon the subjection of others to such beliefs is to promulgate a lie. More important, to simply write off "others" or their art, literature, and other cultural forms without having read or otherwise tried to understand them is to limit the possibility that quality may be determined and traditions defined in new ways that offer better answers than "the classics" alone can provide.

Here, the notion of the class ideal is instructive, for it subjects institutional imperatives and individual inquiries to democratic accountability. Thus, the political responsibility of partisan intellectuals is firmly integrated within the public sphere of the university and wedded to the task of articulating and expanding public knowledge available to the masses. Standards grounded in collective historical memory and accountable to democracy can readily be developed from this stance. This is a matter of (1) placing a specific work within the historical tradition; (2) clarifying and debating the problems it elucidates in reference to both history and democracy; and (3) speculating as to the work's influence on the future, particularly in regard to the movement toward socialist democracy. The point is not to ossify but rather to vivify a cultural tradition that contests the arbitrary exercise of authority and the dominion of illegitimate power. This project, however, calls for a degree of honesty that has been largely absent throughout the current debates; it calls for the frank admission that to deny *anyone* access to the classics—and all other literary forms—is not just an elitist and irresponsible act but a betrayal of public knowledge.

In practice, moving beyond this admission and into the realm of positive public knowledge shaped by a socialist theory of education would mean many things. At this juncture it is necessary to consider some of the more practical implications of the socialist theory of education for democratic reform. These implications entail three broad categories of substantive reform: First, and most important, education is conceptualized as a lifelong process of growth and development limited only by the velvet constraints of democratic accountability. Second, all education must be freely available, universally public, and compulsory through set minimum standards of critical literacy and competency. Third, education is a right, not a privilege, and is predicated on readily accessible public knowledge valued for its own sake and not merely according to the instrumental dictates of the marketplace. *All* education must be free, compulsory up to a set minimum standard, and public. In the current climate, this last is an especially radical mandate. It directly challenges the traditional stratifications within American education by which a small number of private schools are reserved for the children of wealthy elites and many more are dedicated to religious instruction. But it also flies in the face of the currently trendy conservative educational agenda, founded on "choice," which forwards total privatization as the cure-all for the nation's public schools. John Chubb and Terry Moe have been at the forefront of this movement; their *Politics, Markets, and America's Schools* has sparked passionate debate nationwide.[21] Although Chubb and Moe argued that they favor public education, all this means is that they think public funds should be used to pay the bills.[22] Public institutions are the enemy; they see highly bureaucratized, directly politicized public school systems as the stifling antithesis of a creative, innovative private sector, where marketplace choice reigns supreme.

Deborah W. Meier, who argued cogently against Chubb and Moe's emphasis on privatization, suggested in the same article that the concept of choice offers a viable means of progressive reform in public education. She wrote that since "progressives are on the defensive, their concern with equity leads them to attack choice reflexively as inherently elitist." This is a mistake; after all, choice is the foundation of democracy, and "Americans have long supported a dual school system." Social class structures a student's educational experiences; it is foolish to pretend otherwise. The higher up on the socioeconomic scale, the more challenging the curriculum, the more respect for individual students' ideas and personalities, the greater the rigor, the higher the expectations, the less rote and rigid the instructional methods. It is easy to distinguish a school's quality by looking not at whether it is public or private but at who is in attendance, and educational reform must be about changing that criterion. Reform involves not "dumbing down" but making what the wealthy have always valued available to everyone, regardless of status or privilege, for "the rich have always had good public schools as well as good private schools."[23]

As I have argued throughout this book, the primary reason behind such differential education has been the privileging of public knowledge; if "choice" prevails as a euphemism for privatization, then the duality of the educational system will only become more pervasive, further privileging elite forms of knowledge in the process. Clearly, the socialist theory of education, which is premised on expanding and extending publicly available choice through democratic accountability, provides a firm foundation for reforms aimed at eliminating this historic dualism.

Meier described her involvement as the founder of a network of small public schools, located in East Harlem's District 4, that were all based on choice. Over time, the new schools developed "differences in pedagogy, style of leadership, forms of governance, tone and climate."[24] Their small size provided "a level of energy and esprit, a sense of co-ownership that made these schools stand out." Some tried "radically different forms of teaching and learning, testing and assessment, school/family collaboration and staff self government." Overall, the experiment provided not just a hopeful outlook but a significant measure of successful reforms. Whereas only a decade earlier this district had been designated one of the worst in the city, by 1984 it had dozens of schools with "considerable citywide reputations and stature, alongside dozens of others that were decidedly more humane." Problems, of course, remained, but the consensus of observers and students of the district-wide reform was that substantive, lasting changes had been effected. More significant, perhaps, was that a foundation had been laid for new, innovative ideas because professionals at the schools had opportunities to be more directly involved in educational decision making. Although the schools were not cost free, the expenses incurred were relatively small—"less than the cost of one additional teacher for every newly created school."[25] Of course Meier's experience cannot provide a universally valid recipe for educational reform, but what happened in District 4 suggests that privatization is not the only efficient or effective way to set school reform in motion. Furthermore, as Meier pointed out (and as I have argued in this book), public education is fundamental to the task of reviving and maintaining democratic institutions and reconstituting the public sphere.

The District 4 story shows that it is possible to create high-quality public education, which is absolutely necessary to the democratic practices put forward under the socialist ethic and to maintaining "the good life" in a complex, information-based society. But Meier recognized that it will not be easy to make this available to all students in practice, for such dramatic changes would require a drastic rethinking of bureaucratic regulation, if not a wholesale dispensing with existing rules. Change would entail not just toleration of nonconformity and "messiness" but a reconceptualization of educational authority, for those most involved—teachers, administrators, parents—would have to be granted far more power over the day-to-day operations of the schools than they now have. It is impossible to mandate such changes bureaucratically, from the top down; to do so would guarantee "anger and sabotage on the part of unwilling, unready parents and professionals as well as the manipulation of data by ambitious bureaucrats and timid administrators."[26]

The point, of course, is that education premised on expanding opportunities to partake of and create public knowledge—to enhance the possibilities by which ordinary people can shape and form their own affairs—must take place in the public sphere. Public schools today serve primarily to reproduce existing forms of social, economic, and political inequality. Contra Chubb and Moe's claims, the problem with this system is not that it is overly socialized but that it is not socialized enough. The aim of universally available (and compulsory) public education is simple: to give workers and elites the same access to fully autonomous development while democratic accountability is maintained. Why not have high expectations for all our children? Or all citizens?

This question leads directly to the recognition that education is a right, not a privilege, and that knowledge is valuable for its own sake. This has long been central to elite cultural and educational practices, but it has been largely absent elsewhere—as Rifkind's cynical contention that at his Bronx high school "an honor student is somebody who attends class, isn't disruptive, tries to learn, and does all right at reading and arithmetic" painfully demonstrates.[27] We have looked at several examples surrounding "the canon" that demonstrate the high regard that those most excluded from its benefits have placed on such privileged knowledge and cultural forms, and I have suggested that only within a public knowledge founded in the collective can individuals become autonomous. Recent rhetoric to the contrary, the rationale for improving education goes far beyond providing employers with literate workers or bemoaning the fact that American students consistently place at the bottom of international rankings of science and math test scores. Throughout history, people have found freedom, empowerment, and pleasure in literature enjoyed both for its own sake and as a tool for expanding their horizons and gauging critical literacy and intellectual maturity. This aspect of public knowledge simply cannot be ignored.

Up to the present, however, the struggle over public knowledge has been a battle with winners and losers. Who wins and who loses is a fairly direct outcome, as Meier and many others have suggested, of social class. The winners go to Harvard, or Yale, or Stanford; losers study shorthand or refrigeration repair at the local community college. The real issue at stake here returns us to the concept of freely available education and unconstrained forms of cultural and political communication. After all, in order to participate in the forms of "communicative action" Habermas posited as fundamental to democratic practice, people must have had unlimited access to public knowledge. The conservative climate of the past decade has popularized a mythic vision of the United States as a big spender on education. As the story goes, we have been pouring money into public schools and getting little by way of results, so more spending is not the answer to educational reform; in fact, President Bush recently suggested that it ought to be possible to reform America's schools without seriously increasing the education budget. However, a few statistics attest to the illusory nature, if not the sheer foolishness, of such claims.

In terms of gross domestic product (GDP) devoted to education, per capita and per pupil expenditures, pupil-teacher ratios, and teacher salaries, the United States consistently lags behind several other industrialized countries—despite the fact that we have the world's highest standard of living and enroll the most students in our schools.[28] The often repeated claim that the United States is already the world's biggest spender on education has no basis in reality. Better pay and working conditions for teachers across the board could have a tremendous impact on the quality of education, making it easier to recruit and retain talented individuals; so would improved working conditions. Meier and others have pointed out the clear and compelling need for teachers to have more autonomy and a greater voice in governance and control of their schools.[29] The point is that conceptualizing education as a right available to *all* requires a far more substantial commitment to children—indeed, to adults as well—than even these figures might indicate.

A commitment to children's lives involves not just access to knowledge and good teachers; it requires food, clothing, shelter, and safety. None of these are universally available to American children today; indeed, fully one-third of them live in poverty. Unless Americans are willing to shift course, reorienting national priorities so that human life and human dignity carry a higher premium than Patriot missiles and other high-tech weapons of death, it will simply be impossible to make educational reforms meaningful in practical terms. Solutions to the social problems that impinge upon an individual's ability to fully realize his or her talents are often masked by the instrumental logic of capitalism and its technocratic rhetoric. However, the socialist ethic of democratic accountability would subject both the uses and rhetoric of science and technology to public debate, with the technical becoming political and vice versa.[30] Thus, questions of national priorities would become open to *public* debate: Under the democratic imperative of the class ideal, more humane responses to social questions would be forthcoming than we have seen to date. When it comes to top national priorities, Americans usually ignore arguments of cost; this has given us the most sophisticated war machine in the world. To believe that it is impossible, today, to develop the resources necessary to make a serious commitment to children's lives and to education is simply to buy into a lie.

Yet such dishonesty prevails today, especially in the highest echelons of government. Jonathan Kozol drove this point home:

> Two years ago, George Bush felt prompted to address this issue [educational finance]. More spending on public education, said the president, isn't 'the best answer.' Mr. Bush went on to caution parents of poor children who see money 'as a cure' for educational problems. 'A society that worships money ... ,' said the president, 'is a society in peril.'
>
> The president himself attended Phillips Academy in Andover, Massachusetts—a school that spends $11,000 yearly on each pupil, not including the costs of room and board. If money is a wise investment for the education of a future president at Andover, it is no less so for the child of poor people in Detroit. But the climate of the times does not encourage this belief, and the president's words will surely reinforce that climate.[31]

Even more than the lives of children is at stake, however. The ideas of education as a lifelong process and access to public knowledge as a political and cultural *right* have impacts far beyond the marketplace. They call for across-the-board changes in how we conceptualize political and cultural institutions. Precisely what shapes such reforms might take could not, of course, be predetermined or imposed from the top down; within the socialist theory of education, they would represent the outcomes of a process of public, democratic discourse. Meier correctly argued that although most public school systems have evolved into stultifying, factory-style behemoths of bureaucracy, there was no valid reason to assume that this form was inevitable to public education. Others have put forward suggestions for innovation where political and cultural institutions are concerned.

In *Strong Democracy,* for example, Benjamin Barber outlined a plan for an "interactive" communications system by which directly democratic participation in the day-to-day affairs of government could become available to ordinary households through cable television and computer networks.[32] Douglas Kellner described how citizens could develop alternatives to the culture industry's often dismal bill of fare and implement them through public access channels on cable television.[33] Public funds could be used to subsidize publishing and translation, making literature and ideas available internationally on an immediate and broad scale; this would open up a virtually infinite variety of multidimensional cultural prospects. And such suggestions only scratch the surface of possibility; in practice, the range of political and cultural reforms would be as unlimited as the human imagination.

One such route calls into question the limitations currently imposed on human possibility by the lockstep conformity that is a corollary of the capitalist ethic of consumerism. Most Americans today look upon adolescence as a sort of limbo, where young people go when they are too mature to require constant adult supervision yet too numerous to be absorbed by the economy and too unwise in the ways of the world to be granted full rights as adults. Thus, an artificial state of "teenage" has become socially entrenched; little is expected or demanded of teenagers except that they do well in school or (more likely) that they stay out of trouble. For working-class adolescents, the years between, say, thirteen and eighteen are more or less wasted; for those from the middle or upper classes, this holds true up to the age of twenty-one or twenty-two. Experiments in consumerism, sociability, and sexuality occupy the bulk of their time. These abysmally low—but culturally sanctioned and conditioned—expectations send unmistakable messages to the bright minds of youth. By asking much less of young people than their native intelligence and creativity might allow, society gets what it deserves from them— not much.

Educational reforms premised on public knowledge would demand that the current line of demarcation between theoretical knowledge (book learning) and practical knowledge (everything else) be radically redrawn. This entails integrating theory and practice as part of the real world of work and civic responsibility. Why not draw upon the energy and vitality of high school and college age individuals to build, or rebuild, communities? Why not restructure the high school curriculum so that kids can have real opportunities to use what they are learning? The possibilities are endless. Students could spend the morning hours pursuing traditional academic subjects like art, literature, and mathematics and the afternoons rehabilitating housing, on the model of projects like Habitat for Humanity. Flynn recognized long ago that young people need real-world experiences—thus, everyone should learn a trade through hands-on opportunities, perhaps through an apprenticeship system. Or students could alternate academic and community service pursuits along the lines of the quarter systems currently in place in college cooperative education programs.[34] The point is that teenagers can be taken seriously as intelligent and productive people, capable of accomplishing far more than they have usually been expected to. (Of course, one should also restructure work and civic responsibility for everyone, but that takes us a bit farther afield than is possible within the limitations of this book.)

If education were to be truly recast as a lifelong process of becoming, as Henry Adams put it, "a consciously assenting member in full partnership with the society of his [or her] age,"[35] then the present relationship between high school and college education would undergo significant alteration. This relationship is, at present, founded on the notion that students generally enter and exit at a certain age, attaining a specific credential and then proceeding on to the next stage of life without interruption; it reflects the hierarchical organizational forms of corporate capital. There is also an internal hierarchy: Public community and junior colleges designed to serve the vocational needs of the working classes offer far more flexibility in this respect than the elite four-year colleges that serve traditional student populations.[36]

There is no absolutely objective reason why this should be the case, especially in a social order dedicated to implementing and extending democracy in all spheres of life. Thus, a variety of options could be made available; for instance, bright youngsters who meet minimum competency requirements quickly could leave school for a time before proceeding on to the university (or to college, or to advanced trade school) and perform some kind of public service, such as teaching adults literacy skills. A term of national service could be required of all young people before they begin a trade or higher education, with educational or cultural opportunities offered as an incentive for such service. Once again, the possibilities are limitless, once the premise of reform is accepted.

Another avenue of reform in high schools, colleges, and neighborhoods is the concept of "learning communities."[37] In an institutional context, these are curricular structures that link different disciplines around a common theme or question. The aim is to restructure curricula so that courses, or course work, are linked up in ways that enhance not only the coherence of the material under study but also the intellectual interaction between faculty and students. Learning communities are generally associated with "collaborative and active approaches to learning, some form of team teaching, and interdisciplinary themes."[38] Several colleges and universities are currently experimenting with a variety of models, including linked courses or clusters of courses offered by different departments, with faculty roles ranging from the traditional professor to "master learners," who may take courses alongside undergraduate students in areas where they have no prior expertise. The idea is that faculty and students are involved more closely, and often more democratically, as participants in a common project of exploring knowledge within the public sphere that the particular institution represents.[39]

But there is no social mandate that such learning communities be developed within any institutional context; in fact, they evoke the historical precedents for autodidactic collectivity among newly freed African American slaves and middle-class women in the nineteenth century that Gutman and Martin described.[40] A learning community could come into being whenever any group of people share a common interest and the desire to explore it. Within the positive conceptualization of public knowledge that is central to the socialist paradigm for educational thought, all kinds of intergenerational or interclass situations could become the focus of emancipatory (or simply pleasurable) learning experiences in all kinds of settings. Again, what is most important is the emphasis on the collective and public aspects of education for the fullest possible forms of human development.

Critical literacy in this context would become both a tool for comprehending social reality and a vehicle for protesting stupidity. From this partisan standpoint, it becomes possible to attack those elements of existing culture that inhibit the extension of democracy and to put forward new cultural values that affirm freedom and equality in public spheres founded on democratic participation. Such spheres might be schools or universities, learning communities or other community groups, national or international networks or organizations, workplaces, and any other social structures or combinations that meet democratic criteria. Within these public spheres and as various publics interrelate, a constant process of *praxis*-based autonomy and solidarity could be enacted, with the twin goals of testing the limits of freedom and imagining new forms and priorities of choice kept constantly in view.

All of this would require an enormous amount of courage, imagination, and commitment on the part of educators, students, parents, public intellectuals—anyone willing to make a personal investment of time and energy to overcome the limitations of the present. Time, especially, is of the essence—although not necessarily in the sense of efficiency or expediency—for it will be possible to create good schools only if teachers, parents, and students have the time to reach agreement on the necessary changes and to decide whether they want to participate.[41] The tasks would be many, and they would not be easy. But the payoffs would be enormous; as Hannah Arendt suggested at the end of an essay entitled "What Is Freedom?": "The decisive difference between the 'infinite improbabilities' on which the reality of our earthly life rests and the miraculous character inherent in those events which establish historical reality is that, in the realm of human affairs, we know the author of the 'miracles.'"[42] What determinist theories of education overlook is precisely this: It is *people* who make the miracles of history—individuals who, as Arendt eloquently put it, "because they have received the twofold gift of freedom and action can establish a reality of their own."[43] This is the crux of public knowledge and the task of education today: to reconcile freedom and action in the public arena so that we can continue to realize these gifts. So that we can continue to author miracles. So that we can realize what Americans have not yet seen: a truly democratic politics.

# Notes

## Introduction

1. Marilyn Frye, *Willful Virgin: Essays in Feminism* (Freedom, CA: Crossing Press, 1992), 9.

2. hooks suggested "advocacy" as a substitute for the phrase "I am a feminist," which evokes personal aspects of identity, a move that emphasizes "engagement with feminist struggle as political commitment." bell hooks, *Feminist Theory from Margin to Center* (Boston: South End Press, 1984), 29–30.

3. Immanuel Kant, "Perpetual Peace," in *Kant's Political Writings,* ed. Hans Reiss, trans. H. B. Nisbet (Cambridge: Cambridge University Press, 1970), 93–130.

4. Henry Brooks Adams, *The Education of Henry Adams,* ed. Ernest Samuels (Boston: Houghton Mifflin, 1974); Jürgen Habermas, *The Philosophical Discourse of Modernity: Twelve Lectures,* trans. Frederick Lawrence (Cambridge, MA: MIT Press, 1990).

5. See John Dewey, *The School and Society,* 2d ed. (Chicago: University of Chicago Press, 1915); *Democracy and Education* (New York: Macmillan Publishing Co., Inc., 1916; reprint, New York: Free Press, 1966); *The Public and Its Problems* (New York: Henry Holt and Company, 1927; reprint, Athens: Ohio University Press, Swallow Press Books, 1954); and *Reconstruction in Philosophy* (Boston: Beacon Press, 1957).

6. Ira Katznelson and Margaret Weir, *Schooling for All: Class, Race, and the Decline of the Democratic Ideal* (New York: Basic Books, 1985; reprint, Berkeley: University of California Press, 1985); Henry A. Giroux and Peter McLaren, "Teacher Education and the Politics of Engagement: The Case for Democratic Schooling," *Harvard Educational Review* 56 (August 1986), 213–238; Henry A. Giroux, *Schooling and the Struggle for Public Life: Critical Pedagogy in the Modern Age* (Minneapolis: University of Minnesota Press, 1988).

7. For narratives of decline from a right-wing perspective, see Jacques Barzun, *The Culture We Deserve,* ed. Arthur Krystal (Middletown, CT: Wesleyan University Press, 1989); Allan Bloom, *The Closing of the American Mind* (New York: Simon & Schuster, 1987); and Norman Podhoretz, *Breaking Rank: A Political Memoir* (New York: Harper & Row, 1979). The best example of this from a left-wing perspective is Russell Jacoby, *The Last Intellectuals: American Culture in the Age of Academe* (New York: Basic Books, Inc. 1987).

8. Bruce Robbins, introduction to *Intellectuals: Aesthetics, Politics, Academics* (Minneapolis: University of Minnesota Press, 1990), xii.

9. This is not, however, to suggest that universities are without exception *free* of such linkages and concomitant constraints. See Clyde W. Barrow, *Universities and the Capitalist State: Corporate Liberalism and the Reconstruction of American Higher Education, 1894–1928* (Madison: University of Wisconsin Press, 1990). Barrow argued that during the period he studied, a broad political coalition led by business executives and government officials successfully transplanted many of the values and practices of corporate and bureaucratic administration to colleges and universities.

10. See Richard Hofstadter, *Academic Freedom in the Age of the College* (New York: Columbia University Press, 1961); also Laurence R. Veysey, *The Emergence of the American University* (Chicago: University of Chicago Press, 1965).

11. Their contrasting views are summarized in Paulo Freire, *Pedagogy of the Oppressed,* trans. Myra Bergman Ramos (New York: Seabury Press, 1970); and E. D. Hirsch, Jr., *Cultural Literacy: What Every American Needs to Know* (Boston: Houghton Mifflin Company, 1987).

12. For example, Critical Pedagogy supports classroom analysis of and rejection of oppression, injustice, inequality, silencing of marginalized voices, and authoritarian social structures. A general discussion of these points can be found in Michelle Fine, "Silencing in the Public Schools," *Language Arts* 64 (1987); 157–174; Henry A. Giroux, "Radical Pedagogy and the Politics of Student Voice," *Interchange* 17 (1986); 48–69; and Roger Simon, "Empowerment as a Pedagogy of Possibility," *Language Arts* 64 (1987); 370–382. Elizabeth Ellsworth developed an impressive critique of this discourse in "Why Doesn't This Feel Empowering? Working Through the Repressive Myths of Critical Pedagogy," *Harvard Educational Review* 59 (August 1989); 297–394.

13. Adrienne Rich, "Double Monologue," in *Collected Early Poems, 1950–1970* (New York: W. W. Norton & Co., 1993), 158.

## Chapter 1

1. Noah Webster, "On the Education of Youth in America," in *Essays on Education in the Early Republic,* ed. Frederick Rudolph (Cambridge, MA: Belknap Press of Harvard University Press, 1965), 77.

2. See Carl F. Kaestle, *Pillars of the Republic: Common Schools and American Society, 1780–1860,* American Century Series (New York: Hill and Wang, 1983); and Rush Welter, *Popular Education and Democratic Thought in America* (New York: Columbia University Press, 1962). Both discussed the ambivalence of the common school movement, which combined conservative motives such as limitation of the mob and prevention of popular anarchy with notions of freedom and rights.

3. Harvey J. Graff, *The Literacy Myth* (New York: Academic Press, 1979), xxi.

4. The Bacon quotation is from his 1597 religious meditation, *De haeresibus (Of heresies),* 10, quoted in J. A. Simpson, ed., *The Concise Oxford Dictionary of Proverbs* (Oxford: Oxford University Press, 1982), 126–127. The biblical passage is from Proverbs 24:5; the English proverb "Knowledge is power" is identified in H. L. Mencken, ed., *Historical Principles from Ancient and Modern Sources* (New York: A. Knopf, 1942), 638.

5. Thomas Jefferson, "Bill 79 of 1799 for the 'More General Diffusion of Knowledge," in *Early History of the University of Virginia As Contained in the Letters of Thomas Jefferson and Joseph C. Cabell* (Richmond, VA: J. W. Randolph, 1856), 365.

6. Jürgen Habermas, *The Structural Transformation of the Public Sphere: An Inquiry into a Category of Bourgeois Society,* trans. Thomas Burger with the assistance of Frederick Lawrence (Cambridge, MA: MIT Press, 1989).

7. Ibid., 51.

8. Sheldon S. Wolin, "The People's Two Bodies," *Democracy* 1 (January 1981); 11.

9. Ibid., 11–17.

10. Ibid., 19.

11. James D. Richardson, ed., *A Compilation of the Messages and Papers of the Presidents, 1789–1902* (New York: Bureau of National Literature and Art, 1908), 1:220.

12. See Nancy Fraser, "Rethinking the Public Sphere: A Contribution to the Critique of Actually Existing Democracy," *Social Text* 25/26 (Winter 1990); 56–80; Joan Landes, *Women and the Public Sphere in the Age of the French Revolution* (Ithaca, NY: Cornell University Press, 1988); and Mary P. Ryan, *Women in Public: Between Banners and Ballots, 1825–1880* (Baltimore: Johns Hopkins University Press, 1990), for discussions of how women and other groups were excluded from the "public spheres" of eighteenth- and nineteenth-century politics.

13. Joshua Cohen and Joel Rogers, *On Democracy* (New York: Penguin Books, 1983), 49.

14. For an excellent summary of these debates, see Beatrice and Ronald Gross, eds., *The Great School Debate: Which Way for American Education?* (New York: Simon and Schuster, 1985), and Harvey Holtz, Irwin Marcus, Jim Doughtery, Judy Michaels, and Rick Peduzzi, eds., *Education and the American Dream: Conservatives, Liberals, and Radicals Debate the Future of Education,* intro. Henry A. Giroux and Paulo Freire (Granby, MA: Bergin & Garvey Publishers, Inc., 1898).

15. John E. Chubb and Terry M. Moe, *Politics, Markets, and America's Schools* (Washington, D.C.: Brookings Institutions, 1990), 1.

16. Peter Schrag, "The Great School Sell-Off," *American Prospect* (Winter 1993), 34–43.

17. Jonathan Kozol, *Savage Inequalities: Children in America's Schools* (New York: Crown Publishers, Inc., 1991). Samuel G. Freedman, *Small Victories: The Real World of a Teacher, Her Students and Their High School* (New York: Harper & Row, 1990); and Emily Sachar, *Shut Up and Let the Lady Teach: A Teacher's Year in a Public School* (New York: Poseidon Press, 1991), provided representative accounts of such conditions.

18. Kevin Phillips, *The Politics of Rich and Poor: Wealth and the American Electorate in the Reagan Aftermath* (New York: HarperPerennial, 1991). For exemplary left and liberal treatments, see Barbara Ehrenreich, *Fear of Falling: The Inner Life of the Middle Class* (New York: Pantheon Books, 1989); and Thomas Byrne Edsall, *The New Politics of Inequality* (New York: W. W. Norton & Company, 1985).

19. Kevin Phillips, "The Collapse of the Middle Class," *New Perspectives Quarterly* 7 (Fall 1990), 42.

20. Barbara Ehrenreich, "The Hour-Glass Society," *New Perspectives Quarterly* 7 (Fall 1990), 44.

21. Jim Hightower, "You've Got to Spread It Around," *Mother Jones* (May 1988), 56.

22. Phillips, *Politics of Rich and Poor,* 24–25.

23. Walter Dean Burnham, *The Current Crisis in American Politics* (New York: Oxford University Press, 1982).

24. Phillips, *Politics of Rich and Poor,* 25. Also see Frances Fox Piven and Richard A. Cloward, *Why Americans Don't Vote* (New York: Pantheon Books, 1989), for a somewhat different interpretation of this phenomenon.

25. See, for example, the accounts in E. J. Dionne, Jr., *Why Americans Hate Politics* (New York: Simon & Schuster, 1991); Richard N. Goodwin, *Promises to Keep: A Call for a New American Revolution* (New York: Times Books, 1992); William Greider, *Who Will Tell the People: The Betrayal of American Democracy* (New York: Simon & Schuster, 1992).

26. "America's Choice: High Skills or Low Wages!" Report of the Commission on the Skills of the American Workforce, June 1990; Lauro F. Cavazos, address to the LULAC Youth Leadership Convention, May 31, 1990; both quoted in "The Stupidification of America," *New Perspectives Quarterly* 7, no. 4 (Fall 1990), 47.

27. "America's Choice: High Skills or Low Wages!"

28. Ibid.

29. Lawrence Mishell and Ray Teixeira, "The Myth of the Labor Shortage: Jobs, Skills, and Incomes of America's Workforce 2000," Economic Policy Institute, June 18, 1990, quoted in "The Stupidification of America."

30. "American's Choice: High Skills or Low Wages!"

31. Henry Cisneros, "Four Tiered Education," *New Perspectives Quarterly* 7, no. 4 (Fall 1990), 16.

32. Mishel and Teixeira, "The Myth of the Labor Shortage."

33. Cavazos, address to the LULAC Youth Leadership Convention, May 31, 1990.

34. Phillips, *Politics of Rich and Poor,* 22.

35. Cisneros, "Four Tiered Education," 17.

36. Ibid.

37. Edith Rasell and Lawrence Mishel, "Shortchanging Education: How US Spending on Grades K–12 Lags Behind Other Industrial Nations," quoted in "The Stupidification of America," Economic Policy Institute, January 1990, 47.

38. Albert Shanker, "Our Successful Students Are Note Very Successful," *New York Times,* April 16, 1990, E9.

39. See, for example, the discussions in Peter W. Cookson, Jr., and Caroline Hodges Persell, *Preparing for Power: America's Elite Boarding Schools* (New York: Basic Books, Inc., 1985); Steven Brint and Jerome Karabel, *The Diverted Dream: Community Colleges and the Promise of Educational Opportunity in America, 1990–1985*(New York: Oxford University Press, 1989); Jeannie Oakes, *Keeping Track: How Schools Structure Inequality* (New Haven: Yale University Press, 1985); Michael Apple, *Teachers and Texts: A Political Economy of Class and Gender Relations in Education* (London: Routledge and Kegan Paul, 1986); and Julia Wrigley, *Class Politics and Public Schools: Chicago 1990–1950* (New Brunswick, NJ: Rutgers University Press, 1982).

40. Cisneros, "Four Tiered Education," 15.

41. Dewey, *The Public and Its Problems*, 166.

42. Clarence J. Karier, *The Individual, Society, and Education: A History of American Educational Ideas* (Urbana and Chicago: University of Illinois Press, 1986), xviii.

43. Quoted in Eleanor W. Thompson, *Education for Ladies, 1830–1860* (New York: King's Crown Press, 1947), 40.

44. See Paula S. Fass, *Outside In: Minorities and the Transformation of American Education* (New York: Oxford University Press, 1989).

45. Kant, "Idea for a Universal History with a Cosmopolitan Purpose," in Reiss, ed., *Kant's Political Writings*, 41–53; Karl Marx and Friedrich Engels, "Manifesto of the Communist Party," in *The Marx-Engels Reader*, ed. Robert Tucker (New York: W. W. Norton, 1978), 491.

46. Cohen and Rogers, *On Democracy*, 56–57.

47. Robert Bellah, with Richard Madsen, William M. Sullivan, Ann Swidler, and Steven M. Tipton, *Habits of the Heart: Individualism and Commitment in American Life* (Berkeley: University of California Press, 1985; reprint, New York: Harper Perennial, 1986), vii. An individualistic society is "characterized by *privatization* and atomistic social relations, qualities which, if not synonymous with egoism in a narrower sense, always threaten to degenerate into it." Ellen Meiksins Wood, *Mind and Politics: An Approach to the Meaning of Liberal and Socialist Individualism* (Berkeley: University of California Press, 1972), 127.

48. Elizabeth Cagan, "Individualism, Collectivism, and Radical Educational Reform," *Harvard Educational Review* 48 (May 1978), 228.

49. See Michael B. Katz, *Reconstructing American Education* (Cambridge, MA: Harvard University Press, 1987); Ira Katznelson and Margaret Weir, *Schooling for All: Class, Race, and the Decline of the Democratic Ideal* (New York: Basic Books, 1985; reprint, Berkeley: University of California Press, 1985); and Diane Ravitch, *The Great School Wars, New York City 1805–1973; A History of the Public Schools as Battlefield of Social Change* (New York: Basic Books, Inc., 1974).

50. Jonathan Kozol offered a timely and provocative treatment of this issue, beginning from the premise that "what seems unmistakable, but, oddly enough, is rarely said in public settings nowadays, is that the nation, for all practice and intent, has turned its back upon the moral implications, if not yet the legal ramifications, of the *Brown* decision. The struggle being waged today, where there is any struggle being waged at all, is closer to the one that was addressed in 1896 in *Plessy v. Ferguson,* in which the court accepted segregated institutions for black people, stipulating only that they must be equal to those open to white people. The dual society, at least in public education, seems in general to be unquestioned." Kozol, *Savage Inequalities,* 4.

51. Although I am here treating education in the United States, partly because our system possesses several unique developmental features, partly because good comparative studies are lacking, and partly because it is what I know best as a career educator, and the public to which I refer connotes citizenship, or at least residence, in this particular country, I do not mean to limit the terms to an exclusive usage. Taken to the logical limits of an interdependent and rapidly shrinking planet, "public" must

also represent the human population of our globe, as seen from a distance through an orbiting satellite's camera lens.

52. See John Keane, *Public Life and Late Capitalism: Toward a Socialist Theory of Democracy* (Cambridge: Cambridge University Press, 1984), 146.

53. See Robert H. Wiebe, *The Search for Order, 1877–1920* (New York: Hill and Wang, 1967); and Ellen W. Schrecker, *No Ivory Tower: McCarthyism and the Universities* (New York: Oxford University Press, 1986).

54. Rosa Luxemburg, "The Crisis in German Social Democracy" (The Junius Pamphlet: Part 1), in *Selected Political Writings*, ed. Dick Howard (New York: Monthly Review Press, 1971), 325.

55. Oskar Negt and Alexander Kluge, "The Public Sphere and Experience: Selections," trans. Peter Labanyi, *October* 46 (Fall 1988), 60–82; "Selections from *Public Opinion and Practical Knowledge: Toward An Organizational Analysis of Proletariat and Middle Class Public Opinion*," *Social Text* 25/26 (Winter 1990), 24–32; and *Public Sphere and Experience: Toward an Analysis of the Bourgeois and Proletarian Public Sphere* (Minneapolis: University of Minnesota Press, 1993).

56. Michael Harrington, *Socialism Past and Future* (New York: Plume/Penguin Books, Inc., 1990), 28.

57. Distinctions must be drawn, however, between the need to maintain, in the words of the young Marx, "a ruthless critique of everything existing," and Theodor Adorno's "negative dialectics," within which it is, indeed, impossible to develop any positive standpoint. Karl Marx, "Letter to Ruge, 1843," in *The Marx-Engels Reader, 2d ed.*, ed. Robert Tucker (New York: W. W. Norton and Company, 1978), 13; and Theodor W. Adorno, *Negative Dialectics*, trans. E. B. Ashton (New York: Continuum, 1983).

58. Stephen Eric Bronner, *Socialism Unbound* (New York: Routledge, 1990), 147.

59. Ibid., xxii–xxiii.

60. Ibid., 157.

61. Rosa Luxemburg, "In Memory of the Proletariat Party," in *Selected Political Writings*, ed. Dick Howard, 201.

62. Bronner, *Socialism Unbound*, 166–168.

63. Ibid., 155.

64. Ibid., 156.

65. Henry A. Giroux and Peter McLaren, introduction to *Critical Pedagogy, the State, and Cultural Struggle*, eds. Henry A. Giroux and Peter McLaren (Albany: SUNY Press, 1989), xii.

## Chapter 2

1. Henry Brooks Adams, *The Education of Henry Adams*, ed. Ernest Samuels (Boston: Houghton Mifflin company, 1974), 4.

2. See Earnest Samuels, *Henry Adams* (Cambridge, MA: Belknap Press of Harvard University, 1989), for the most complete discussion of these issues. A critical literary interpretation is found in R. P. Blackmur, *Henry Adams*, ed. Veronica A. Makowsky (New York: Da Capo Press, 1980). Other biographical information may be found in Patricia O'Toole, *The Five of Hearts: An Intimate Portrait of Henry Adams and His Friends, 1880–1918* (New York: Clarkson Potter/Publishers, 1990), and Eugenia

Kaledin, *The Education of Mrs. Henry Adams* (Philadelphia: Temple University Press, 1981).

3. For example, Adams's sketching Harvard College as a "negative force" that "taught little, and that little ill" in his brilliant chapter on that institution, while entirely of a piece with his general depiction of a life ill trained to cope with modern science and politics, is, in Samuels's opinion, extremely misleading: "Nothing could have been farther from the fact. The four years at that maligned institution touched Adams's mind at so many points and so pervasively that even had he been a willing debtor he could hardly have listed his full obligation." Samuels, *Henry Adams,* 8–9; Adams, *Education,* 55.

4. The comparison to Rousseau was made directly by Adams, in the preface to *Education.* See Adams, *Education,* xxix. Also see Henry Brooks Adams, *Mont-Saint-Michel and Chartres* (Privately printed: Washington, DC, 1904).

5. Adams, *Education,* 225.

6. Adams's description of the Grant administration is scathing. He is equally caustic in reference to Theodore Roosevelt: "Roosevelts are born and never can be taught." Adams, *Education,* 255–283 and 419. Gore Vidal's series of Washington novels also provides insights, reminiscent of Adams, into the degeneration of public life during this period. See Gore Vidal, *Empire: A Novel* (New York: Random House, 1987), and *Hollywood: A Novel* (New York: Random House, 1990).

7. Adams, *Education,* 12.

8. Ibid., 5.

9. Ibid., 421.

10. Ibid., 423.

11. Ibid., 320.

12. Blackmur, *Henry Adams,* 103–107.

13. O'Toole, *Five of Hearts,* 17.

14. Adams, *Education,* 497.

15. Habermas, *Structural Transformation.*

16. Ibid., 143.

17. Douglas Kellner, *Television and the Crisis of Democracy* (Boulder, CO: Westview Press, 1990), 12.

18. Stuart Ewen, *Captains of Consciousness: Advertising and the Social Roots of the Consumer Culture* (New York: McGraw-Hill, 1977).

19. Kellner, *Television and the Crisis of Democracy,* 12.

20. See especially the papers collected in Craig Calhoun, ed., *Habermas and the Public Sphere* (Cambridge, MA: MIT Press, 1992). Also see those in "The Phantom Public Sphere," *Social Text* 25/26 (1990); John Forester, ed., *Critical Theory and Public Life* (Cambridge, MA: MIT Press, 1985); and David Rasmussen, ed., *Universalism vs. Communitarianism: Contemporary Debates in Ethics* (Cambridge, MA: MIT Press, 1990)>

21. Michael Schudson made a strong argument to the contrary, concluding that "it does not appear that in any general sense rational-critical discussion characterized American politics in the colonial era. The politically oriented riot was a more familiar form of political activity than learned discussion of political principles." Although at times compelling, this argument fails to elaborate the relationship between historical

conditions and politics; Schudson's focus is on a limited criterion of "rationality" rather than on the social, economic, and cultural conditions for an effective public sphere. Thus he does not really challenge the larger, general (and to my mind accurate) patterns of historical development presented here. See Michael Schudson, "Was There Ever a Public Sphere? If So, When? Reflections on the American Case," in Calhoun, *Habermas and the Public Sphere,* 142–163, 160.

22. Alexis de Tocqueville, *Democracy in America* (1831; reprint New York: Macmillan Company, 1969), 242–243.

23. To Tocqueville's credit, however, he was impressed by the participation of women—who, although granted no public political voice, were often nevertheless quite informed and articulate about politics. For a discussion of how this "private sphere" practice became institutionalized with the concept of "Republican Motherhood," see Linda Kerber, *Women of the Republic: Intellect and Ideology in Revolutionary America* (New York: W. W. Norton & Company, Inc., 1986).

24. See Habermas, *Structural Transformation,* 124.

25. Mary O'Brien, *The Politics of Reproduction* (London: Routledge & Kegan Paul, 1981), 99. Furthermore, the situation is exacerbated by the way in which public "debates" are distorted even before the first word is uttered. Since virtually all sources of information readily available to any discussion of public affairs and events are derived from privately owned media, and these operate according to the instrumental logic of capital, the question of just how freely the "marketplace of ideas" can operate today comes to the fore.

26. Hannah Arendt, *The Human Condition* (Chicago: University of Chicago Press, 1958), 28.

27. Ibid., 32–33.

28. Ibid., 38.

29. Ibid., 29.

30. Ibid., 38.

31. Ibid., 41.

32. Ibid., 59. I have not added "and women" to the generic "men" here because, given the context, it is clear that the sexual division of labor is to be ordered so that it is women who are to *provide* the shelter and warmth in the private sphere; given this, they would thus not experience the same deprivations as men in the face of the colonization of this sphere by "society." See Christopher Lasch, *Haven in a Heartless World: The Family Besieged* (New York: Basic Books, 1977), for a related line of argument.

33. Susan Moller Okin, "Gender, the Public and the Private," in David Held, ed., *Political Theory Today* (Stanford, CA: Stanford University Press, 1991), 68.

34. Ibid., 69.

35. *Oxford English Dictionary, 2d ed.* (Oxford: Clarendon Press, 1989), 12: 778.

36. Anne Philips, *Engendering Democracy* (University Park: Pennsylvania State University Press, 1991), 103–104.

37. Ibid., 95.

38. Iris Marion Young, "Impartiality and the Civic Public: Some Implications of Feminist Critiques of Moral and Political Theory," in Seyla Benhabib and Drucilla Cornell, eds., *Feminism as Critique* (Minneapolis: University of Minnesota Press, 1987), 57–76.

39. Clearly, the questions raised by Habermas's work on the public sphere are largely beyond the scope of this project. However, they provide the focus for some fascinating contemporary scholarship. See, for example, the articles collected in "The Phantom Public Sphere," *Social Text* 25/26 (1990)—especially Fraser, "Rethinking the Public Sphere"; Calhoun, *Habermas and the Public Sphere*; Forester, *Critical Theory*; Rasmussen, *Universalism vs. Communitarianism*.

40. Adams, *Education*, 21.

41. Elizabeth Fox-Genovese, *Feminism Without Illusions: A Critique of Individualism* (Chapel Hill: University of North Carolina Press, 1991), 38.

42. Arendt, *The Human Condition*, 55.

43. Fox-Genovese, *Feminism Without Illusions*, 219.

44. Deborah W. Meier, "Myths, Lies, and Public Schools," *The Nation* (September 21, 1992), 271.

45. Kozol, *Savage Inequalities*, 137–138.

46. Horace Mann, *Twelfth Annual Report of the Board of Education, Together with the Twelfth Annual Report of the Secretary of the Board* (Boston, 1849), 84, cited in Lawrence A. Cremin, *The Transformation of the School: Progressivism in American Education 1876–1957* (New York: Vintage, 1964), 9.

47. Ralph Waldo Emerson, "Education," in *Selected Prose and Poetry*, ed. Reginald L. Cook (New York: Rinehart, 1954), 208.

48. Jeannie Oakes, *Keeping Track: How Schools Structure Inequality* (New York: Yale University Press, 1985), 197.

49. Ibid., 4.

50. See, for example, representative works like Pierre Bourdieu and Jean-Claude Passeron, *Reproduction in Education, Society, and Culture*, trans. Richard Nice (London: Sage Publications, Ltd., 1990); Samuel Bowles and Herbert Gintis, *Schooling in Capitalist America: Educational Reform and the Contradictions of Economic Life* (New York: Basic Books, Inc., 1976).

51. Bowles and Gintis, *Schooling in Capitalist America*.

52. Paul Willis, *Learning to Labour: How Working Class Kids Get Working Class Jobs* (Lexington, MA: D. C. Heath, 1977).

53. Michael W. Apple, "Ideology, Reproduction, and Educational Reform," *Comparative Educational Review* 22 (1978), 367–387.

54. Bourdieu and Passeron, *Reproduction*.

55. Private schools in general have attracted some public and scholarly attention: James S. Coleman, Thomas Hoffer, and Sally Kilgore. *High School Achievement: Public, Catholic, and Private Schools Compared* (New York: Basic Books, 1982); Denis Doyle, "The Storm Before the Lull: The Future of Private Schooling in America," in John H. Bunzel, ed., *Challenge to American Schools: The Case for Standards and Values* (New York: Oxford University Press, 1985); Cookson and Persell, *Preparing for Power*; Amy Gutmann, *Democratic Education* (Princeton: Princeton University Press, 1987).

56. David Halberstam, *The Best and the Brightest* (New York: Random House, 1969), 51.

57. C. Wright Mills, *The Power Elite* (London: Oxford University Press, 1959), 64–65.

58. *Groton School Bulletin,* 1981–1982, 15; cited in Cookson and Persell, *Preparing for Power,* 74.

59. Cookson and Persell, *Preparing for Power,* 74–75.

60. Ibid., 84.

61. Ibid., 169.

62. Herbert C. Gutman, "Schools for Freedom: The Post-Emancipation Origins of Afro-American Education," in *Power and Culture: Essays on the American Working Class,* ed. Ira Berlin (New York: Pantheon Books, 1987), 260.

63. Theodora Penny Martin, *The Sound of Our Own Voices: Women's Study Clubs, 1860–1910* (Boston: Beacon Press, 1987).

## Chapter 3

1. Walt Whitman, "Democratic Vistas" (1871), in *Walt Whitman: Complete Poetry and Collected Prose* (New York: Library of America, 1982), 960; Dewey, *The Public and Its Problems.*

2. Dewey, *The Public and Its Problems,* 111.

3. Ibid., 126.

4. Ibid., 111.

5. Ibid., 126.

6. Ibid.

7. Besides articulating a notion of public knowledge and emphasizing "the public sphere," Dewey also anticipated Habermas's theory of communicative action. See Dewey, *The Public and Its Problems,* 142.

8. Jürgen Habermas, *Autonomy and Solidarity: Interview with Jürgen Habermas,* ed. Peter Dews (London: Verso, 1986), 151.

9. J. Donald Butler, *Four Philosophies and Their Practice in Education and Religion,* 3d ed. (New York: Harper and Row, Publishers, Inc., 1968), 405. These rather grandiose claims should be contrasted with Robert B. Westbrook's recent sympathetic reassessment of Dewey's influence: "Although perhaps every public school district has at least one teacher who had read Dewey and tried to teach as he would have had him or her teach, his critics have vastly overestimated his influence. American schools remain far from the interesting and dangerous outposts of a human civilization he would have had them be." Robert B. Westbrook, *John Dewey and American Democracy* (Ithaca: Cornell University Press, 1991), 543.

10. Dewey, *Democracy and Education,* 107.

11. Ibid.

12. Dewey, *The Public and Its Problems,* 166.

13. Ibid., 167.

14. Many "progressive" educators who invoked Dewey's name distorted his ideas to the point that they were no longer recognizable. In his last book on education, *Experience and Education,* published in 1938, Dewey sharply criticized proponents of "child-centered" education, with whom he was often quite wrongly identified. John Dewey, *Experience and Education* (New York: Macmillan, 1938). Also see Patricia Albjerg Graham, *Progressive Education: From Arcady to Academe* (New York: Teachers College Press, 1967), and Laurence Cremin, *Transformation of the School,* 201–215, 240–347.

15. Ralph Barton Perry, *The Thought and Character of William James* (Cambridge, MA: Harvard University Press, 1948), 281.

16. Karier, *The Individual, Society, and Education.* 125.

17. Peirce believed that an individual's character was shaded by his or her participation in community life: "A person is not just absolutely an individual. His thoughts are what he is 'saying to himself,' that is, is saying to that other self that is just coming into life in the flow of time. When one reasons, it is that critical self that one is trying to persuade; and all thought whatsoever is a sign, and is mostly of the nature of language." Peirce, *Collected Papers of Charles Sanders Peirce,* ed. Charles Hartshorne and Paul Weiss (Cambridge, MA: Harvard University Press, 1931–1958), 7: 319.

18. See, for instance, "The Function of Cognition," in William James, *Pragmatism and the Meaning of Truth* (Cambridge, MA: Harvard University Press, 1978), 179–198.

19. Richard J. Bernstein, *Praxis and Action: Contemporary Philosophies of Human Activity* (Philadelphia: University of Pennsylvania Press, 1971), 201.

20. Cornel West, *The American Evasion of Philosophy: A Genealogy of Pragmatism* (Madison: University of Wisconsin Press, 1989), 5.

21. See, for example, the treatments in Richard J. Bernstein, ed., *Perspectives on Peirce: Critical Essays on Charles Sanders Peirce* (New Haven: Yale University Press, 1965); Bernstein, *Praxis and Action;* and West, *The American Evasion of Philosophy.*

22. Jürgen Habermas, *Knowledge and Human Interests,* trans. Jeremy J. Shapiro (Boston: Beacon Press, 1971), 91.

23. Peirce, *Collected Papers,* 7: 319.

24. Peirce, "How to Make Our Ideas Clear," *Collected Papers,* 5: 407.

25. Peirce, *Collected Papers,* 5: 13.

26. Habermas, *Knowledge and Human Interests,* 100–101.

27. Ibid., 118.

28. Ibid., 137.

29. Ibid.

30. Karier, *The Individual, Society, and Education,* 127. See also William James's letter to President Eliot of Harvard, March 3, 1895, quoted in Perry, *Thought and Character of William James,* 283.

31. Even neopragmatist Richard Rorty complained of "a tendency to overpraise Peirce." What Rorty disliked about Peirce, as opposed to James and Dewey, is that Peirce remained a Kantian, or "the most convinced that philosophy gave us an all-embracing ahistorical context in which every other species of discourse could be assigned its proper place and rank." Richard Rorty, *Consequences of Pragmatism: Essays, 1972–1980* (Minneapolis: University of Minnesota Press, 1982), 160–161.

32. Merle Curti, *The Social Ideas of American Educators, With a New Chapter on the Last Twenty-five Years* (Totowa, NJ: Littlefield, Adams and Company, 1978), 443.

33. William James, *The Principles of Psychology* (New York: Henry Holt and Company, 1923); *Talks to Teachers on Psychology: And to Students on Some of Life's Ideals* (New York: W. W. Norton and Company, 1958); *Psychology: Briefer Course* (New York: Henry Holt and Company, 1920).

34. Clark Kerr, *The Uses of the University,* 3d ed. (Cambridge, MA: Harvard University Press, 1982), 137–139.

35. John Dewey, "The Pragmatism of Peirce," supplementary essay in Charles S. Peirce, *Chance, Love and Logic*, ed. Morris R. Cohen (New York: George Brazillier, Inc., 1956), 307.

36. Curti, *The Social Ideas of American Educators*, 448.

37. James, *The Principles of Psychology*, 121. See also Curti, *The Social Ideas of American Educators*, for a discussion of James's social conservatism, especially 429–437.

38. James, *Talks to Teachers*, 18.

39. William James, *Pragmatism and the Meaning of Truth* (Cambridge, MA: Harvard University Press, 1978), 169.

40. Ibid., 97.

41. Ibid., 106, 54.

42. Ibid., 169.

43. Benito Mussolini, interview with Dr. Andre Revesz, in *Sunday Times* (London), April 11, 1926. Quoted in Perry, *The Thought and Character of William James*, 317.

44. James, *Pragmatism*, 32.

45. Richard Bernstein, *Praxis and Action*, 172–173.

46. John Dewey, *Philosophy and Civilization* (New York: Capricorn Books, 1963), 34.

47. Dewey, *The Public and Its Problems*, 149.

48. John Dewey, "Creative Democracy—The Task Before us," *Classic American Philosophers*, ed. Max Fisch (New York: Appleton-Century-Crofts, 1951), 394.

49. Dewey, *Democracy and Education*, 328. Emphasis in original.

50. Dewey, *The Public and Its Problems*, 175.

51. Ibid., 157.

52. Ibid., 184.

53. John Dewey, *Individualism Old and New* (New York: Capricorn Books, 1929), 171.

54. John Dewey, *Liberalism and Social Action* (New York: G. P. Putnam's Sons, 1935), 50.

55. John Dewey, *Problems of Men* (New York: Philosophical Library, 1946), 58.

56. John Dewey, "The Ethics of Democracy," in Dewey, *The Early Works, 1882–1898* (Carbondale: Southern Illinois University Press, 1969), 1: 246.

57. Robert B. Westbrook, *John Dewey and American Democracy* (Ithaca: Cornell University Press, 1991), 49–50.

58. John Dewey, "The School as Social Centre," in Dewey, *The Middle Works, 1899–1924* (Carbondale: Southern Illinois University Press, 1976), 2: 93.

59. John Dewey, "Ethical Principles Underlying Education," in Dewey, *The Early Works*, 5: 59–60.

60. Dewey, *Democracy and Education*, 89–90.

61. Ibid., 134.

62. In the *Prison Notebooks*, Gramsci referred to common sense as "a generic form of thought common to a particular period and a particular environment," describing how "it holds together a specific social group, it influences moral conduct and the direction of the will." Antonio Gramsci, *Prison Notebooks* (New York: International

Publishers, 1971), 330, 333. Also see Rachel Sharp, *Knowledge, Ideology, and the Politics of Schooling: Toward a Marxist Analysis of Education* (London: Routledge and Kegan Paul, 1980), 106, for a discussion of ideology as a social formation.

63. Dewey, *Democracy and Education*, 260.

64. Marx, "On the Jewish Question," in Tucker, *The Marx-Engels Reader*, 35.

65. Habermas, *Knowledge and Human Interests*, 137.

66. Dewey, *Democracy and Education*, 83.

## Chapter 4

1. See Samuels, *Henry Adams*, and O'Toole, *The Five of Hearts*, for detailed discussions of this speculation.

2. Henry Brooks Adams, *Democracy: An American Novel* (New York: NAL Penguin, 1983), 17.

3. Patricia O'Toole noted that "names do not sit lightly on the characters of *Democracy*; the "Rat" and the "Peon" signified, and Adams expressed his resentment of the rising financial power of American and European Jews by naming a Jewish character Schneidekoupon—literally, 'coupon clipper,'" a derisive term for one who lives on investments." See O'Toole, *The Five of Hearts*, 75.

4. Adams, *Democracy*, 24.

5. Ibid., 47.

6. Ibid., 102.

7. Ibid., 33.

8. Ibid., 49, 50.

9. Ibid., 50.

10. Ibid., 188.

11. For a succinct discussion of the complexities and evolution of the word "democracy" in English, see Raymond Williams, *Keywords: A Vocabulary of Culture and Society* (New York: Oxford University Press, 1983), 93–98.

12. Ellen Meiksins Wood, *The Retreat from Class: A New "True" Socialism* (London: Verso, 1986), 134.

13. Howard Zinn, *Declarations of Independence: Cross-Examining American Ideology* (New York: HarperPerennial, 1991), 150.

14. See Richard Kluger, *Simple Justice: The History of Brown v. Board of Education and Black America's Struggle for Equality* (New York: Vintage, 1977).

15. See National Commission on Excellence in Education, *A Nation at Risk: The Imperative for Educational Reform* (Washington, DC: Government Printing Office, 1983), for the first—and most famous—articulation of this perspective. Also see Gross and Gross, *The Great School Debate*, for a comprehensive collection of articles on both sides of the controversy provoked by *A Nation at Risk*.

16. Marian Wright Edelman, "Kids First!" *Mother Jones* 11 (May/June 1991), 31.

17. Ibid., 32.

18. See Colin Greer, *The Great School Legend: A Revisionist Interpretation of American Public Education* (New York: Basic Books, 19720; Clarence Karier, *Shaping the American Educational State* (New York: Free Press, 1975); Paul Violas, *The Training of the Urban Working Class* (Chicago: Rand McNally, 1978); Joel Spring,

*Education and the Rise of the Corporate Liberal State* (Boston: Beacon Press, 1972); and Bowles and Gintis, *Schooling in Capitalist America.*

19. See Martin Carnoy, and Henry M. Levin, *Schooling and Work in the Democratic State* (Stanford, CA: Stanford University Press, 1985); Katznelson and Weir, *School for All;* Wrigley, *Class, Politics, and Public Schools;* Aronowitz, Stanley, and Henry Giroux, *Education Under Seige: The Conservative, Liberal, and Radical Debate Over Schooling,* Critical Studies in Education Series (South Hadley, MA: Bergin & Garvey Publishers, Inc.), 1985.

20. Carnoy and Levin, *Schooling and Work,* 77.

21. Meiksins Wood, *The Retreat from Class,* 138.

22. Michael Walzer, *Spheres of Justice: A Defense of Pluralism and Equality* (New York: Basic Books, Inc., 1983), 28.

23. Benjamin R. Barber, *Strong Democracy: Participatory Politics for a New Age* (Berkeley: University of California Press, 1984), 219.

24. Ibid., 232.

25. Habermas, *Structural Transformation.*

26. Barber, *Strong Democracy,* 235.

27. Benjamin R. Barber, *An Aristocracy of Everyone: The Politics of Education and the Future of America* (New York: Ballantine Books, 1992).

28. Fox-Genovese, *Feminism Without Illusions,* 38.

29. John Rawls, *A Theory of Justice* (Cambridge, MA: Belknap Press of Harvard University Press, 1971), 253.d

30. Ibid., 129.

31. Ibid., 37.

32. Amy Gutmann, *Democratic Education* (Princeton: Princeton University Press, 1987), 3.

33. Ibid., 12.

34. Ibid.

35. Ibid.

36. Ibid., 12–13.

37. Ibid., 17.

38. Ibid., 42.

39. Less sanguine views of the state have seen it as intervening instrumentally on behalf of capitalist social and economic reproduction; see, for example, Bowles and Gintis, *Schooling in Capitalist America.* A more balanced, although also more complex, view was that of Carnoy and Levin: "The educational system is not an instrument of the capitalist class. It is the product of conflict between the dominant and the dominated. The struggle in the production sector, for example, affects schools, just as it conditions all State apparatuses. Furthermore, because the State, including the educational system, is itself the political arena, schools are part of social conflict. Education is at once the result of contradictions and the source of new contradictions. It is an arena of conflict over the production of knowledge, ideology, and employment, a place where social movements try to meet their needs and business attempts to reproduce its hegemony." Carnoy and Levin, *Schooling and Work,* 50.

40. Ibid., 115.

41. Ibid., 117.

42. J. Anthony Lukas, *Common Ground: A Turbulent Decade in the Lives of Three American Families* (New York: Vintage Books, 1986).

43. Cookson and Persell, *Preparing for Power.*

44. Bronner, *Socialism Unbound,* 153–155.

45. I refer to those debates surrounding the "canon" of higher education or promoting "excellence" in the nation's public schools. See, for example, the essays collected in Gross and Gross, *The Great School Debate,* and Robert L. Stone, ed., *Essays on The Closing of the American Mind* (Chicago: Chicago Review Press, 1989).

46. In addition to Habermas, see the discussion of the proletarian public sphere in Negt and Kluge, "The Public Sphere and Experience" and "Selections."

47. Shirley Brice Heath, *Ways with Words: Language, Life and Work in Communities and Classrooms* (New York: Cambridge University Press, 1983).

48. Ibid., 365.

49. Bronner, *Socialism Unbound,* 156.

50. Ibid., 157.

51. Ibid., 159, 161.

## Chapter 5

1. See Russell Jacoby, *The Last Intellectuals: American Culture in the Age of Academe* (New York: Basic Books, 1987).

2. See Roger Kimball, *Tenured Radicals: How Politics Has Corrupted Our Higher Education* (New York: HarperPerennial, 1991); Charles J. Sykes, *Profscam: Professors and the Demise of Higher Education* (Washington, D.C.: Regnery Gateway, 1988); and Charles J. Sykes, *The Hollow Men: Politics and Corruption in Higher Education* (Washington, D.C.: Regnery Gateway, 1990).

3. Adams, *Education,* 348.

4. Richard Hofstadter, *Anti-Intellectualism in American Life* (New York: Alfred A. Knopf, 1970), 177.

5. Adams, *Education,* 320.

6. Hofstadter, *Anti-Intellectualism in American Life,* 145.

7. Ibid., 157–159.

8. Ibid., 159.

9. Adams, *Education,* 265.

10. J. P. Nettl, "Ideas, Intellectuals, and the Structures of Dissent," in Philip Rieff, ed., *On Intellectuals* (New York: Doubleday & Company, Inc., 1969), 87.

11. Julien Benda, *The Treason of the Intellectuals (La Trahaison des Clercs),* trans. Richard Aldington (1928; reprint, New York: W. W. Norton and Company, Inc., 1969).

12. Robbins, introduction to *Intellectuals,* xv.

13. See, for example, Adams, *Education;* José Ortega Y Gasset, *Man and Crisis,* trans. Mildred Adams (New York: W. W. Norton and Company, Inc., 1958), *Mission of the University,* trans. Howard Lee Nostrand (Princeton: Princeton University Press, 1944), *The Revolt of the Masses,* trans. anonymous (New York: W. W. Norton and Company, Inc.), 132.

14. Bloom, *The Closing of the American Mind,* and Jacoby, *The Last Intellectuals.*

15. See especially the arguments in "Introduction: Our Virtue," and "Values," in Bloom, *The Closing of the American Mind,* 25–43, 194–216.

16. Ibid., 380.

17. See Martha Nussbaum, "Undemocratic Vistas," *New York Review of Books* (November 5, 1987), 21–22.

18. Bloom, *The Closing of the American Mind,* 336–382. Martha Nussbaum's comment on Bloom's extremely narrow reading of the legacy of "Western civilization" is especially pertinent here: "His special love for these books [the "great books" of ancient philosophy] has certainly prevented him from attending to works of literature and philosophy that lie outside the tradition they began. For he makes the remarkable claim that 'only in the Western nations, i.e., those influenced by Greek philosophy, is there some willingness to doubt the identification of the good with one's own way.' This statement shows a startling ignorance of the critical and rationalist tradition in classical Indian thought, of the arguments of classical Chinese thinkers, and beyond this, of countless examples of philosophical and nonphilosophical self-criticism from many parts of the world." Nussbaum, "Undemocratic Vistas," 22.

19. See, for example, the reviews and essays collected in Stone, *Essays on The Closing of the American Mind;* also Jacoby, *The Last Intellectuals.*

20. Jeffrey Escoffier, "Pessimism of the Mind: Intellectuals, Universities, and the Left," review of *The Closing of the American Mind: How Higher Education Has Failed Democracy and Impoverished the Souls of Today's Students,* by Allan Bloom, and *The Last Intellectuals: American Culture in the Age of Academe,* by Russell Jacoby, *Socialist Review* 18 (Jan.–March 1988), 124.

21. Jacoby, *The Last Intellectuals,* ix.

22. Lynn Garafola, review of *The Last Intellectuals,"* *New Left Review* 169 (May/June 1988), 125.

23. Jacoby, *The Last Intellectuals,* 185.

24. As Robbins put it, "The subject of intellectuals has been about as gender-neutral as pro football." Jacoby himself was no exception; a quick count of the names indexed in *The Last Intellectuals* shows 359 identifiable as male and only 27 as female (29 if you count *Marjorie Morningstar* and *Mother Jones*—the periodical, not the person). Robbins, introduction to *Intellectuals,* xvii.

25. Ibid., 77.

26. Garafola, review of *The Last Intellectuals,* 126.

27. Barbara Ehrenreich, "The Professional-Managerial Class Revisited," in Robbins, *Intellectuals,* 177.

28. Ibid., 177–178.

29. Noam Chomsky, "The Responsibility of Intellectuals" (1966), in *The Chomsky Reader,* ed. James Peck (New York: Pantheon Books, 1987), 60.

30. Tom Wolfe, *The Bonfire of the Vanities* (New York: Bantam Books, 1988), 27.

31. See, for example, the descriptions in Phillips, *The Politics of Rich and Poor;* Edsall, *The New Politics of Inequality;* and Ehrenreich, *Fear of Falling.*

32. Jacoby, *The Last Intellectuals,* 235.

33. See Honoré de Balzac, *Lost Illusions,* trans. Herbert J. Hunt, (New York: Viking Penguin, Inc., 1988 [1837–1843]); Jean-Jacques Rousseau, "Discourse on the Sciences and Arts (First Discourse)," in *The First and Second Discourses,* trans. Roger

D. and Judith R. Masters (New York: St. Martin's Press, 1964), 31–74; Gustave Flaubert, *A Sentimental Education: The Story of a Young Man,* trans. Douglas Parmée (New York: Oxford University Press, 1989).

34. Habermas, *Structural Transformation.* Robbins described Habermas's engagement in one recent controversy: "Jürgen Habermas, who had done much to sustain and elaborate the language of legitimacy and is also a great living example of an incontrovertibly 'public' intellectual, has taken an admirable public role in the German *Historikerstreit* over revisionist readings of Nazism. In that debate, the academic historians who were in effect apologizing for the Nazis could insist that, as a mere philosopher, Habermas lacked appropriate expertise. Their stronger and stranger argument, however, has been a version of the poststructuralist one: suspicion of all claims to legitimacy before a nonacademic public. ... At least for those who take Habermas' side against the revisionist historians, this would seem an argument for intellectuals *not* to forsake their efforts at legitimation. It is too easy for the right to claim legitimacy for itself, discrediting its opponents as an elite of 'specific,' self-interested outsiders." Robbins, introduction, to *Intellectuals,* xxiii–xxiv. Also see Jürgen Habermas, *The New Conservatism: Cultural Criticism and the Historians' Debate,* ed. and trans. Shierry Weber Nicholsen (Cambridge, MA: MIT Press, 1989).

35. Although a discussion of Habermas's work from the standpoint of gender is beyond the scope of this chapter, Joan Landes's contention that the bourgeois public sphere was essentially, and not just contingently, masculinist, bears mention here. Landes took Habermas to task for not paying adequate attention to the way in which the eighteenth-century public sphere was shaped by gendered categories and overtly sexist strategies, like Rousseau's ideology of republican motherhood. Joan B. Landes, *Women and the Public Sphere in the Age of the French Revolution* (Ithaca: Cornell University Press, 1988), 7, 129.

36. Karl Jaspers, *The Idea of the University,* trans. H.A.T. Reiche and H. F. Vanderschmidt (London: Peter Owen, 1959).

37. See representative works by reproduction theorists on education: Pierre Bourdieu and Jean-Claude Passeron, *Reproduction in Education, Society, and Culture,* trans. Richard Nice (London: Sage Publications, Ltd., 1990); Samuel Bowles and Herbert Gintis, *Schooling in Capitalist America: Educational Reform and the Contradictions of Economic Life* (New York: Basic Books, Inc., 1976).

38. See the discussions in Katznelson and Weir, *Schooling For All,* and Giroux, *Schooling and the Struggle for Public Life.* Hofstadter's treatment of the historical foundations of the concept of academic freedom is excellent: Hofstadter, *Academic Freedom in the Age of the College.*

39. Kerr, *The Uses of the University,* 114.

40. Daniel Bell, *The Coming of Post-Industrial Society: A Venture in Social Forecasting* (New York: Basic Books, Inc., 1976), 245–246.

41. For an extended discussion of the growth of research universities in America, see Roger L. Geiger, *To Advance Knowledge: The Growth of American Research Universities, 1900–1940* (New York: Oxford University Press, 1986). For an excellent analysis of the linkages between university research, the state, and capital interests, see Barrow, *Universities and the Capitalist State.*

42. Oscar Negt and Alexander Kluge, "The Public Sphere and Experience: Selections," trans. Peter Labanyi, *October,* 46 (Fall 1988), 60–82; "Selections from *Public*

*Opinion and Practical Knowledge: Toward an Organizational Analysis of Proletariat and Middle Class Public Opinion,*" *Social Text* 25/26 (Winter 1990), 24–32; and *Public Sphere and Experience: Toward an Analysis of the Bourgeois and Proletarian Public Sphere* (Minneapolis: University of Minnesota Press, 1993).

43. Veysey, *The Emergence of the American University,* 36.

44. Page Smith, *Killing the Spirit: Higher Education in America* (New York: Viking Penguin, 1990), 74.

45. Daniel Bell, *The Reforming of General Education: The Columbia College Experience in Its National Setting* (New York: Columbia University Press, 1966), 14.

46. Committee on the Objectives of a General Education in a Free Society, 1945, *General Education in a Free Society: Report of the Harvard Committee* (Cambridge, MA: Harvard University Press, 1945).

47. Bell, *The Reforming of General Education,* 14.

48. *Involvement in Learning: Realizing the Potential of American Higher Education,* Report of the Study Group on the Conditions of Excellence in American Higher Education, sponsored by the National Institute of Education, October 1984.

49. The past thirty years have seen the growth, in Randall Collins's phrase, of a "credentialized society," where degrees or certificates granted by colleges and universities serve as rites of passage. Randall Collins, *The Credentialed Society* (Berkeley: University of California Press, 1978). For an extended discussion of the concept of cultural capital, see Bourdieu and Passeron, *Reproduction in Education, Society, and Culture.* Also see Stanley Aronowitz, "Academic Freedom: A Structural Approach," in Craig Kaplan and Ellen Schrecker, *Regulating the Intellectuals: Perspectives on Academic Freedom in the 1980s* (New York: Praeger, 1983), 79–90.

50. Alexander Cockburn, "Bush & P.C.," *The Nation* 27 (May 1991), 691.

51. Dinesh D'Souza, *Illiberal Education: The Politics of Race and Sex on Campus* (New York: Free Press, 1991); Roger Kimball, *Tenured Radicals: How Politics Has Corrupted Our Higher Education* (New York: HarperPerennial, 1991); Charles J. Sykes, *Profscam: Professors and the Demise of Higher Education* (Washington, DC: Regnery Gateway, 1988) and *The Hollow Men: Politics and Corruption in Higher Education* (Washington, DC: Regnery Gateway, 1990); and John Searle, "The Storm over the University," *New York Review of Books* (December 6, 1990), 39.

52. See *A Nation at Risk* for the best articulation of the "big business" connection. National Commission on Excellence in Education, *A Nation at Risk: The Imperative for Educational Reform* (Washington, DC: Government Printing Office, 1983).

53. William Bennett, "'To Reclaim a Legacy': Text of Report on Humanities in Higher Education," *Chronical of Higher Education* 28 (November 1984), 16–21; Diane Ravitch and Chester Finn, Jr., *What Do Our 17-Year-Olds Know?* (New York: Harper and Row, 1988); Bloom, *The Closing of the American Mind;* D'Souza, *Illiberal Education;* Hirsch, *Cultural Literacy.*

54. Kimball, *Tenured Radicals;* Sykes, *Profscam* and *The Hollow Men.*

55. As one review of D'Souza's book put it recently: "Things are bad, perhaps, but compared with what? In 1960, a year well within the memories of most senior professors and university administrators, ninety-four per cent of college students were white. ... Of the students making up the remaining six per cent, a third attended all black or predominantly black institutions. Sixty-three per cent of college students

were men; almost nine of every ten Ph.D.s awarded were awarded to men; and nearly eighty per cent of university faculty were men. Some of the most distinguished private colleges in the country did not admit women, and there were several public universities (not to mention private ones such as Duke) that did not admit black students. ... *Isn't it possible that, even assuming all the good will in the world ... what was taught and how it was talked about did not reflect the interests and perspectives of the people who were not there?*" Louis Menard, "Illiberalisms," *New Yorker* (May 28, 1991): 104.

56. D'Souza, *Iliberal Education*, 246–249.

57. Ellen Meiksins Wood, "The Uses and Abuses of 'Civil Society,'" in *The Retreat of the Intellectuals: Socialist Register, 1990*, ed. Ralph Miliband and Leo Panitch (London: Merlin Press, 1990), 60.

58. Stephen Eric Bronner, "Tasks of the Socialist Intellectuals," *Enclitic* 10 (Spring/Fall 1988), 79.

59. For a succinct political critique, see Bronner, "The Challenge of Postmodernism," *Socialism Unbound*, 169–172. Also see Habermas, *The Philosophical Discourse of Modernity*, and Peter Dews, *Logics of Disintegration: Post-Structuralist Thought and the Claims of Critical Theory* (London: Verso, 1987). For an extended (and much less critical) discussion of postmodernism and educational theory, see "Postmodernism and the Discourse of Educational Criticism," in Stanley Aronowitz and Henry A. Giroux, *Postmodern Education: Politics, Culture, and Social Criticism* (Minneapolis: University of Minnesota Press, 1991), 57–86.

60. A. Bartlett Giamatti, *A Free and Ordered Space: The Real World of the University* (New York: W. W. Norton and Company, 1990), 115–116.

61. Herbert G. Gutman, *Power and Culture*, and *Work, Culture and Society in Industrializing America: Essays in American Working-Class and Social History* (New York: Vintage Books), 1977.

62. Ernst Bloch, *The Principle of Hope*, vol.1, trans. Neville Plaice, Stephen Plaice, and Paul Knight (Cambridge: MIT Press, 1986), 131.

63. Václav Havel, "I Take the Side of Truth: An Interview with Antoine Spire," in *Open Letters: Selected Writings, 1965–1990* (New York: Vintage Books, 1992), 248.

## Chapter 6

1. The course was "Reading and Linguistics," offered by Carol Chomsky at Harvard Graduate School of Education, fall 1977. See Carol Chomsky, "Reading, Writing, and Phonology," and "Stages in Language Development and Reading Exposure," in *Thoughts on Language/Language and Reading*, Reprint Series #14 (Cambridge, MA: *Harvard Educational Review*, 1980), 51–71, 201–229. Both articles address spontaneous reading as the outcome of "language play" through the use of invented spellings, and so on; also see Courtney Cazden, *Classroom Discourse: The Language of Teaching and Learning* (Portsmouth, NH: Heinemann, 1988).

2. James Paul Gee, "The Legacies of Literacy: From Plato to Freire Through Harvey Graff," review of *The Legacies of Literacy: Continuities and Contradictions in Western Culture and Society* by H. J. Graff, *Harvard Educational Review* 58 (May 1988), 195–212.

3. Lawrence Cremin, *Traditions of American Education* (New York: Basic Books, Inc., 1977), 31.

4. Ibid., 31–32.

5. Ibid., 127.

6. Harvey J. Graff, *The Legacies of Literacy: Continuities and Contradictions in Western Culture and Society* (Bloomington: Indiana University Press, 1987); also see Graff, *The Literacy Myth: Literacy and Social Structure in the Nineteenth-Century City* (New York: Academic Press, 1979).

7. Cited in Carlo M. Cipolla, *Literacy and Development in the West* (London: Penguin Books, Ltd., 1969), 65–66.

8. Carl F. Kaestle, with Helen Damon-Moore, Lawrence C. Stedman, Katherine Tinsley, and William Vance Trollinger, Jr., *Literacy in the United States: Readers and Reading Since 1880* (New Haven: Yale University Press, 1991), 27.

9. Gee, "The Legacies of Literacy," 196.

10. Freire, *Pedagogy of the Oppressed.*

11. Gee, "The Legacies of Literacy," 196.

12. Habermas, *Knowledge and Human Interests.*

13. See Michel Foucault, *Madness and Civilization: A History of Insanity in the Age of Reason* (New York: Pantheon, 1965) and *Power/Knowledge: Selected Interviews and Other Writings, 1927–1977* (New York: Pantheon, 1980); and Karl Mannheim, *Man and Society in an Age of Reconstruction* (New York: Harcourt, Brace and World, 1940).

14. Noam Chomsky, *Topics in the Theory of Generative Grammar* (The Hague: Mouton, 1966); Jürgen Habermas, *The Theory of Communicative Action, Vol. 1: Reason and the Rationalization of Society,* trans. Thomas McCarthy (Boston: Beacon Press, 19840, and *The Theory of Communicative Action, Vol. 2: Lifeworld and System: A Critique of Functionalist Reason,* trans. Thomas McCarthy (Boston: Beacon Press, 1987).

15. Mortimer J. Adler, *The Paideia Proposal: An Educational Manifesto* (New York: Macmillan Publishing Co., Inc., 1982), 5.

16. Dewey, *Individualism, Old and New,* 10.

17. Simon Tisdall, "Poverty Timebomb Ticks on in US Cities," *Guardian* (February 6, 1990), 4.

18. Robert D. Hamrim, "Sorry Americans—You're Still Not 'Better Off.'" *Challenge: Magazine of Economic Affairs* 31 (September/October 1988), 50–51.

19. See Edsall, *The New Politics of Inequality,* especially chapter 5, and Ehrenreich, *Fear of Falling.*

20. Kaestle et al., *Literacy in the United States,* 28.

21. Bell, *Post-Industrial Society,* 43.

22. Ibid., 27.

23. Ibid., 175.

24. Suzanne De Castell and Allan Luke, "Models of Literacy in North American Schools," in Suzanne De Castell, Allan Luke, and Kieran Egan, eds., *Literacy, Society, and Schooling: A Reader* (Cambridge: Cambridge University Press, 1986), 87, 101.

25. Ibid, 104.

26. Max Horkheimer and Theodor Adorno, *Dialectic of Enlightenment* (New York: Seabury, 1972 [1947]).

27. See Freire, *Pedagogy of the Oppressed; Education for Critical Consciousness* (New York: Seabury Press, 1973); *Pedagogy in Process: The Letters to Guinea-Bissau,* trans. Carman St. John Hunter (New York: Seabury Press, 1978); *The Politics of Education: Culture, Power, and Liberation,* trans. Donaldo Macedo (South Hadley, MA: Bergin & Garvey, Publishers, Inc., 1985); and Paulo Freire and Donaldo Macedo, *Literacy: Reading the Word and the World* (South Hadley, MA: Bergin & Garvey Publishers, Inc., 1987).

28. Freire, *The Politics of Education,* 162.

29. Ibid., 102.

30. Freire and Macedo, *Literacy,* 35.

31. Ibid., 35.

32. Peter Elbow, "The Pedagogy of the Bamboozled," in *Embracing Contraries: Explorations in Learning and Teaching* (New York: Oxford University Press, 1986), 87.

33. Gee, "The Legacies of Literacy," 195–212.

34. Freire and Macedo, *Literacy,* 76, 87–88.

35. Ibid., 54.

36. Gee, "The Legacies of Literacy," 208.

37. Bloom, *The Closing of the American Mind,* 21.

38. Hirsch, *Cultural Literacy,* 113.

39. Stanley Aronowitz and Henry A. Giroux, "Schooling, Culture, and Literacy in the Age of Broken Dreams: A Review of Bloom and Hirsch," *Harvard Educational Review* 58 (May 188), 182.

40. Robert Scholes discussed the conservative agenda that shaped the differences and commonalities in Bloom and Hirsch: "Hirsch wants to save us through information. He thinks that knowing about things is more important than knowing things. Bloom, on the other hand, thinks that the only thing that can save us is a return to really knowing and experiencing the great books, especially the great works of political and social philosophy that follow in the train of Plato's *Republic.* Hirsch concerns himself with what every American student should know, whereas Bloom is concerned only about a tiny elite. Together, they set the conservative agenda for American education. Hirsch will make sure that everyone knows that the classics are and respects them, while Bloom will see to it that an elite can be defined by actually knowing these classics. In this way, the masses will be sufficiently educated to respect the superior knowledge of their betters, who have studied in a few major universities. Both Hirsch and Bloom emphasize certain kinds of traditional learning, but it is important to recognize that the attitude they take toward this learning is very different. For Bloom nothing less than a prolonged, serious engagement with the great books themselves can save the souls of our students. For Hirsch, just knowing the names of the great books and authors will suffice. Both Hirsch and Bloom share, however, a nostalgia for a not very closely examined past in which things were better." Robert Scholes, "Review. Three Views of Education: Nostalgia, History, and Voodoo," *College English* 50 (1988), 323–324.

41. Hirsch, *Cultural Literacy,* 56–57.

42. See, for example, Basil B. Bernstein, *Class, Codes, and Control* (London: Routledge and Kegan Paul, 1971); Heath, *Ways with Words.*

43. Hirsch, *Cultural Literacy,* 155.

44. Hirsch has provided a partial response to criticism regarding the arbitrary and discrete choices on his lists. See E. D. Hirsch, James S. Trefil, and Joseph P. Kett, *The Dictionary of Cultural Literacy* (Boston: Houghton Mifflin, 1993).

45. Scholes, "Three Views of Education," 331.

46. James Paul Gee, "Orality and Literacy: From *The Savage Mind* to *Ways with Words,*" *Journal of Education* 171, no. 1 (1989), 55; Heath, *Ways with Words.*

47. Heath, *Ways with Words,* 386.

48. Ibid., 11.

49. Ibid., 369.

50. Ibid., 363–364.

## Chapter 7

1. Elizabeth Gurley Flynn, "Education and the School System (1906)," in Rosalyn Fraad Baxandall, ed., *Words on Fire: The Life and Writing of Elizabeth Gurley Flynn* (New Brunswick, NJ: Rutgers University Press, 1987), 81.

2. Ibid., 79.

3. Ibid., 79–80.

4. Ibid., 82, 83.

5. Wolfe, *The Bonfire of the Vanities* 27.

6. Ibid., 229–231.

7. Habermas, *Structural Transformation;* Negt and Kluge, "The Public Sphere" and "Selections."

8. Jürgen Habermas, *Toward a Rational Society: Student Protest, Science and Politics,* trans. Jeremy J. Shapiro (Boston: Beacon Press, 1970), 108.

9. Ibid., 57.

10. Ibid., 61.

11. Nathan Gardels, "Comment/The Education We Deserve," *New Perspectives Quarterly* 7 (Fall 1990), 2–3.

12. Seyla Benhabib, "Modernity and the Aporias of Critical Theory," *Telos* 49 (Fall 1981), 56.

13. See Habermas, *The New Conservatism* and *Theory and Practice.* For Wolin's metaphor of dissonance, see Wolin, "The People's Two Bodies," 11.

14. Habermas, *The Theory of Communicative Action,* Vol. 1 and Vol. 2.

15. Ibid., Vol. 1, chap. 2, 143–271.

16. Jürgen Habermas, *Moral Consciousness and Communicative Action,* trans. Christian Lenhardt and Shierry Weber Nicholsen (Cambridge, MA: MIT Press, 1990).

17. Bronner, "Tasks of the Socialist Intellectuals," 80.

18. See, for example, the arguments presented by David Montgomery, *The Fall of the House of Labor: The Workplace, the State, and American Labor Activism, 1865–1925* (Cambridge: Cambridge University Press, 1987).

19. Hazel V. Carby, "The Politics of Difference," *Ms* (September/October 1990), 85.

20. Kennett Love quoted Tom Lamont of the American University in Cairo (AUC): "the decision of the Nobel Prize committee was based chiefly on the ten novels republished in English by AUC. The Prize has made them hot and scarce items. The press runs before the Prize were small, the copies on the market were few, and they were snapped up when Mahfouz's fame leaped over the great Arabic language barrier." Kennett Love, "How I Won The Nobel Prize (for Naguib Mahfouz)," *Poets & Writers,* v. 17, n. 4, July/Aug. 1989, 22. Also see Menahem Milson, "A Great 20th-Century Novelist," *Commentary,* June 1991, 34–38; Milton Viorst, "Man of Gamaliya," *New Yorker,* July, 1990, 32–53.

21. Chubb and Moe, *Politics, Markets, and America's Schools.*

22. Ibid., 193–194.

23. Deborah W. Maier, "Choice Can Save Public Education," *Nation* (March 4, 1991), 226.

24. Ibid., 268.

25. Ibid.

26. Ibid.

27. Wolfe, *The Bonfire of the Vanities,* 231.

28. Albert Shanker, "Where We Stand," *New York Times* (May 5, 1991), E7. Shanker cited a study by economist F. Howard Nelson, "International Comparison of Public Spending on Education," completed for the American Federation of Teachers.

29. See, for instance, Maier, "Choice Can Save Public Education"; Chubb and Moe, *Politics, Markets, and America's Schools;* Susan Moore Johnson, *Teachers at Work: Achieving Success in Our Schools* (New York: Basic Books, Inc., 1990).

30. See Habermas, *Toward a Rational Society;* Benhabib, "Modernity and the Aporias of Critical Theory," 56.

31. Kozol, *Savage Inequalities,* 205. President Bush's remarks were quoted in a White House press release, April 13, 1989.

32. Barber, *Strong Democracy,* 274–281.

33. Kellner, *Television and the Crisis of Democracy.*

34. Harry C. Boyte, "Beyond Community Service: Turning Youth on to Politics," *Nation* (May 13, 1991), 626–628.

35. Adams, *Education,* 4.

36. Brint and Karabel, *The Diverted Dream.*

37. Faith Gabelnick, Jean MacGregor, Roberta S. Matthews, and Barbara Leigh Smith, *Learning Communities: Creating Connections Among Students, Faculty, and Disciplines* (San Francisco: Jossey-Bass Inc., Publishers, Number 41, Spring 1990).

38. Ibid., 5.

39. Ibid., 32–37.

40. See Gutman, *Power and Culture,* and Martin, *The Sound of Our Own Voices.*

41. Maier, "Choice Can Save Public Education," 271.

42. Hannah Arendt, "What Is Freedom?" in *Between Past and Future: Eight Exercises in Political Thought* (New York: Viking Press, 1968), 171.

43. Ibid.

# About the Book
# and Author

This timely volume explores the present-day implications of the traditional American belief in public education as a vehicle for extending democratic politics. In light of the current debates about public schools, are they still the key to upward mobility? Can they still serve to create a civic consciousness?

Elizabeth A. Kelly defends the role of public education against its critics and throws light on such issues as privatization, voucher systems, the role of public intellectuals, critical literacy, and educational reform. She unabashedly offers a renewed vision of public schooling as the locus of public knowledge and political democracy, a vision that will appeal to those who are not prepared to abandon the ideals of either democracy or public education.

Generously conceived, clearly argued, and gracefully written, *Education, Democracy, and Public Knowledge* is important reading not just for students of democracy and of education but for all those concerned with the future of American education.

Elizabeth A. Kelly is assistant professor of political science at DePaul University.

# Index

Academic Marxism, 85
Active experimentalism, 48
Adams, Charles, 27
Adams, Clover Hooper, 29
Adams, Henry
  autobiography of, 27–33
  on bourgeois public sphere, 32–33
  on democratic politics, 63–64, 76,
    128
  John Dewey and, 5–6, 47–48
  elitism of, 82, 143(n3)
  on Harvard College, 137(n3)
  on individualism vs. collectivity, 36
  on intellectual decline in America,
    79–81
  public knowledge and, 44–45
Adams, John, 27
Adams, John Quincy, 27, 80
Adler, Mortimer, 102
Adolescents, education of, 128
Adorno, Theodor, 82, 106, 136(n57)
Advertising industry, 31
Advocacy, feminism and, 131(n2)
African Americans
  exclusion of, from public sphere, 20,
    133(n12)
  population growth of, 19
  slavery and, 44, 129
  university faculties and, 91–92
  wages for, 17
  See also Race
Alger, Horatio, 103
Apple, Michael, 40–41
Apprenticeship system, 128
Arendt, Hannah, 33–34, 36–37, 130

Aristocracy of Everyone, An (Barber),
  69
Asian-Americans, population growth
  of, 19

"Back to basics" movement, 21
Bacon, Francis, 12
Baldwin, James, 86
Barber, Benjamin, 7, 68, 69
Barrow, Clyde W., 132(n9)
Behaviorism, literacy and, 106–107,
  112
Bell, Daniel, 85, 89, 90, 104
Bellow, Saul, 122
Benda, Julien, 81
Benhabib, Seyla, 119
Bernstein, Basil, 110
Bernstein, Richard, 50
"Bill for the More General Diffusion of
  Knowledge" (Jefferson), 12
Blacks. See African Americans
Bloch, Ernest, 95
Bloom, Allan, 82–84, 87, 109, 113,
  121, 146(n18)
Blum, Leon, 82
Body politic
  democracy and, 13–14
  modernity and, 120
  pragmatism and, 48
Bonfire of the Vanities, The (Wolfe), 87,
  116–117
Bourdieu, Pierre, 41
Bourgeoisie
  Henry Adams's critique of, 29

public sphere of, 5–6, 13, 30–32, 35–
    36, 69, 87–88, 139(n39), 147(n35)
  *See also* Class polarization; Middle
    class
Bowles, Samuel, 40, 43, 144(n39)
Bronner, Stephen Eric, 1, 8–9, 22, 24,
    25, 75
*Brown v. Board of Education,* 22, 38,
    135(n50)
Buckley, William, 82
Burnham, Walter Dean, 16
Bush, George, 4, 126, 127
Business linkages, of universities,
    132(n9)

Cagan, Elizabeth, 21
Capitalism
  class polarization and, 23, 67
  communitarianism and, 70
  liberal competitive vs. monopoly, 31
  pragmatism and, 58–61
  socialism and, 23–24, 76, 93
  universities and, 89
Capitalist democracy
  Henry Adams's critique of, 28
  class polarization and, 67
  defined, 14–15
  education and, 17–19, 67, 118–119
  formal vs. substantive equality in, 39
  political democracy and, 58–61, 65,
    118
  *See also* Capitalism; Democracy
Carby, Hazel V., 121
Carnoy, Martin, 67, 144(n39)
Caste system, American, 103
Children
  democratic education and, 65–66
  linguistic styles of, 111–112
  living conditions of U.S., 66, 126
Choice, educational, 123–124
Chomsky, Noam, 86, 102
Chubb, John, 123, 125
Citizenship, community and, 68
Civic education, 69–70
Civil rights movement, 90
Classics, cultural access to, 122–123

Class polarization
  in American society, 15–16, 103–104
  capitalism and, 23, 67
  democracy and, 76–77
  denial of, 102–103
  economic equality and, 15–16
  educational reproduction and, 40–41,
    59
  education and, 17–19, 22, 59, 74–75,
    123–124, 144(n39)
  intellectualism and, 83–84
  labor and, 74–75, 77
  literacy and, 104–112
  neighborhood provincialism and, 22
  politics and, 16
  private schools and, 42
  public knowledge and, 105, 108–109,
    120–121
  socialism and, 23–25, 77
  wage inequities and, 66
  *See also* Elitism; Power; Privilege
Clemenceau, Georges, 81
*Closing of the American Mind, The*
    (Bloom), 82–83, 146(n18)
Cohen, Joshua, 14, 21
Collective memory, 36–37
Collectivity
  individualism vs., 36–37
  learning communities and, 129
  liberty and, 25
  socialism and, 75
College education
  costs of, 18
  job opportunities and, 17
  *See also* Universities
Collins, Jackie, 86
Collins, Randall, 148(n49)
Commonality, subjectivity vs., 55
Common school movement, 12,
    132(n2)
Common sense, 58, 60, 142(n62)
Communication
  democratic society and, 120, 126
  literacy and, 109
Communicative action, 48, 120, 126,
    140(n7)

Communitarianism
  capitalism and, 70
  individualism vs., 68–69
  neorationalism vs., 70–71, 74
  socialism vs., 75
Community
  American democracy and, 47
  citizenship and, 68
  collective memory and, 36–37
  common culture and, 68–69
  Dewey's "Great Community," 48,
    49–50, 57
  education and, 5, 48–49
  individual character and, 141(n17)
  learning communities and, 129
  socialism and, 58
Conscious assent, 27
Consequentialism, 51
Conservative counterrevolution, 92–93
Constitution, public education and, 12
Consumerism, 87
Cookson, Peter W., Jr., 42, 43, 73
Cooperation, individualism vs., 21, 104
Cooperative education programs, 128,
  129
Corporate linkages, of universities,
  132(n9)
Cosmopolitanism, intellectual, 80
Credentialism, 91, 148(n49)
Cremin, Lawrence, 99, 100
Critical literacy, 8, 130
  *See also* Literacy
Critical Pedagogy movement, 8,
  132(n12)
Cultural capital
  acquisition of, 111
  elite private schools and, 42
  social reproduction and, 41, 59
*Cultural Literacy* (Hirsch), 109
Cultural literacy movement, 21
Culture
  class ideal and, 122
  as commodity, 31
  communitarian view of, 68–69
  literacy and, 111–114
  public sphere and, 30–31, 87

Curriculum
  public knowledge and, 120
  in socialist education, 76–77
  university, 90, 95–96
  *See also* Education
Curti, Merle, 53

Debate, public
  on democratic education, 74,
    145(n45)
  distortion of, 138(n25)
  on national priorities, 126–127
  in universities, 94–95
Decisionism, 55
Declaration of Independence
  equality and, 65
  formalization of democracy and, 13
Decter, Midge, 85
*Democracy: An American Novel*
  (Adams), 63–64
Democracy
  American politics and, 63–64
  body politic and, 13–14
  class polarization and, 76–77
  communitarian theories of, 68–70
  education and, 12–13, 26, 28, 58–61,
    65, 71–72
  etymology of word, 143(n11)
  formalized, 60–61
  industrial, 58
  literacy and, 12, 113
  political vs. capitalist, 58–61, 65, 118
  pragmatism and, 56–61
  private schools and, 72–73
  public knowledge and, 4–5, 19, 37,
    60–61, 118
  public schools and, 6–7
  socialism and, 22–25, 75–77, 126–
    127
  universities and, 88–89, 95–96
  *See also* Capitalist democracy
*Democracy and Education* (Dewey), 49
Democratic education
  equality and, 65–66
  moral vs. political ideals in, 71–72
  neorationalism and, 70–73
  socialism and, 67–68, 75–77

*See also* Education; Socialist
   education
"Democratic Vistas" (Whitman), 47
Development, human. *See* Human
   development
Dewey, John
   Henry Adams and, 5–6
   educational philosophy of, 48–50,
      58–59, 102, 140(nn 9, 14)
   pragmatism of, 47–52, 56–61,
      140(n7)
   on public knowledge, 19
Dreyfus affair, 81, 82
D'Souza, Dinesh, 92, 148(n55)

Economic democracy, 58–60
Economic polarization. *See* Class
   polarization
Economics, American
   class polarization and, 15–16, 103
   of college education, 17–18
   public education and, 126–127,
      153(n28)
   wage inequities in, 66
Edelman, Marian Wright, 66, 119
Education
   American vs. foreign, 18, 126
   capitalist democracy and, 17–19, 67,
      118–119
   class polarization and, 4, 17–19, 22,
      59, 74–75, 123–124, 144(n39)
   community and, 5, 48–49
   critical literacy and, 8, 130
   democracy and, 12–13, 26, 28, 58–
      61, 65, 71–72
   Dewey's philosophy of, 48–50, 58–
      59, 102, 140(nn 9, 14)
   economic support for, 126–127,
      153(n28)
   elective system in, 90
   elitism and, 83–84, 88, 95, 123,
      151(n40)
   equality in, 65
   general vs. specialized, 90–91
   human growth and, 48–49
   in inner-city schools, 116–117
   intellectuals and, 82–83

William James's view of, 53–54
   as lifelong process, 128–129
   literacy and, 8, 74–75, 107–109
   moral ideal of, 71–72
   philosophy and, 56
   poverty and, 38
   pragmatism and, 6, 48–53, 56–61
   privilege and, 37–43, 59
   public knowledge and, 5–6, 14, 19–
      21, 96, 120, 125–126, 135(n51)
   public sphere and, 89, 91, 95–96, 130
   social function of, 53–54
   socialism and, 5–6, 22–26, 58, 67–
      68, 75–77, 117–119, 124
   social reproduction and, 40–41
   universities and, 88–89
   wages and, 17
   *See also* Democratic education; Public
      education; Socialist education
Educational choice, 123–124
Educational publishing, 106–107
Educational reform
   American individualism and, 21
   creation of system for, 38
   democracy and, 26, 59
   neoconservativism and, 92
   pragmatism and, 59–61
   strategies for, 123–125, 128–130
Educational reproduction, 40–41, 59
"Education and the School System"
   (Flynn), 115
*Education of Henry Adams, The*, 5, 27–
   33, 82
Egalitarianism, American myth of, 102–
   103
Ehrenreich, Barbara, 22, 86
Elbow, Peter, 108
Elective system, 90
Electoral college, 47
Eliot, Charles W., 90
Elitism
   education and, 83–84, 88, 95, 123,
      151(n40)
   intellectualism and, 81–82, 87
   in universities, 83–84, 88, 93, 95,
      148(n55)
   *See also* Class polarization; Privilege

Emancipation, education and, 44, 119
Emerson, Ralph Waldo, 39, 117
Empire of Reason, 13
Empiricism, critique of, 25
Employment
    college degree and, 17
    education and, 11, 119
    educational empowerment and, 44
    *See also* Labor
Engels, Friedrich, 104
Enlightenment
    Declaration of Independence and, 13
    Dewey's ideals of, 56
    Kant's definition of, 44
    socialism and, 23, 76
Equality
    American myth of, 102–103
    in education, 37–40
Escoffier, Jeffrey, 84
"Ethics of Democracy, The" (Dewey), 58
Ethnicity
    economic polarization and, 19
    educational quality and, 38
    literacy and, 74–75
    neighborhood provincialism and, 22
    political exclusion and, 20
    university faculties and, 91–92

Facts, knowledge vs., 110
Faculty, university, gender differences in, 91–92
Family values agenda, 94
Fascism, relativism and, 55
Feminism
    advocacy and, 131(n2)
    public/private dichotomy and, 35–36
    *See also* Gender differences; Women
Flynn, Elizabeth Gurley, 115–116, 119, 128
Formal equality, 39
Formalized democracy, 60–61
Foucault, Michel, 102
Freire, Paulo, 101, 107–109, 112
Friedman, Milton, 86
Fromm, Erich, 22
Frye, Marilyn, 3

Full partnership, 27

Garafola, Lynn, 85
Garrity, Arthur, 73
Gee, James, 98, 109
Gender differences
    labor and, 33, 35, 138(n32)
    public intellectuals and, 85, 146(n24)
    university faculties and, 91–92
    *See also* Feminism; Women
*General Education in a Free Society*, 90
Generalists
    intellectuals as, 86
    specialists vs., 90–91
Giamatti, A. Bartlett, 94
Gilder, George, 82
Gintis, Herbert, 40, 43, 144(n39)
Government
    education and, 28
    interactive communications with, 127
    society and, 79
Graff, Harvey, 99–100
Gramsci, Antonio, 59, 142(n62)
Grant, Ulysses S., 80, 137(n6)
"Great Community," of John Dewey, 48, 49–50, 57
Gross National Product (GNP), education expenditures and, 18, 126
Growth, human. *See* Human development
Gutman, Herbert, 44, 129
Gutmann, Amy, 7, 70–72

Habermas, Jürgen
    on bourgeois public sphere, 5–6, 13, 30–32, 35–36, 69, 87–88, 139(n39), 147(n35)
    communicative action theory of, 48, 120, 126, 140(n7)
    on language, 102
    on political democracy, 45, 118
    on pragmatism, 48, 51, 52
    as public intellectual, 86, 87, 147(n34)
Habitat for Humanity, 128
*Habits of the Heart* (Bellah), 21

Halberstam, David, 41–42
Harrington, Michael, 22, 24
Harvard College
    Henry Adams on, 137(n3)
    elective system at, 90
Havel, Václav, 96
Heath, Shirley Brice, 74–75, 110, 111–
    112
Higher education. *See* Universities
High school education
    historical view of, 37–38
    job opportunities and, 11, 17
High-status knowledge, 40–41
Hightower, Jim, 16
Hirsch, E. D., 109–110
Hispanics, population growth of, 19
History, knowledge of, 12–13
Hofstadter, Richard, 80
Holt, Henry, 63
Hook, Sidney, 85
hooks, bell, 3, 131(n2)
Horkheimer, Max, 82, 106
Human development
    education and, 48–50
    pragmatism and, 51

Ideas
    marketplace of, 138(n25)
    putting to work of, 55
    social construction of, 59–60
*Idea of the University, The* (Jaspers), 88
*Illiberal Education* (D'Souza), 92
Individualism
    American culture and, 21, 135(n47)
    collectivity vs., 36–37
    communitarianism vs., 68–69
    cooperation vs., 21, 104
    educational reform and, 21
    truth and, 54–55
Industrial democracy, 58
Information society, 104–105
Inner-city schools, education in, 116–
    117
Instrumentalism
    socialism and, 76
    universities and, 89
Intellectual cosmopolitanism, 80

Intellectuals
    class polarization and, 83–84
    decline of, 79–81, 87
    elitism and, 81–82, 87
    gender and, 85, 146(n24)
    generalist vs. specialist, 86
    left-wing, 81, 84–85, 93–94
    politics and, 79–82, 86, 96, 122
    public knowledge and, 7, 85–86
    right-wing ideals and, 81–82
    truth and, 81–82, 86, 95–96
    types of, 81
    universities and, 82–84, 88–96
Interdependency, 56
Interdisciplinary learning, 129
Intimacy, public sphere and, 50
Isolationalism, 21
Ivy League colleges, 43

Jacoby, Russell, 7, 82, 84–87, 96
James, William
    educational views of, 53–54
    as humanist, 82
    pragmatism of, 6, 50–52, 54–55
Jaspers, Karl, 88
Jaures, Jean, 82
Jefferson, Thomas, 12–13
Job opportunities. *See* Employment

Kantian theories, 70–71, 141(n31)
Kant, Immanuel, 20, 44
Karier, Clarence J., 19
Kellner, Douglas, 127
Kennedy, John F., 110
Kennedy, Joseph P., 73
Kennedy, Paul, 86
Kerr, Clark, 53, 89
Kimball, Roger, 92
King, Stephen, 86
Knowledge
    background, 110–111
    facts vs., 110
    information and, 105
    literacy and, 101–102, 105, 107
    as power, 12, 101–102
    privilege and, 43, 122, 125

society and, 89
  *See also* Public knowledge
Kozol, Jonathan, 22, 38, 127, 135(n50)
Kristol, Irving, 85, 86

Labor
  class differences and, 74–75, 77
  gender differences and, 33, 35,
    138(n32)
  socialist education and, 77
  *See also* Employment
Lamont, Tom, 153(n20)
Landes, Joan, 147(n35)
Language
  class stratification and, 110–112
  social practice and, 102
  *See also* Literacy
*Last Intellectuals: American Culture in
  the Age of Academe, The* (Jacoby),
  7, 82, 84–87
Latin Americans, population growth of,
  19
*L'Aurore*, 81
Learning communities, 129
Left-wing ideals
  intellectuals and, 81, 84–85, 93–94
  university radicals and, 92–94
  *See also* Right-wing ideals
Levin, Henry M., 67, 144(n39)
*Liberalism and Social Action* (Dewey),
  57
Liberty, collectivity and, 25
Literacy
  behaviorism and, 106–107, 112
  class polarization and, 104–114
  critical, 8, 130
  culture and, 111–114
  deficiencies in, 17
  definitions of, 99
  democracy and, 12, 113
  education and, 8, 74–75, 107–109
  knowledge and, 101–102, 105, 107
  myth of, 99–100, 101
  politics of, 98–114
  privilege and, 105–106
  public knowledge and, 8, 100, 108–
    114

race and ethnicity and, 74–75, 113
  skills training and, 106–107, 110
  social change and, 98–100, 108
  working-class jobs and, 74–75
  *See also* Education
Local autonomy, 39
Lorde, Audre, 86
Love, Kennett, 153(n20)
Lukas, J. Anthony, 73
Luxemburg, Rosa, 23, 25, 93

Machine age
  "the eclipse of the public" and, 57
  social institutions and, 47–48
McKinleyism, 29
Mahfouz, Naguib, 122
Mailer, Norman, 85
"Manifesto of the Intellectuals," 81
Mannheim, Karl, 102
Mann, Horace, 39
Marcuse, Herbert, 22
Market metaphor, 18
Martin, Theodora Penny, 44, 129
Marxism
  academic, 85
  Henry Adams and, 28
  cultural change and, 120
  political democracy and, 61
  pragmatism and, 48, 56–57
  public knowledge and, 20
  socialism and, 23–24
  in universities, 92
Marx, Karl, 104, 119, 136(n57)
Mead, Margaret, 86
Media
  distortion of public debate by,
    138(n25)
  public influence of, 31, 87–88
Meier, Deborah W., 37–38, 124–125,
    126, 127
Meiklejohn, Alexander, 90
Meritocracy
  information society and, 104–105
  public education and, 39–40
  *See also* Social reproduction
Michener, James, 86

Middle class
  economic transformation of, 15–16
  learning methods of, 111–112
  *See also* Bourgeoisie; Class
    polarization
Mill, John Stuart, 77
Mills, C. Wright, 42, 85
Minorities. *See* African Americans;
    Ethnicity; Race; Women
Modernity
  body politic and, 120
  Dewey's critique of, 56–58
Moe, Terry, 123, 125
Monopoly capitalism, 31
Moral ideals, 71–72
Multiculturalism, 121
Multinational corporations, 23
"Multiversity," 89
Mussolini, Benito, 55

National Commission on Excellence in
    Education, 37
*Nation at Risk* report, 37
Native Americans, 20
Negative dialectics, 136(n57)
Neighborhood provincialism, 22, 38–39
Nelson, Linda, 1
Neoconservatism, educational reform
    and, 92
Neo-Kantian theories, 70–71, 75
Neorationalism
  communitarianism vs., 70–71, 74
  democratic education and, 70–73
*New York Review of Books,* 92
*New York Times,* 115
Nobel Prize for Literature, 122,
    153(n20)
Nussbaum, Martha, 146(n18)

Oakes, Jennie, 39–40
O'Brien, Mary, 33
Okin, Susan Moller, 34–35
*On the Jewish Question* (Marx), 61
Ortega y Gasset, José, 82
O'Toole, Patricia, 143(n3)
*Oxford English Dictionary,* 35

*Paideia Proposal, The* (Adler), 102
Parochial schools
  democracy and, 73
  studies on, 41
  *See also* Private schools
Passeron, Jean-Claude, 41
*Pedagogy of the Oppressed* (Freire),
    107, 108
Peirce, Charles Sanders, 6, 50–53,
    141(nn 17, 31)
Perry, Ralph Barton, 50
Persell, Caroline Hodges, 42, 43, 73
*Phaedrus* (Plato), 109
Phillips, Anne, 35
Phillips, Kevin, 15–16
Philosophy
  active experimentalism and, 48
  William James's popularization of,
    53, 55
  provincialism and, 146(n18)
  as theory of education, 56
Piven, Frances Fox, 86
Plato, 77, 109
*Plessy v. Ferguson,* 135(n50)
Podhoretz, Norman, 85
Polis, 33
Political correctness, 68
Political democracy, 58–61
Political economy, 13–14
Politics
  Henry Adams's view of, 29, 63–64,
    76
  class polarization and, 16
  higher education and, 90–91
  of literacy, 98–114
  morality vs., 71–72
  of pragmatism, 59–61
  public intellectuals and, 79–82, 86,
    96
  society and, 29, 79–81
*Politics, Markets, and America's
    Schools* (Chubb & Moe), 123
Poor, American. *See* Poverty, American
Positivism
  literacy and, 106
  pragmatism and, 52
Postindustrialism, literacy and, 105

Post-modern relativism, critique of, 93
Poverty, American
  economic changes and, 15–16
  education and, 38
  *See also* Class polarization
Power
  education and, 41–43
  knowledge as, 12, 101–102
  literacy and, 99, 101
  *See also* Elitism; Privilege
Power elite, 41–43
"Pragmaticism," 50
Pragmatism
  body politic and, 48
  capitalism and, 58–61
  democracy and, 56–61
  of John Dewey, 47–50, 51, 56–61
  education and, 6, 48–53, 56–61
  Marxism and, 48, 56–57
  origins of, 50–51
  politics of, 59–61
  public knowledge and, 6, 50–61
  relativism and, 55
  scientific method and, 51–52
Prejudice, public knowledge and, 20
*Preparing for Power* (Cookson & Persell), 42
Prep schools, 41–43
  *See also* Private schools
*Principles of Psychology* (James), 53
Print media
  public intellectuals and, 88
  *See also* Media
*Prison Notebooks* (Gramsci), 142(n62)
Privacy, defined, 33
Private schools
  democracy and, 72–73
  power elite and, 41–43, 123
  privilege and, 41–42, 72–73
  religious education and, 73
  *See also* Public schools
Private sphere
  public sphere vs., 33–36
  women and, 33–36, 138(nn 23, 32)
  *See also* Public sphere

Privatization
  individualism and, 21, 135(n47)
  of public schools, 4, 15, 123–124
Privilege
  education and, 37–43, 59
  knowledge and, 43, 122, 125
  literacy and, 105–106
  private schools and, 41–42, 72–73
  public knowledge and, 20, 37–41, 42–43, 60, 124
  socialist educational theory and, 76–77
  *See also* Class polarization; Elitism; Power
Provincialism
  cultural, 122
  education and, 22, 38–39
  philosophy and, 146(n18)
  universalism and, 76–77
*Psychology: Briefer Course* (James), 53
Psychology, 53
"Public," etymology of word, 35
Public education
  development of system of, 12–13
  educational choice and, 123
  inequality of, 38–39
  meritocracy and, 39–40
  privatization of, 4, 15, 123–124
  reforming, 124–125
  *See also* Public schools
*Public and Its Problems, The* (Dewey), 19, 47
Public intellectuals. *See* Intellectuals
Public knowledge
  accessibility of, 122–123, 127
  Henry Adams's example of, 30
  class polarization and, 105, 108–109, 120–121
  collective memory and, 36–37
  communitarianism and, 68–71, 74
  curriculum and, 120
  democracy and, 4–5, 19, 37, 60–61, 118
  education and, 5–6, 14, 19–21, 69–70, 96, 120, 125–126, 135(n51)
  human development and, 49–50
  intellectuals and, 7, 85–86

literacy and, 8, 100, 108–114
neorationalism and, 70–74
politics and, 59–60, 69–70
pragmatism and, 6, 50–61
prejudice and, 20
privacy vs., 33
privilege and, 20, 37–41, 42–43, 60, 124
socialism and, 5–6, 22–26
subjectivity and, 55
truth as, 52
universities and, 88–89, 118, 122
*See also* Knowledge
Public opinion, 31
Public participation, 69–70
Public schools
criticism of, 15
inequality of, 38–39
middle-class flight from, 73
privatization of, 4, 15, 123–124
*See also* Private schools; Public education
Public sphere
bourgeois, 5–6, 13, 30–32, 35–36, 69, 87–88, 137(n21), 139(n39), 147(n35)
culture and, 30–31, 87
decline of, 47–48, 57
education and, 89, 91, 95–96, 130
exclusion of women from, 20, 33–36, 133(n12), 138(n23), 147(n35)
gender differences and, 35
modern capitalism and, 69
private sphere vs., 33–36
the state and, 31
universities and, 89, 91, 95–96, 130
*See also* Private sphere

Race
economic polarization and, 19
educational quality and, 38
literacy and, 74–75, 113
neighborhood provincialism and, 22
political exclusion and, 20
university faculties and, 91–92
Radicals, university, 92–93
Rahv, Philip, 85

Rawls, John, 7, 70–72
Reading, spontaneous, 149(n1)
Reagan, Ronald, 4
Reflective equilibrium, 72
Reflexivity, 8, 61
*Reforming of General Education: The Columbia College Experience in Its National Setting, The* (Bell), 90
Relativism
critique of post-modern, 93
pragmatism and, 55
Religious education, 73
Republican Motherhood, 138(n23)
*Republic* (Plato), 109
Rhetoric, action vs., 65–66
Rich, Adrienne, 9, 86
Rich-poor polarization. *See* Class polarization
Right-wing ideals
intellectualism vs., 81–82
university radicals and, 92–93
*See also* Left-wing ideals
Robbins, Bruce, 81
Robbins, Harold, 86
Rogers, Joel, 14, 21
Roosevelt, Theodore, 137(n6)
Rorty, Richard, 141(n31)
Rousseau, Jean Jacques, 28, 137(n4)

Samuels, Ernest, 27, 137(n3)
Sartre, Jean-Paul, 86
*Savage Inequalities* (Kozol), 22, 38
Scholes, Robert, 111, 151(n40)
*Schooling in Capitalist America* (Bowles & Gintis), 144(n39)
*Schooling and Work* (Carnoy & Levin), 144(n39)
"School as Social Centre, The" (Dewey), 58
Schools. *See* Education; Private schools; Public schools
Schudson, Michael, 137(n21)
Scientific method, 51–52
Searle, John, 92
Segregation, 38–39
Sexual politics, labor and, 33, 35, 138(n32)

Shanker, Albert, 153(n28)
Silko, Leslie Marmon, 86
Skills training, literacy and, 106–107, 110
Slaves
    education of, 44
    learning communities of, 129
Smith, Adam, 77
Social change
    common sense and, 58
    literacy and, 98–100, 108
Social institutions, machine age and, 47–48
Socialism
    capitalism and, 23–24, 76, 93
    class polarization and, 23–25, 77
    communitarianism vs., 75
    community and, 58
    defined, 25
    democracy and, 22–25, 75–77, 126–127
    education and, 5–6, 22–26, 58, 67–68, 75–77, 117–119, 124
    Marxism and, 23–24
    public knowledge and, 5–6, 22–26
    universities and, 90
Socialist education
    curriculum in, 76–77
    *See also* Democratic education; Education
Socialization
    class differences and, 111–112
    education as process of, 53–54, 125
    in public schools, 125
    in universities, 88
Social reproduction
    education and, 40–41, 119
    task of schools as, 67
Society
    influence of state on, 31
    knowledge and, 89
    politics and, 29, 79–81
    public realm and, 33–35
Specialists
    generalists vs., 90–91
    intellectuals as, 86
Spontaneous reading, 149(n1)

Stamp Act crisis, 99
State, influence of, 31
"Storm over the University, The" (Searle), 92
*Strong Democracy* (Barber), 127
*Structural Transformation of the Public Sphere, The* (Habermas), 30–32
Students, university, composition of, 91
Study clubs, 44
Subjectivity, truth and, 54–55
Substantive equality, 39

*Talks to Teachers* (James), 53
Team teaching, 129
Teenagers, education of, 128
*Tenured Radicals* (Kimball), 92
*Theory of Communicative Action, The* (Habermas), 120
Tocqueville, Alexis de, 21, 32, 77, 138(n23)
*Toward a Rational Society* (Habermas), 118
Town meetings, 56
Trilling, Lionel and Diana, 85
Truth
    individual experience and, 54–55
    as inherently public, 52
    intellectualism and, 81–82, 86, 95–96

Universalism, 76–77
Universities
    capitalism and, 89
    corporate linkages of, 132(n9)
    costs of attending, 17–18
    critical discourse in, 7, 88–89, 94–95
    critique on education in, 82–83
    curriculum in, 90, 95–96
    democracy and, 88–89, 95–96
    elitism and, 83–84, 88, 93, 95, 148(n55)
    faculty in, 91–92
    as "knowledge factories," 89
    left-wing intellectuals in, 92–94
    public debate in, 94–95
    public intellectuals and, 84–85, 92–96

public knowledge and, 88–89, 118, 122
public sphere and, 89, 91, 95–96, 130
socialist perspective on, 90
socioeconomic function of, 88
specialized vs. general education in, 90–91
*See also* College education
Upward mobility, 103
*Uses of the University, The* (Kerr), 53

Veysey, Laurence R., 90
Vidal, Gore, 137(n6)
Vocational education, 128–129
"Voodoo education," 111
Voting
class polarization and, 16
democracy and, 59

Wages
education and, 17
inequities in U.S., 66
Walzer, Michael, 7, 68
Washington, George, 14
*Ways with Words* (Heath), 111
Wealthy, American
economic changes and, 15–16
*See also* Class polarization; Elitism; Privilege
Webster, Noah, 12, 117
Westbrook, Robert, 58, 140(n9)

West, Cornel, 51
Whitman, Walt, 47
*Why Johnny Can't Read*, 100
Williams, Raymond, 22
Willis, Paul, 40
Wilson, Edmund, 85
Wolfe, Tom, 87, 116–117
Wolin, Sheldon, 13–14, 120
Wollstonecraft, Mary, 35
Women
exclusion of, from public sphere, 20, 33–36, 133(n12), 138(n23), 147(n35)
learning communities and, 129
private sphere and, 33–36, 138(nn 23, 32)
study clubs for, 44
university faculties and, 91–92
*See also* Feminism; Gender differences
Women's movement, 90
Wood, Ellen Meiksins, 22, 64, 135(n47)
Working class
learning methods of, 112
need for literacy by, 74–75
*See also* Class polarization
Workplace, democracy in, 59, 76
World's Columbian Exposition (1893), 29

Zinn, Howard, 65